Edward Hay

History of the Irish insurrection of 1798

giving an authentic account of various battles

Edward Hay

History of the Irish insurrection of 1798
giving an authentic account of various battles

ISBN/EAN: 9783741134524

Manufactured in Europe, USA, Canada, Australia, Japa

Cover: Foto ©Thomas Meinert / pixelio.de

Manufactured and distributed by brebook publishing software (www.brebook.com)

Edward Hay

History of the Irish insurrection of 1798

CONTENTS.

	PAGE
INTRODUCTION	ix–lviii
Geographical Description of the County of Wexford	1
Institution of the Volunteers of Ireland	12
Meeting of the County on the 22nd of September, 1792	17
Do. do. on the 11th of January, 1793	19
Riots in the year 1793	23
Meeting of the County on the 23rd of March, 1795, on the Recall of Earl Fitzwilliam	30
Loss of the former Independence of the County of Wexford	32
Melancholy Effects produced by the Riots in the County of Armagh, in 1795	36
Causes of the present State of Ireland	40
Conduct of the Troops in Ireland censured by Sir Ralph Abercromby, Commander-in-Chief	46
Proclamation of Sixteen Parishes in the County of Wexford, 28th of November, 1797	49
Conduct of the North Cork Militia on their arrival in the County of Wexford	54
The whole of the County of Wexford Proclaimed on the 27th of April, 1798	58
Meeting of the Magistrates of the County, 23rd of May	69
Sudden Insurrection on the 27th of May	84
Battle of Oulart, on the 27th of May	85
Battle at Enniscorthy, 28th of May	86
Retreat of the Troops to Wexford—General Confusion	90
Deputation to the Insurgents on Vinegar Hill	95
Defeat at the Three Rocks—Surrender and Abandonment of Wexford to the Insurgents, on the 30th of May	101
Conduct of the Troops on their Retreat to Duncannon Fort	112
General Arrangements of the Insurgents	125
Abandonment of Gorey—Conduct of the Inhabitants	128
Battles of Newtownbarry and Ballycanow, on the 1st of June, 1798	130

CONTENTS.

	PAGE
Lord Kingsborough, Captains O'Hea and Bourke taken Prisoners, 2nd of June	133
Battle of Clough or Tubberneering, 4th of June	140
Battle of Ross, 5th of June	143
Dreadful Abomination at Scullabogue	148
Battle of Arklow, 9th of June	170
Attack at Borris	179
Proposals of Accommodation from Lord Kingsborough, 14th of June	183
Skirmish at Tinehaly, 16th of June	188
Insurgents surprised on Lacken Hill—their Retreat, 19th	190
Critical Situation of Wexford—Dreadful Massacre!	193
Battle of Horetown or Fooks's-Mill, 20th	215
Battle of Enniscorthy, 21st	216
Wexford Surrendered to Lord Kingsborough—his Conduct and Dispatches	219
Major-General Moore's Approach to Wexford, 21st	228
Pursuit of the Insurgents from Gorey, and their Progress out of the County	235
Trials and Executions in Wexford	238
Progress of the Wexford Insurgents in the Counties of Carlow and Kilkenny	243
Progress of the Wexford Insurgents in the County of Wicklow	246
Progress of the Wexford Insurgents closed by Surrender	252
Commanders and Court-Martials Appointed	253
Conduct of General Hunter—his superior Discrimination	257
Intended Extermination of the Inhabitants of the Macomores	259
Conduct of the People on the Landing of the French at Killala	268
Conflagration of a Protestant Church and Catholic Chapels	280
Conclusion	290

CONTENTS.

APPENDIX.

	PAGE
I. Speech of Captain Sweetman, 22nd September, 1792	291
Account of the County Meeting at Wexford	310
Resolutions of the Catholics of Wexford	312
II. Requisition of the Magistrates of County of Wexford	313
Resolutions of the County Meeting, January 11th, 1793	313
III. Certificate of Solomon Richards, Esq.	315
Certificate of Martha Richards	319
Affidavit of Mr. Taylor, an Englishman	319
IV. Extract from the Debates of the House of Lords, 10th of July, 1793	321
V. Resolutions of the Catholics in Wexford, July 30th	322
VI. Requisition to the High Sheriff and Magistrates of the County of Wexford	324
Resolutions at the County Meeting, 23rd of March, 1795, on the Recall of Earl Fitzwilliam	326
Petition to the King	328
Address to his Excellency Earl Fitzwilliam	330
VII. Lord Gosford's Address to the Magistrates of the County of Armagh, with the Resolutions entered into, on the 28th of December, 1795	332
VIII. General Orders of Sir Ralph Abercromby, 26th of February, 1798	335
IX. Oaths during the Insurrection	337
X. The Address of the Inhabitants of the Macomores to Major Fitzgerald	339
The Address of the Inhabitants of the Macomores to General Hunter	339
Letter to Major Fitzgerald	341
XI. Affidavit of Mr. Stephen Lett, jun.	341
Letter from Lieutenant Murphy	343
Affidavit of Edward Roche	343
Letter from Captain Bourke	345
Letters from Lord Kingston and Major Fitzgerald	349
Affidavit of Mrs. Breen	351
Letter from Armstrong Browne, Esq.	353
XII. Testimony of Doctor Jacob	354
XIII. Letter to the Rev. Mr. Gordon, with his Answer	357
Conclusion	361

INTRODUCTION.

I WOULD not obtrude myself on public attention were I not earnestly solicited by numerous and respectable friends' (who have at length prevailed) to give a genuine account of the transactions in the County of Wexford, during the Insurrection, in the year 1798; in order to counteract the baleful effects of the partial details and hateful misrepresentations, which have contributed so much to revive and continue those loathsome prejudices that have, for centuries, disturbed and distracted Ireland. It is conceived, that a fair and impartial account, by dissipating error, may operate as a balm to heal the wounds of animosity; for let the candid reader be of what political principles he may, I am confident he must be sensible, that no adherent of either of the contending parties in this unhappy country, can in justification feel himself authorized to assert, that his own party was perfectly in the right, and the other egregiously in the wrong; and yet there are partisans to be found on either side endeavouring to maintain that this is actually the case. But if these zealots could be induced calmly to listen to the melancholy tales of enormity that can unfortunately be told of both parties, they might be prevailed upon to relax a little in their prejudices. If the spirit of intolerance and retaliation be still held up, no kind of social intercourse or harmony can exist in Ireland. With a view, therefore, of establishing concord, by showing from what has happened, that it will be of universal advantage to forget the past, and to cultivate general amity in future, I have undertaken the arduous task of endeavouring to reconcile; pointing out errors by a genuine relation of facts, and I hope this may eventually prevail upon neighbours of all descriptions to cherish the blessings of union and mutual benevolence, which cannot fail of banishing from their breasts every rankling idea, and must prevent the possibility of their ever again becoming the easy tools of political speculation, which unfortunately hitherto encouraged hatred and variance, and ended in the miserable debility and depression of all.

Did I know any other person willing and able to give a more circumstantial account of what has fatally happened in the County of Wexford (which is the only part of Ireland I at present undertake to treat of), I would cheerfully resign my documents into his hands; but as I have been most peculiarly circumstanced, as an eye-witness of many remarkable transactions, the information cannot be so well handed over, and might not be produced with such good effect at second-hand. I conceive it therefore necessary to give some account of myself, as most of my readers could not possibly otherwise be sensible of the many opportunities I had of being perfectly informed of the state of the country, which certainly did not fall to the lot of many other persons.

INTRODUCTION.

My family have been established in Ireland since the reign of Henry II., as my ancestor came over with Strongbow, and was allotted a knight's share of lands in the southern part of the County of Wexford, which his descendants possessed until the revolution in Ireland about the middle of the seventeenth century, when there was but one estate in the whole county left unalienated by Cromwell. My ancestor had not the good fortune to be the person undisturbed; but he acquired a property in another part of the county, where his descendants have ever since resided. Born of Catholic parents, and being reared in the principles of that religion, occasioned my banishment at an early age for some years from my native country, as my parents wished to procure me a collegiate education in a foreign land, to which the rank and respectability of my family entitled me, but which the laws of my country denied me at home.

After having pursued a course of study for several years in France and Germany, I returned to my native soil, fully sensible of my civil degradation as a Catholic, and I therefore sought all the legal and constitutional means in my power in the pursuit of Catholic Emancipation. The liberality of the times contributed much to the relaxation of the Penal Laws, passed from time to time against the Catholics of Ireland; and they were at length induced to lay their grievances at the foot of the throne, as the most effectual source of redress. They were in part relieved, but many oppressive causes of complaint still remained, and many modes of procuring their abolition were resorted to. A various train of circumstances occurred to produce the circular letter of the sub-committee of the Catholics of Ireland in 1792, and pursuant to its tenor, delegates for all the counties and principal towns were chosen to represent them in the General Committee. I had the honour of being elected a delegate for the County of Wexford, and I exerted myself in that situation with all the energy and ability in my power.

The declaration adopted by the Catholic Committee in March, 1792, was subscribed by a multitude of signatures, and those of the County of Wexford I was instrumental in procuring. I attended my duty in the General Committee of the Catholics of Ireland, where a petition to his Majesty was framed and signed, in November, 1792; and a vindication of the cause of the Catholics of Ireland, containing an exposition of their objects and motives, was adopted; and afterwards published and authenticated. In consequence of royal interposition, by the King's gracious recommendation, the Parliament of Ireland (which almost unanimously rejected a petition of the Catholics in 1792), was induced considerably to extend their privileges in 1793. I attended a subsequent meeting of the General Committee, at which an address of gratitude, for his gracious interposition, was voted to his Majesty, and a similar one to the Lord Lieutenant, expressive of the earnest loyalty of the Catholics, and requesting the former to be transmitted, was drawn up, approved of, and presented by deputation to Lord Westmoreland.

Along with the repeal of the most odious of the Penal Laws, a new oath to be taken by the Catholics to avow their loyalty, was framed by Parliament. All the delegates and a great number of other Catholic gentlemen, anxious to avail themselves of the earliest opportunity of displaying their gratitude for the newly-acquired privileges, and eager to satisfy the public mind as well as to set an example to the whole nation, attended in the Court of King's Bench, on Saturday, the 19th of April, 1793, where they took the oath and subscribed the special declaration prescribed to them; and this was by the appointment of Lord Chief Justice Clonmell, on whom a deputation from the General Committee had previously waited for that purpose.

The magic of royalty, in earnestly recommending *"the union of all descriptions of subjects,"* having lately proved so effectual in altering the conduct of Parliament to the Catholics, the erection of a statue of the King was voted as a monument of Catholic gratitude; but this, along with other honourable engagements adopted by the General Committee, was superseded by illiberal and calumnious outcries raised against the conduct and intentions of the Catholic body, so as to preclude the possibility of carrying into effect the plan of subscription formed for these purposes. I was, however, determined to proceed in the County of Wexford, but was at length obliged to give up the object, in consequence of the baleful operation of party prejudice; and thus did the enemies of the Catholics, under the mask of loyalty, defeat the execution of a project that would exhibit the conduct of the Catholics in a point of view too meritorious for their wishes.

Very serious disturbances took place in a part of the County Wexford, in the month of June, 1793; but they were soon suppressed by the exertions of the country gentlemen, who formed "an Association for the Preservation of the Peace." I constantly attended their meetings, and I believe it will be allowed, that my conduct and endeavours proved as effectual as that of any other to restore public tranquillity.*

In January, 1795, while Lord Fitzwilliam was Viceroy, I procured a great number of signatures to a petition to Parliament, from the Catholics of the County of Wexford, and in the same month I was one of those that presented an address from them to his Excellency. When his lordship's recall was announced from the Government of Ireland, a meeting of the freeholders and other inhabitants of the County of Wexford was convened on the 23rd of March of the same year, when a petition to his Majesty was unanimously agreed to, and I was appointed one of the delegates to present it to the King. I had been as far as Dublin to take ship for England, when it was thought advisable to have the petition subscribed by as many persons as possible, and while my brother delegates proceeded to London, I returned to the County of Wexford, and considering that I was the chosen delegate of Protestants as well as of Catholics, I took the precaution of consulting the

---

* See Mr. Richards' Certificate in Appendix, No. III.

principal Protestant gentlemen of the county first, to prevent the possibility of misrepresentation, or of denominating my pursuit the business of party; and I was so successful as to procure, in the space of one week, twenty-two thousand two hundred and fifty-one signatures to the petition, with which I then proceeded to London, and had the honour to present it, along with my brother delegates, to his Majesty, at a public levee, at St. James's, on the 22nd of April, 1795; and we met a most gracious reception.*

I think it necessary to mention that I was invited, in the most earnest and flattering manner, to become a member of political societies, both in England and Ireland; but these invitations I declined, in consequence of a resolution which I had formed, of never becoming a member of any political society whatsoever; and to this I have ever since most scrupulously adhered. I proposed a plan for the enumeration of the inhabitants of Ireland to Lord Fitzwilliam, which met with his strongest approbation, and but for his recall he would have patronized the undertaking, and done everything in his power to facilitate its execution. I had this plan long in agitation, and was induced to enter on the business particularly from a consideration that, by the current statements, the population of Ireland was vastly underrated. Some years ago, the Established clergy had made returns of the population of their several parishes, by order of Government, and I had the

* See Appendix, No. VI.

curiosity to inquire into the returns made of the population of the parishes in my own neighbourhood, and these I found really correct, according to the general mode of calculation; but as my curiosity led me to number every individual, I found them very defective as to the actual state of the population, both in the total and comparative numbers.

While in England on my delegation, this plan for estimating the population of Ireland was seen at Lord Fitzwilliam's by the Right Hon. Edmund Burke, who was thereby induced to do me the honour of soliciting my acquaintance; and after a minute investigation of its nature and extent, he earnestly encouraged me to proceed, as he considered it would be productive of the greatest possible benefit to Ireland. Backed by the authority and flattering opinion of so much genius, and sanctioned also by the countenance of Lord Fitzwilliam and a great number of other enlightened men in England, I was induced on my return to Ireland to use every exertion to put it forward, and met such encouragement from dignity and distinction, that I submitted my plan to the inspection of the Royal Irish Academy, who were much pleased with it as an essential branch of a statistical inquiry which they had then in contemplation to promote. This produced the pleasing consequence to me of being proposed to the Academy by the present President, and I had the honour of being unanimously admitted a member of that learned and respectable body. Certainly, had not the misfortune of the times prevented my success, this must have been considered as honourable and remarkable an undertaking as any individual could have accomplished, and the nature of the encouragement I met with, induced me to print a great number of copies of the plan, and to procure a sufficiency of ruled paper for writing out the returns from every part of Ireland, as in Appendix. I am thus led to publish the whole plan, on the present occasion, to show the falsity of the prejudiced arguments adduced by reference to a part; especially as I conceive that it wants only to be known to show the futility of such arguments. But I have by no means dropped the idea of bringing this scheme to perfection, nor do I think that my labours, even as far as I have proceeded, are not likely to be useful to my country; for although I have not been able to go to the extent proposed, yet the returns which have been made to me are sufficient to give a much more certain account of the population of Ireland, than can be collected from any other statement that has appeared. I have been favoured with authentic copies of all the documents on which the late Mr. Bushe grounded his return of the inhabitants of this country, which has gained him so much credit; and I can positively affirm that he was not in any degree possessed of such various and detailed accounts as those which, on my plan, have been returned to me; and I shall feel highly obliged to any person, who, according to this scheme, shall make me a return of one or more parishes, through the country at large, or of a street or streets in any town or city, together with any remarks tending to show the increase or decrease of population since the year 1795. I shall also feel extremely thankful to any person, who at that period proceeded in any degree on this plan, for letting me have the result of that inquiry, whether returned to me formally or not; as I can the more readily compare the former and present accounts, on getting them together, than by the trouble of searching out the original returns. If it can be established beyond a possibility of doubt, that there are vastly more inhabitants in Ireland than they are at present supposed to be (and this I have good reason to believe is the case), surely the national consequence must be enhanced, and our importance in the scale of nations raised in proportion; and as I already feel a well-founded expectation that I shall be enabled to perfect this desirable object, I hope it will induce every real lover of his country to make me those returns, which the simplicity of the plan will enable any person to execute in his own neighbourhood; and I trust I have already given such proofs of the sincerity of my intentions, as to entitle me to this information from any friend to the country, as it is self-evident, that this plan does not in any degree partake of party spirit, but is merely concerned with general information.

How can the wants of a nation be properly supplied if the extent of its population be not accurately known? or how can the redundancy of one nation be applied to the benefit of another, where this important fact is not ascertained? For example's sake, the crops of Ireland, in the year 1801, were supposed to be better able to supply the wants of its inhabitants than those of Great Britain were to supply her own at that period. How was it possible to ascertain this but from surmise? In England it was a measure of Parliamentary inquiry to ascertain the state of the population exactly. Why should not the like policy obtain with respect to Ireland? Surely, since the union of both nations has been formed, Ireland is entitled to the same advantages with England. In short, a knowledge of the real state of any country is of such material importance to any one wishing to promote its welfare, as to be evident on first contemplation, since without it conjecture must supply the place of certainty, and so perhaps occasion material error and confusion.

As this object is of such national consequence, I hope my countrymen will be kind enough to furnish the means to render me able, as I am willing, to make them acquainted with their real importance; and in proportion to the extent of documents will be the accuracy of the result. But I esteem even a partial return of such moment, that I earnestly request no person inclined to promote so desirable an object may withhold his particular information; for such communication may in time occasion the entire plan to be brought to perfection; and as I mentioned before, it is astonishing how a few returns from different parts of Ireland, according to this model, will contribute to ascertain its true state better than it has been ever hitherto accomplished.

Different motives of private concern induced me to resolve to quit Ireland, in the year 1797, and to go to reside in America; and this I purposed to do as soon as the regulation of my affairs would permit me. I was mostly in the County of Wexford in the latter end of 1797, and beginning of 1798; but my attendance in Dublin was sometimes necessary upon law business, which I at length flattered myself I had finally got rid of by compromise. In the latter end of April therefore I took leave of my friends, as my proposed short stay in Ireland would not allow me the opportunity of seeing them again; as I had determined to go immediately to England, and from thence to America. In this project I was most unhappily disappointed, as a part of the compromise, which was, that my furniture should be taken at a valuation, was not complied with; and I was therefore reluctantly obliged to remain in the country, until I could, as I thought, dispose of them by auction, which I advertised would take place on Monday, the 28th of May. I am thus particular, to counteract the malevolent insinuations of my enemies, and as it was this disappointment that occasioned my detention in the County of Wexford until the commencement of the disturbances; by which I lost all my furniture, and all else that could be taken from me, except what I had on my back, and about my person.

Had I any possible intimation of the calamities that ensued, I most undoubtedly would have preferred settling my property even at a loss, and securing the value, to waiting to be detained against my will in that unfortunate country; and I would thus have escaped enduring those sufferings and persecutions that afterward fell to my lot. The particulars of the situation I was in previous to, and at the breaking out of the Insurrection comes more properly in my general account. Until the 28th of May I got on board a ship in Wexford harbour, and did all in my power to induce the captain to sail for England; and on its being objected that there was not a sufficiency of provisions on board the "Adventure," which was the name of the ship, just then arrived with a cargo of coals, I proposed we should shift on board another vessel belonging to the same proprietor, which had cleared out off the Custom-house Quay laden with oats, which I represented would, in case of necessity, supply our wants during our passage; but the low state of the ebbing tide and contrary winds prevented either of these ships, both being heavily laden, from possibly crossing the bar of Wexford harbour, which they could not do but at high tide.

Frustrated in every wish to leave the country, before and after the Insurrection broke out, what could I do but submit to my evil fate, and remain in a place delivered up, and abandoned, by those who should have been its natural protectors, to the mercy of an uncontrollable multitude? My popularity in the country, and my intimacy with the greater number of its gentlemanly inhabitants, of whom many remained in Wexford, placed me in a very unenviable situation. It made my friends imagine that I possessed a plenitude of power, and induced them to apply to me for protection from popular fury, either personally or through some one of their family. I never hesitated, on these occasions, to risk my own life to preserve that of others, and never heard or saw of any one in danger, that I did not use every effort for their preservation. If greater expectations were formed of me than what I could effect, I have to regret the limitation of my power. I most solemnly declare, that during the Insurrection, I never omitted a single opportunity of being as serviceable as in my power, by administering comfort to the afflicted and distressed, or every assistance I could to those in danger. Some are found grateful enough to acknowledge the fact. There were *three gentlemen* apprehensive I might resent former conduct, but when misfortune intervened I threw away resentment. One of them had, upon previous occasion, treated me so ill, that I had determined to chastise him to the utmost of my power; but they all now acknowledge that, forgetful of personal injury, I risked my life for the preservation of theirs. My conduct during the Insurrection, as far as it is necessary to be known, properly belongs to the history of the times; and so I shall proceed to a relation of my persecutions and sufferings.

Lord Kingsborough and his officers conceived themselves under such obligations to me, that at their entreaty I lived in the same house with them, from the surrender of the town until the 29th of June, when they departed for Waterford. Being well aware of malice and obloquy, I constantly expressed a desire, during their stay, to be brought to trial, for any allegation that might be framed against me; and I am now confident, that had it been possible to procure any proof against me, it would by no means be neglected. But this being impracticable, even in such crazy times, other means of deep malignity were resorted to, and these, as well as I am hitherto acquainted with them, I shall endeavour to describe. My former intention of going to America was by no means lessened, but augmented, by the scenes of which I had so recently been witness to in my native country. I accordingly persisted in my resolution, and was determined to get out of the country as speedily as possible. The committee that had been appointed by Lieutenant-General Lake, to act as a kind of council to General Hunter, then in command in Wexford, and to grant passes, now began to practise their malicious arts against me, which they avoided before, being apprehensive, if not well aware, that their schemes would be counteracted and defeated, if attempted to be put in execution, while the officers, who were acquainted with my conduct, remained in Wexford. I received a note from the chairman of this committee (and it was delivered to me by one of the body, whom I then considered as my friend), desiring I would write to him, stating what I would wish to be done, and that my request would be taken into immediate consideration. This induced me to write to them, intimating the desire I had so often expressed, of going to America, adding, that I wished to set off the next day in order to sail in a ship then in the harbour of Dublin; and this determination I would, in all probability, have since put in execution, but that I considered it might have given freer sanction to the calumnies so industriously raised against me. This consideration has detained me in Ireland, as here I was the better enabled to vindicate my honour, and this, indeed, my persecutors have completely effected, quite in contradiction to their inclinations and wishes.

The *immediate consideration* of the committee was, in consequence of *premeditation* to send back the gentleman, who brought me the note and took my answer, to *arrest* me. This he did at my lodgings, where I was publicly known to be since the Insurrection, and two yeomen were there placed as a guard over me. This whole conduct, from several circumstances of which I have since come to the knowledge, was certainly *preconcerted*. Had I been sent to gaol, it would have been productive of a trial by Court-Martial, and this was a benefit which they did not wish to allow me, as they were well aware of the sentiments of the officers, whom I would have summoned back to Wexford. Besides, some individuals among them were most ungratefully induced to forward the vile proceedings against me, as they were apprehensive I might call on them as witnesses, when their loyalty may have been called in question, were they to do justice to my conduct; and it may also have been manifested, that whatever honour some of them now possess, is owing to their taking my advice in preference to their own; as if they escaped *piking* on the one side, they may have been *hanged* on the other, and with much more justice than several who have forfeited their lives on the occasion. To transport me without further inquiry was therefore considered more advisable. Several, who had been tried and sentenced to transportation, were taken on the 3rd of July from the gaol and put on board a sloop which had been twice condemned during the Insurrection, and which had sunk within a foot of her deck, and was only pumped out that morning. Afterward a guard was sent to my lodgings, and I was marched down to the Custom-house Quay, in the most conspicuous manner, and put on board this horrid hulk, without any trial or further investigation!

Two sloops had been prepared as prison-ships during the Insurrection; one of them, however, was immediately condemned as unfit for that service, and afterward, on the occasion of Lord Kingsborough and his officers being put on board for a few hours, she was again, on the inspection of the butchers of Wexford, pronounced unfit for the reception of a *pig*. After this second condemnation the *Lovely Kitty* (for so this infernal vessel was called) was hauled to one side of the harbour, where, from her leaky state, she sunk within a foot of her deck, and so escaped firing when the other sloop which had been used as a prison-ship was burned. This was the vessel the Wexford Committee ordered to be their prison-ship; and accordingly, on the 3rd of July, she was hauled into the channel, a little dry straw was shaken over that which had remained in her hold for a month before, and the prisoners then were sent on board. Our walking on the fresh litter soon made it as wet as the dung underneath, so that it was impossible to sit or lie without imbibing the moisture; nor, indeed, could we have the comfort of resting against her sides, as the planks were water soaked, and the effervescence of putrid malt, accumulated between her timbers, was so strong as even to turn silver black in our pockets in the course of a few hours. The stench was, besides, insupportable, and there was such an infestation of rats that some of the prisoners were bitten by them. The weather at the time was mostly warm, and this raised such an exhalation that, small as the vessel was, we could scarcely see each other from either end of the hold. If it rained, the deck was so open that it was impossible, in any part of the ship, to avoid being wetted; and, contrary to the usual state of leaky vessels (where the bilge water is not offensive), we were nearly suffocated while she was pumping. In our own defence we were obliged to be continually at the pump, to prevent our being overflowed; and, though our last occupation at night, we were always summoned to the same task early every morning; the water, by this time, having got above the double flooring, a cautionary plan always used in vessels employed in the transportation of malt.

Among the twenty-one doomed to this dreadful and loathsome confinement (which I believe not to be paralleled by any dungeon in the world) there were desperate villains and scums of the earth—a circumstance more degrading and offensive to a liberal mind than any other punishment, when unable to avoid such intercourse, and this was the case aboard the *Lovely Kitty*, whose burden was but about fifty tons. This aggravation was verily and avowedly intended by the merciless persecutors; for when one of them was told on his coming on board of our desperate situation, *I heard him* assert that "*we had no reason to complain, since the vessel had been fitted out by the rebels, she was good enough for us!*"

Our guards were at first seven yeomen of the Shilmalier infantry, afterward called *Ogle's Loyal Blues*. These were relieved every twenty-four hours, and, indeed, they were apparently humane. One of them was an apprentice to a carpenter who used to work at my father's, and offered to be particularly kind to me. He promised to bring me my bed, and represented it would not become wet through in the course of the night, but that he would continue to dry it in the day-time, in which he hoped to be assisted by another young man, his fellow-apprentice, and proposed to arrange it so as that they would every day mount guard alternately. He, however, said that he could not act without the permission of his captain, the Right Hon. George Ogle. With this gentleman I formerly kept company, as our families were neighbours, and visited each other. I therefore thought, as well as from the favourable opinion which he before constantly expressed of me, that his prejudice or bigotry could not make him forget good manners so far as not to answer a letter from me on such an occasion. I did, of course, address him one, but certainly not in the strain of a prisoner, which I knew I ought not to be, but as one gentlemen would write to another, giving an account of my distressing and unmerited situation. This letter the Right Hon. George Ogle laid before the Wexford Committee, and declared that he would not permit any of his corps to go on such an errand. Of this I was informed by a letter from the secretary of the Committee, which I preserve for the inspection of the curious. It was intimated that if I wanted my bed the Committee would grant a pass to any other messenger I could procure to bring it to me; but this was impossible at the time, as military law existed in such rigour, and it was a great while afterwards before I could procure a bed to be brought to me. The good-natured yeoman who offered me his kind service was checked by his captain for demeaning himself by speaking to the prisoners, and he soon after quitted the corps in disgust, and enrolled himself with a captain more congenial to his disposition and feelings.

I applied to General Hunter to be liberated under a general proclamation which he had published, and he asked the Committee by what authority I had been at all confined. He was there informed, contrary to all truth, that I had petitioned for transportation; and the answer I received from him in consequence of this misinformation was, that it exceeded his power to liberate me. I instantly memorialled the General a second time, stating that I had never the most distant idea of petitioning for transportation, and solicited enlargement or trial. Upon this the General again applied to the Committee; and they had the effrontery to repeat and insist on their former assertion, persisting in falsehood to sanction their iniquitous proceeding. The General, not being as yet sensible of the extent of their persecuting spirit, and naturally, conceiving that the principal gentlemen of the county, who composed the Committee, would not assert a lie, was induced to give them credence in preference to a prisoner; but still, from the consideration of my statement, he advised me to address the Lord Lieutenant, and that he would forward it with his strongest recommendation. I accordingly did so, but, as misrepresentation respecting me was practised in every quarter, to prevent a detection of the original villainy, I had no better success then with his Excellency.

I cannot omit mentioning a fellow-prisoner of mine on this occasion—Master James Lett, thirteen years old (but little for his age), a near relative of Mr. Bagnal Harvey, was a child of such undaunted spirit and courage that he manifested a most heroical disposition at the battles of Ross and Fooks's-mill, and was after the Insurrection taken up and put in gaol. He was threatened to be hanged if he did not sign a petition for transportation presented to him as a great favour, and as a further inducement he was told that he would be let go off with Mr. Hay (this intimation was signified to Master Lett before I was arrested, or had written to the chairman of the Wexford Committee, which letter was *their excuse* for their premeditated scheme to entrap me). The little hero signed the paper required, and on my being dropped down into the hold of the *Lovely Kitty*, where he was before me, he clung to me and exclaimed, "*I don't care where I go, when I am to be with you!*" If nothing else was attracting in the child, surely in this instance I could not be insensible to such pathetic feeling. Captain Keen, of the Royal Navy, hearing of this wonderful boy, asked him whether he would be glad to go with him, which he consented to, and in a day or two after he was conducted by the captain on board the *Chapman*, and where, I understand, he was intended for a midshipman. I rejoiced in the release of my little companion, but had the mortification of seeing him brought in a few days back to the infernal prison-ship!—His return is said to be occasioned by the representations of *the Committee* to Captain Keen, " That he had no right to release any prisoner, as they claimed the exclusive privilege of *the management of their prisoners!*" On my removal to the gaol the child grieved immoderately, which, being made known to General Hunter, he was ordered to be sent to me. Notwithstanding many applications had been made for his release, they were counteracted through the representations of *the Committee;* and to the eternal shame of those concerned—*persons of distinction* were the promoters!

In January, 1799, a writ of *habeas corpus* was obtained, and Master Lett was brought by the Sub-Sheriff of the County of Wexford, from Wexford gaol to the Court of King's Bench, in Dublin, and on inquiry for the prisoner he was held up on a man's arm, to the utter astonishment of Lord Kilwarden, and thus was prejudice scouted out of the court by his liberation. This, I believe, unexampled case, took place in the presence of a full attendance of the gentlemen of the Bar, who had crowded to see such a phenomenon, as from the child's appearance it was thought he wanted the superintendence of a nurse more than a gaoler.

After a few days the Wexford yeomen infantry were appointed to guard the prison-ship, and were restricted not to depart for twenty-four hours. Among them were gentlemen of my acquaintance, from whose society I experienced much comfort in my calamitous situation; but the loathsome station of duty soon deprived me of this alleviation of suffering. All those of the better sort rejected the hateful service, and paid smartly for substitutes. The hirelings considered spirits as the only specific against contagion, and the use of them did not improve the manners of the lowest description of yeomen. Two of our guards died in consequence of sickness contracted in this service, but none of the prisoners, although some got dangerously ill.

In consequence of the opinion of a most eminent physician in Dublin, that it would be more humane to order me to be shot than to leave me in such a situation, being made known to General Lake, through General (now Sir John) Craddock, he sent down orders to inquire more particularly into the state of my case;

and General Hunter accordingly sent Doctor Jacob to visit me. The result was, that after five weeks' confinement in such a mansion of wretchedness, I was removed to the gaol; but my health had become so impaired that, I much fear, it may never be perfectly re-established. Doctor Jacob paid me two visits. I paid him for his attendance and wished him to continue; but such was my lot that, however much I stood in need of it, I could not procure medical assistance!—In my own conception this neglect was occasioned by a complaint of the hardship of my case to Doctor Jacob, upon which he promised to bring me a copy of what I had written to the Committee, which they alleged to be a petition for transportation. He brought me an application of mine to General Hunter, which he said was the only paper that he could see or find relative to me; and he afterward avoided me, lest in visiting me he might let out anything that should lead to a detection of the schemes of the Committee. I could not even afterward procure his attendance as a magistrate, on discovering in the gaol of Wexford the murderer of Mr. Nowlan, of Greek Street, in Dublin, whence he had fled, but was apprehended as a stranger, not being able to give a good account of himself, and lodged in prison. Apprehensive that this man might be let out, I sent to Doctor Jacob, as Mayor of Wexford, to state to him the reasons for his detention until I could get an answer of a letter I had written to Dublin. But Doctor Jacob did not attend; yet so right was I, that on my information the man was ordered to Dublin, where he turned King's evidence against his accomplices, who were accordingly brought to trial, condemned, and executed. The same reason, I do suppose, operated on the doctor, on this as well as former occasions; and, had it not been for the gaoler, who prevailed on the military commander to detain this fellow, who had been taken up only as a suspicious stranger, he might have escaped.

Brigade-Major Fitzgerald was sent to me from General Hunter, to inquire particularly into my situation, and I demonstrated it to him, from most authentic and convincing documents, in such a manner, that I can't convince the world of his conviction of the iniquitous practices of the Committee against me better than in his own words, in a letter written to me at a subsequent period, which is inserted in the Appendix, No. XI.

I presented in all thirteen or fourteen memorials to be liberated or tried, but the active malevolence of my persecutors prevented them from being attended to. In the month of January, 1799, I made an application to be removed to Dublin. A writ of *habeas corpus* was accordingly issued from the Court of King's Bench, ordering the Sheriff of the county to bring me up, and a notice was served on the Attorney-General to come forward if he had any charge against me. This was, however, superseded by a secretary's warrant being sent to General Grose; he detained me upon it, and, although I then became a State prisoner,

I had none of the advantages or indulgences allowed people in that situation, and of which, from my state of health, I stood in utmost need. The suspension of the *Habeas Corpus* Act obliged me to put up with my situation, and I must have remained a prisoner, God knows how long, had not my persecutors overshot their mark, by endeavouring to smuggle me off in a manner contrary to every law known or enacted in this country; not resting content with having me a State prisoner, from which situation I could not have extricated myself, if not enabled by their iniquity.

The prisoners which had been first tried by Court-Martial in Wexford, and sentenced to transportation, previous to the passing of the law that legalised trial by Court-Martial, were held over till the Spring Assizes of 1799. My name was returned in the Crown book as under sentence of transportation, and I should have been sent off immediately after the Assizes, along with all the rest of the proscribed, had I not made an application, by letter, to Judge Chamberlain, denying that I had ever been tried or petitioned for transportation; and that, as he himself had granted a writ of *habeas corpus*, to have me removed to Dublin, the January before, I considered myself under his protection, and that of the Court of King's Bench, and hoped that my situation, as unfortunate as unmerited, which I was ready to prove, would induce him not to sanction any sentence of transportation against me. My letter was delivered to him as he was going into Court, and he held it in his hand, while he publicly declared from the bench, that "although he did not usually attend to private letters in his judicial capacity, yet he had received a letter from Mr. Hay, a prisoner then confined in the gaol of Wexford, and that, if the contents of it were true, his situation must be deplorable indeed; and he added, that if nothing appeared against him, he would liberate him next day." The letter, at the request of the Grand Jury, was delivered to them, and it was now found absolutely necessary, for my detention, to procure informations against me. Accordingly a magistrate came down to the gaol, and called for a *noted informer* (since condemned to be hanged for murder, but whose sentence was commuted to transportation for his services), brought him into the gaoler's apartments, in an adjoining house, called the bridewell, over which I was confined, and the ceiling under me was so bad, that listening with attention, I could hear a great deal of what passed below stairs. In such a situation, it is natural to suppose I availed myself of this advantage, and could distinctly hear the informer threatened to be hanged if he would not swear against me; and it was promised that his life should be spared if he would. Conversation followed now and then in a higher tone, so that I was able to understand that the informer would not swear to the examinations first proposed and brought ready written, in the magistrate's own hand-writing, and he now, out of fury and disappointment, tore them to pieces. Threats, however, at last prevailed on the murderer to swear to other examinations framed in a more palatable form against me. The name of another gentleman I also heard mentioned; but the point of swearing against him was not insisted on. When the magistrate departed, I asked to be let out to walk, and accosted the informer on meeting him, to know how was it possible for him to swear anything against me? He told me, that as he had heard me say I was not afraid of anything that might be sworn against me, he thought it no harm, as it was to save his own life; and that certainly what he had sworn could not affect mine. After minutely relating the story of his being so obliged to swear (and which perfectly coincided with what I was able to hear), he put me in the way of getting the scraps of the torn examinations, which I immediately set about arranging, and have them now pasted together in regular order, as an existing, incontrovertible proof of the subornation, and unravelling the whole of the nefarious plot formed against me, as well as exposing the atrocious deed of the magistrate. This I meant to have proved on my trial, by producing the identical magistrate, and putting the document into his hand for avowal. But my lawyers would not suffer me to produce any evidence, when Counsel for the Crown gave up the prosecution; otherwise the public would have been in possession of several transactions in a far fuller manner than I can set forth at present. I was nine months confined before any charge on oath was made against me; and this, it must be thought, was sufficient time to bring forth any human conception, and ought then to have naturally entitled me to a political delivery.

The Grand Jury now found bills of indictment against me for high treason. There were several ladies and gentlemen at tea with me, and some of my fellow prisoners (who were afterward honourably acquitted) in the evening, when a gentleman came to visit me, as he had done several times before, and in the presence of the whole company, he declared that he had been *hooked in* to prosecute me. He mentioned, that while listening to the trials in the Court-house, he was summoned before the Grand Jury, where he was questioned about a conversation he had unguardedly held respecting me, which it was represented as his duty to swear to, and he was bound over to prosecute. He, however, imagined that what he had sworn could not injure me, and he then related to us many other circumstances that completely did away what he had said before the Grand Jury. Several others also came and informed me, that upon being summoned and sworn before this tribunal, they were asked if they knew anything concerning me during the Insurrection; and that they acknowledged they did with gratitude, as I had saved their lives or properties, or comforted them in one way or other in their afflictions. It was then put to them on their oaths whether I could do so without having great authority? But this they considered I had not, as they declared that it was for giving them information of their danger, and advising them how to act, they were indebted to me, and on stating that they knew nothing against me, they were dismissed. I was brought down to the Court-house to be arraigned, and when the indictment was read, I declared myself ready for trial upon getting a list of the witnesses to be produced against me. This Mr. Justice Chamberlain ordered to be given to me, but said I should not be tried those Assizes, and would not listen to any argument I could urge, but instantly remanded me back to gaol. I have been informed, and have good reason to believe, that my persecutors represented "they had not entertained an idea that I should not be transported, and were therefore totally unprepared to proceed against me; and that what made me so anxious to hurry on my trial was, that the evidence they had to produce against me was not in Wexford; but that, against the ensuing Assizes, they hoped to be able to convict me!"

Some time after this, in the summer of 1799, a distinguished gentleman of property, and constant Grand Juror of the County of Wexford, mentioned publicly in the canal passage boat on his way to Dublin, that "Mr. Hay wanted several times to be tried by Court-Martial, which was unfortunately prevented, as a military tribunal would pay too much attention to ladies and officers as witnesses for Mr. Hay; but that a Wexford jury would not be so squeamish. It was a providential circumstance that Mr. Hay had himself demanded a trial by jury, as it would inevitably prove *fatal* to him, instead of the boon of transportation intended for him." This and many such declarations the assertors are since ashamed of.

On all occasions that I possibly can, I avoid mentioning names, as I consider several have been led into error, through party prejudice, which compliment I hope may secure the concurrence of many gentlemen in promoting union and harmony among all descriptions of their countrymen. I regret the character of an historian obliges me to mention some, however, on my part, free from any intention of personality or offence, but a correct statement of facts from authorities I deemed undeniable. However, should I have been led into any involuntary error, and if any gentleman should think himself injured, I shall be proud to be undeceived, and shall be happy on a candid investigation to do ample justice to him, by declaring truth in the most conspicuous manner. On the other hand, the times have been such, that I have omitted many at their own request, whose meritorious actions might be recorded to their honour, which, along with other unavoidable wants, may, when prejudice is dissipated, be published at a future period.

Six magistrates of the county afterwards formed themselves into an inquisitorial court, consisting of the Right Hon. George Ogle, James Boyd, Richard Newton King, Edward Perceval, Ebenezer Jacob, M.D.; and John Henry Lyster, Esqrs. They assembled at the house of James Boyd, and summoned hundreds before them, whom they swore to give such information as they could concerning the rebellion. About fifty persons have informed me, that they were principally questioned concerning me, and upon their acknowledging that they were indebted to me for life, property, or consolation, as the case may have been, they were strictly questioned, evidently with a view to criminate me, whether I could have done so without great power or authority with the insurgents; but the consciences of these persons on their oaths did not warrant them to make such a deduction; and on being finally interrogated whether they knew anything against me, and their answering in the negative, they were dismissed. These persons also informed me, that they had heard several others to declare, that they had been questioned about me, and even some who had no personal knowledge of me whatsoever; so that I have strong reason to believe, that no means were left untried to criminate me. My conduct has certainly undergone stricter investigation than that of any other person in Ireland, and such, as I believe, that of the most unexceptionable of my persecutors would not pass through unblemished; while mine is irreproachable in the utmost degree, having passed with unimpeached honour the ordeal of the Wexford inquisition. We read of nothing that has gone such lengths in foreign countries. Even the inquisitors are by duty and oath to seek out all evidence as well for as against their prisoners!

The Summer Assizes, in 1799, began in Wexford on Monday the 24th of July, and being brought up that day to be arraigned, I was asked whether I was ready for trial. This question, I said, I would answer when furnished with a list of the witnesses to be produced against me. This Baron Smith (now Sir Michael Smith, Master of the Rolls), the sitting judge, ordered to be delivered to me, and it was sent to me that evening by Mr. William Harvey, the Agent for the Crown. On receipt of this I sent off several witnesses whom I had summoned, but for whose attendance I now considered myself to have no occasion. At last my long wished for trial came forward, on Thursday the 27th of July, and although I was advised that I might have availed myself of the defectiveness of the indictment in point of form, and although I might also have protected myself by the Amnesty Act, if necessary, yet I disdained to adopt such subterfuges, and declared myself ready to meet the whole of the charges against me. Two only, out of the four witnesses named to me, were brought forward; but their cross-examination completely did away anything injurious that could be inferred from their direct testimony. One of these was William Carty, the informer, who afterwards pleaded guilty to an indictment for murder, and was condemned to death, which sentence, in consideration of his services, was commuted for transportation to Botany Bay; and although half what he had sworn was false, and invented to criminate me, yet in the event it turned out so much to my honour, that my counsel thought it not necessary to impeach his credit, which I was well prepared to do, he being the principal evidence for the Crown.

Although it be obvious to infer, that furnishing me with a list of the witnesses, was a palpable consent to produce no others against me but those named therein, yet on the disappointment of the failure in the evidence of the two first, other witnesses, not named in the list with which I was furnished, were produced; and the most material of them was sworn of the jury then trying me; and to him I certainly would have objected, had I not been thrown off my guard by the trick practised for that purpose. I was, therefore, totally unprepared to rebut or explain any evidence he might offer, as, on receiving the list, I had sent off witnesses whose testimony would have particularly borne upon anything he could allege. I must, however, excuse Counsellor O'Driscol, the leading Counsel for the Crown, from having any concern in this vile transaction, as he most honourably declared, that he was astonished I had not been furnished with this man's name, as the purport of his evidence was set forth in his brief, which he held up and pointed to; however, he said duty obliged him to insist upon his being examined, for that although it was the privilege of prisoners accused of high treason in England, that no other witnesses but those named in the lists furnished, should be produced against them, yet the law did not entitle them to such an indulgence in Ireland. Notwithstanding all these disadvantages, I was honourably acquitted. Baron Smith declared in his charge, that I had undergone the most virulent persecution, that my loyalty was unimpeachable, and that if the jury attempted to find me guilty, as some juries had acted contrary to law and justice at those Assizes in Wexford, I might take advantage of the Amnesty Bill, by moving arrest of judgment, and that I should be instantly discharged, so that they might as well give me at once the acquittal I deserved.

I walked about the town publicly that evening, and on the ensuing days, until the judges and lawyers left Wexford on the conclusion of the Assizes. On Saturday evening, the 29th of July, however, General Grose arrested me in the street, and gave me in charge to the gaoler, then along with him. I remonstrated; but was informed by the General, that it was represented to him, that he could not leave me at liberty until he knew the Lord Lieutenant's pleasure, as the Secretary's Warrant, by which I was before detained, had been directed to him. I urged my honourable acquittal, which the General acknowledged, but still he would not leave me at liberty. I then requested, that, if he considered it necessary to detain me, he would make the town my prison, and might consider my honour as his best security, but that I would procure him any other security he would require. This request was not complied with, and I was conducted back to my former situation in the gaol, and lodged there without any kind of indulgence above any other prisoner. After a lapse of four days, however, the General permitted me to walk out, followed by a military sergeant. A near relation of mine, on my arrest, set off for Waterford where the astonishment of all the gentlemen of the Leinster Bar was excited upon hearing of my apprehension after such an acquittal as that of which they had been witnesses, particularly Counsellor O'Driscol, the leading Counsel for the Crown on my trial, who offered to prove and substantiate my honourable acquittal in any manner that my lawyers might suggest. A memorial to the Lord Lieutenant was now framed in my behalf, referring to Baron (now Sir Michael Smith, Master of the Rolls), and to Justice Chamberlain, for the truth of its contents; and praying that no reference should be made to the Wexford gentry, who had already alleged so many falsehoods against me, but to any liberal man, of independent mind, at all acquainted with the circumstances of my case. This memorial was presented to his Excellency Marquis Cornwallis, by the Earl of Donoughmore, at whose residence he was then on a visit. The consequence was, that orders were immediately sent to General Grose to liberate me, and I was then released from a confinement altogether of thirteen months.

I went to England in November, 1799, and remained there until the month of February, 1800. Four days after my arrival in Ireland, a forged letter was written in my name to Doctor Jacob, in so ungentlemanly a style as I hope I shall never be guilty of, against the measure of the Union. This letter was also one of the dark contrivances of my persecutors (who have never come forward against me in an open or manly manner), and was evidently fabricated in order to get me confined, and this I fortunately discovered time enough to prevent its execution. A Member of Parliament, belonging to a strong party in favour of the Union, luckily for me, drank a little more than ordinary, and declared that he understood I had spent some time in England, where I had paid visits to noblemen of the first distinction, and had concerted plans against the Union. These sentiments of opposition I had luckily discovered in a letter to Doctor Jacob, but that I should be taken care of and secured; that certainly my talent for procuring signatures could not be denied, but that I should have no opportunity of exerting it, as I should be taken up to prevent the danger to be apprehended from my opposition in the County of Wexford. This plot I had the good fortune to discover, as the information was conveyed to me with all the anxiety of friendship, and I found it to be but too true. My object then was to wait on persons of distinction, well acquainted with my determination, *as a Catholic, not to interfere about the Union*, and I was promised their utmost interest and protection, should any sinister measure against me be attempted. Without this precaution against an intended blow, of which my friend got intelligence by mere accident, I should have been taken up and confined without knowing why or wherefore; as it was touching Government at the time in the tenderest point; and had the appearance of *zeal for the Union* under the mask of the basest imposition. I now wrote to Doctor Jacob to send me the letter, that it might enable me to find out its author, but was not favoured with an answer, although I had learned that the doctor had declared that I did not write the letter, which, I believe, he perfectly knew on receiving it. An officer, who was a friend of mine, was going down to the Spring Assizes of Wexford, in April, 1800, and I commissioned him to wait on the doctor, to let him know, that if he would not produce the letter, I should consider him as its author and treat him accordingly. In consequence of this, the doctor condescended to write to me, excusing himself for not having answered my letters sooner, not being able to find the forgery, which he then enclosed to me; the author I have not yet been able to discover.*

This is a curious specimen of party prejudice. Those who had influence could have any one for whom they entertained a personal dislike, taken upon the score of public justice; and too many instances of the kind occurred, suggested by private malice. The circumstance of my discovering this letter in time was rather fortunate, as it secured me powerful support in case of any future attempt. The times were such, however, that I considered it better to be peculiarly cautious and circumspect, to prevent the possibility of my actions being misrepresented; and I even thought it prudent to overlook many things which I should have properly noticed at any other period. But, as I had dreadful experience of the hardship of confinement, I was not willing to risk again being in the same pre-

---

* SIR,—Allow me to acknowledge the favour of two letters from you on the subject of one which I some time since received from Dublin, to which your name was, as I am convinced, forged; if I could sooner have found the forgery, I should have immediately, according to your desire, enclosed it to you.

I am, Sir,
April 20th, 1800. Your obedient humble servant,
EBEN. JACOB.
To EDWARD HAY, Esq.

dicament, although I could defy the utmost malice of my enemies, if they would dare openly to avow themselves; but during the suspension of the *Habeas Corpus* Act, no man could be secure from the rancour of party spirit, which I fear it will still take much time to allay, before numbers are brought back to their sober senses. I have had constant opportunities of observing the baleful effects of being led away by party. I have known men, whom I believe to be naturally well inclined, if their dispositions were not warped by the virulence of such companions as they think it necessary to associate with, lest their loyalty may be otherwise impeached, join in acts of outrage and excess; varying their conduct according to the temper of their associates, or the circumstances that may occur, and condescending now and again to speak only to individuals whom it was happy for them to meet in the hour of misfortune, and to whom they owe any share of character they still retain; but so lost to all sense of gratitude, that the mere condescension of speaking is never exhibited in the presence of certain individuals, or where there may be any possibility of its being observed by such characters. As for myself, I was so calumniated and reviled during my confinement, when I had not the power of counteraction, that evil rumour wrought so much on some of my former acquaintances as to occasion their assuming the appearance of not knowing me; but I was even with them in pitying their pusillanimity and littleness. I was well prepared for such occurrences, and I have made it an invariable rule with myself, not to appear to know any former acquaintances, until first known by them; considering that my misfortunes entitle me to the first compliment; and some have after a time returned to former civility, and excused themselves on being undeceived, as having being misled by false information. Indeed the spirit of mistaken loyalty was so zealous, that it induced many to fabricate lies which required numberless others to support them. Nay, the public mind was so led astray, that truth itself, by various misconstructions, was perverted into absolute falsehood. I remember on my first coming to Dublin after my acquittal, that several persons told me how distressing it was to them to hear many falsehoods related of particular instances of which they had themselves been witnesses, but which their timidity prevented them from contradicting. On my mentioning that I would not act in a manner that might sanction falsehood, by remaining silent in the presence of its known assertors, I was entreated not to give them as authority.

I have afterward chanced to fall into company with these retailers of fabricated reports, and on my mentioning facts as they happened, but which I was informed they had previously misrepresented, they remained as silent as those who some time before were overawed by their arrogance. Others of my acquaintance anxiously inquiring about the heroism and magnanimity of their friends, have been vastly disappointed at my not confirming the accounts they had before received, and my being in truth obliged to declare the contrary. Upon being informed that the facts were reported quite otherwise, I always answered by expressing a desire to be confronted with the narrators, where it would be easy to judge who told truth. So many and so various have the impositions on the public been, that it is truly astonishing how such a compilation of falsehoods could be fabricated and heaped together; and it would, indeed, be a Herculean task to attempt to answer them, as it would in general take ten times the extent of a false story to disprove and set it aside; so that it would be too tedious and tiresome for public perusal, and would prove an endless source of controversy and contradiction. I therefore do not enter the lists against any one, but endeavour to give a true statement of what has happened, without attempting to palliate or falsify; and I request the reader to consider that I have been an eye-witness of some of the principal events, and therefore could not readily be imposed upon. I have, besides, the corroboration of persons of all parties to support me in such a manner as to prove convincing to every one inclined to hearken to truth; and I am sure it must prove grateful to every benevolent mind to be convinced, that all the horrors perpetrated in the year 1798 were the consequence of party prejudice, now generally supposed to have been urged forward from political motives to weaken the country, by setting the people by the ears. Troops were at first employed, as it were to crush disturbances, in order to put down one party; and those on the other side were not aware of their situation until a power was established superior to all parties; and the bitterest complaints have been made by the opposers of the Union, that they themselves contributed most without knowing it until it was too late, to carry that measure. A dissertation on the Union is not my present object; I only want to make all ranks and degrees of my countrymen sensible that union and harmony among themselves will prevent the possibility of their being put down by any power on earth. Every point of view in which this desirable object is put, must contribute to show its heavenly principle, and I hope this may have due weight to cause sincere endeavours for its accomplishment.

What I consider most lamentable in Ireland is the dreadful prevalence of religious prejudice and its baleful consequences. This is so inculcated, even in infancy, that it is scarcely to be eradicated by any future conviction or experience, however evident its mischief and absurdity. I shall endeavour to exemplify this by a comparison, of the aptness of which everyone must be sensible. Among the many odious and lamentable impressions made on the tender minds of children, when in the care of ignorant and illiterate persons, none is so general as the terror of ghosts and hobgoblins, related to make them obedient. Although this all-powerful remedy may for the moment diminish the trouble of the keepers by making the children more subservient, yet it often prevents the parents from coming to the knowledge of any thing it may dictate. I believe it has come within the observation of everyone that there are persons of the most undoubted courage who would be afraid to go up stairs in the dark, although they would face a cannon in the day-time; and of this weakness they cannot divest themselves, although they may be long convinced of the absurdity of such notions; for so deep a root do false ideas take in the infant mind, that mature good sense and conviction are unable to shake off their shackles. So it is with all early impressions. How lamentable then is it to inculcate prejudice in the tender mind of youth, so as to make them imbibe bigoted sentiments almost with their milk; enslaving their understanding in such a manner, that it can scarcely ever become free from their influence. I venture to hope that this admonition may have the effect of making parents endeavour to prevent their children from being led astray by such hateful impressions in early life, that they may be brought to maturity unbiassed by any prejudice, and thus may judge of things impartially of which they must be otherwise utterly incapable. Parents cannot be so selfish as not to wish their children as much happiness as possible, or as they can at all procure them, and to this it materially contributes (and it is a duty incumbent on all who have the care of children) to prevent false impressions. Should this salutary precept be carefully attended to, we may hope to see the rising generation grow up free of those prejudices which have, unfortunately for Ireland, produced such dreadful consequences. What a melancholy reflection is it that any person should be reared and educated with the belief that the great majority of his countrymen have vowed his destruction! Does not such a conception naturally inculcate all kind of distrust, blasting all confidence, and destroying the happiness that would result from harbouring more charitable opinions? Such notions it is not at all wonderful to find strongly rooted in vulgar minds, that have not had the benefit of a good education; but it is truly a national grievance, that men of the first rank and rearing should be brought up with such horrid and absurd prejudices. I have heard some of the most dignified and exalted personages in Ireland declare that great pains had been taken in the course of their education to impress their minds with an inveterate dislike to Roman Catholics; and that so forcibly dictated were these bigoted precepts, that they firmly believed them to be true, and that it was not without great exertion of mind they were afterwards able to bring themselves to keep company with people of that communion. The terrors, however, diminished by more frequent intercourse, and in proportion as this was cultivated, they became sensible of the inculcated error and of the absurdity of the prejudice against their countrymen, and at length became the greatest supporters of the Catholic cause. As for myself, although I now profess the Roman Catholic religion, I should not be of that communion one single hour were the principles such as they are represented; but Catholics, I know, abhor and detest the principles that prejudice has thought proper to attribute to them. Had those absurdities any other than a speculative existence in the minds of fanciful and designing men, wishing to bring public sentiment to second their views, would the Parliament have voted a free exercise of their religion? If Catholics did not reverence oaths, what could keep them from enjoying the honours of the State, since an oath would completely qualify them ? Or, if they were as represented, would such monsters be suffered to exist, instead of being protected and cherished by King, Lords, and Commons? I will only observe that the greatest villains and hypocrites generally assume the mask of religion, as the robber does that of honesty, in order to cover sinister design; and they are both, for private advantage, adepts in the art of deception. History furnishes too many dreadful examples of the shocking effects of religious bigotry; but it is the misapplication of religion, and not its essential principles, that urge inordinate fury. Of this we have had a striking example in our own days The riots in London in 1780, when the mob was unquestionably composed of Protestants and Dissenters, forming an immense multitude, were excited for the avowed destruction of Pope and Popery. It was impossible that their views could be mistaken, as they proceeded not only in avowed enmity to the Catholics themselves, by destroying their property, by burning their houses and places of worship, but they even demolished the houses of Members of Parliament who had supported a Bill previously passed for the relief of the Catholics of England; and, although the same spirit was manifested at Edinburgh, Bath, Bristol, and other parts of England, yet the Parliament did not seem aware of the object of the rabble. The last riots in Birmingham are also of the same nature, and tend to prove that religion is only the pretext generally assumed to cover the greatest enormities; but it is not all to be inferred that the religion of any Christian sect inculcates such principles as their adherents exhibit by their actions, otherwise it might be said with equal feasibility that the Christian religion encourages sin, because Christians commit sin; but the parable of the good Samaritan, one would think, should do away all prejudice between all sorts of Christians. Were I absurd enough to advance that the Protestant religion inculcated the destruction of Catholics, and that it could be clearly demonstrated from many examples, but particularly could be adduced from the acts and avowals of the people of the capital of the Church of England, as before stated, I think I should be more justifiable than those who venture to assert (what is very astonishing that many are led to believe) that Catholics are vowed for the destruction of Protestants. In the transactions even of the year 1798 in the County of Wexford such a principle was not maintained, but the contrary manifested by every public avowal; but in different parts of England and Scotland, and in Ireland itself, in the County of Armagh, in the year 1795, dreadful sentiments appeared against Catholics. There are truly individual monsters of all parties who would destroy everyone not of their own way of thinking, were they not restrained in their evil inclinations by fear or force; and their principles are unfortunately too widely diffused, and encouraged by those who, without actually committing murder themselves, frequently occasion its committal by subtle assertion and implication of principles too dreadful to be admitted among Christians!

I shall not by any means pretend to excuse any bad action, let it originate from what cause it may; and, although I maintain that the Catholic religion inculcates the principles of charity and general morality as much as any other on earth, I shall condemn the bad actions of Catholics as much, if not more, than those of any other religious persuasion. My whole object in giving this account to the public is to promote union and harmony, as much as it lies in my power, among all descriptions of my countrymen; and if I knew of any other and better mode to effect this desirable object, I certainly would adopt it. But I conceive it mainly necessary to give an account of what I think I am master of now, and for this reason it is that I confine myself for the present to the County of Wexford, where, quite contrary to my inclinations and wishes, I was so critically placed as to be an eye-witness of what passed. But this enables me now to be the better judge of hearsay evidence, let it come from what quarter it may; and I hope my execution of this sketch will procure such satisfactory intelligence as will enable me to give a general history of Ireland, with the causes leading to elucidate the events of that unfortunate period of 1798. To accomplish this, I call on my countrymen in general for assistance; and, although it would be impossible for me to relate every transaction that happened, it will, however, be necessary that I shall be in possession of many occurrences that may tend to prove the leading features of a general account; for particular instances, though not recited, will hold their place essentially upon a general principle. I trust this will prove a sufficient apology to those who have favoured me with documents, which the limits of my present work would not permit me to give at full length; however, their advantage and use in the compilation have been very great; so that what might, at first view, appear a trivial circumstance, I shall be glad to have an opportunity of perusing. I also hope that the precaution I have already recommended may be used: of sending it to a friend in Dublin, who may be good enough to apply to my printer, where my address may be known and forwarded to me without any disappointment, where, on delivery, he may get it inserted in a book, which is to be kept for that purpose, with his address as well as that of the writer, in order, that if any further explanation should be required, I may not be at a loss where to apply. All this precaution is easy to be taken by such as may be kind enough to transmit matter of information; and what would be little trouble to each individual would save me immense labour in detail. I hope, therefore, I shall be excused for being so particular, as I wish to lose as little time as possible in contributing my mite for general information.

Had I not the conciliation of all my countrymen very much at heart, I should not venture on the arduous undertaking of giving a history of the present times. The various and contradictory materials produced by contending parties have existed to that degree that the same occurrence is represented, as prejudice and interest operate in as opposite views as light and darkness. I cannot hope to please partisans of any description, nor shall I attempt it. The cool and dispassionate philanthropist I flatter myself will approve of my intentions, and lend his assistance in endeavouring to dissipate the cloud of prejudice that has overpowered the good sense of many of my countrymen; and through those sentiments I may obtain the indulgence of the public, which I stand so much in need of.

Now that peace is established with all foreign powers, it behoves every well-disposed person to cultivate its blessings at home. I, therefore, hope this will induce many to step forward to promote my present undertaking. As for my own part, I confess I considered it prudent not to lay my account before the public until I was secure from the malevolence of those from whom I had good reason to apprehend danger, as my persecution might be renewed if I ventured to arraign the supposed justice and merits of my persecutors before I could be certain of not

e

being sacrificed to party spirit, which, I presume, I have sufficiently shown to have been violently and unwarrautably exerted against me; and if the account of it shall in any wise contribute to promote the union and consequent happiness of my countrymen, I shall endeavour to forget my sufferings in the blessings which such an event must ensure to Ireland.

HISTORY

OF THE

Irish Insurrection of 1798.

BEFORE entering on the narrative of the late insurrection in the county of Wexford—the causes that produced it, and its calamitous consequences—I think it necessary to give a general sketch of its geography and local circumstances, together with a short topographical outline of its boundaries, principal rivers, harbours, and remarkable places, to render references more easy and obvious; adding the estimate of its computed population in 1788, stated by Mr. Bushe, in the Transactions of the Royal Irish Academy, and published in 1790.

The county of Wexford is a maritime tract on the south-eastern coast of Ireland, taking the utmost limits within the fifty-third degree of north latitude, and between the sixth and seventh of longitude west from London; being about thirty-nine miles long, from north to south, and twenty-four broad, from west to east; bounded on the north mostly by the county of Wicklow, and in a very small part (towards the west) by the county of Carlow; on the east and south, by that part of the Atlantic Ocean, denominated the Irish Sea, or St. George's Channel; and on the west, from north to south, partly by the county of Carlow, and partly by the Barrow, a fine navigable river, deemed second only to the Shannon in Ireland, which divides it from the counties of Kilkenny and Waterford. In a direction from south-west to north-east, the boundaries of the county of Wexford, between it and the county of Carlow, are the long ridges of mountains called Black Stairs and Mount Leinster, which are divided by the defile of Scollagh-gap, the only high-road into it from the Barrow to the Slaney, at Newtownbarry, which, together with Clonegal two miles farther up, is situated partly in the county of Carlow, and partly in the county of Wexford; but, southward of the county of Wicklow, a chain of lofty mountains, opening with different defiles, rivers and high hills, form a strong natural barrier to the county of Wexford, which, thus physically fortified by sea and land, appears naturally formed into a district, which it has certainly been by all ancient divisions of the country, whether ecclesiastical, civil, or military. The bishopric of Ferns, one of the oldest in Ireland, founded in the latter end of the sixth century, is nearly co-extensive with the county, only a small strip of land about Carnew, in the county of Wicklow, forming a part of the diocese of Ferns, while the see of Glendalough includes two parishes in the neighbourhood of Coolgreny, in the county of Wexford. The English adventurers having first landed here under Fitzstephen, in the reign of Henry the Second of England, to assist in the restoration of M'Morragh, King of Leinster, it became the strongest military station of the invaders, while they were endeavouring to establish themselves in the country, and was one of the first demarked counties of the English Pale.

Wexford is sixty-four miles distant from Dublin, —called by the old natives Loch-Garmain, by the Danish invaders *Weifsford*, and after them by the English, Wexford,—is the capital, or shire and assizes town of the county, situated in a hollow beneath a rising hill, with a southern aspect, at the mouth of the beautiful river Slaney, which rises in the county of Wicklow, takes a southern direction, with little variation, from Newtownbarry, till it passes some miles below Enniscorthy, then shapes its course from west to east, and empties itself by the harbour of Wexford, into the Irish Sea, or St. George's Channel. This harbour is formed by two narrow necks of land, bending towards each other like two arms closing after an extension from the body, which appearance the river's mouth assumes by its banks, not very unlike the old Piræus of Athens. The extremities of these peninsulas, denominated the Raven on the north, and Roslare on the south, form the entrance into the harbour, which is about half a mile broad, defended by a fort erected at the point of Roslare. The harbour itself, in superficial appearance, and from the view of a delightfully expanded sheet of water, must be considered extremely beautiful; but unfortunately, it is so shallow, that vessels drawing more than eleven feet of water, cannot enter it, being impeded by a bar which is continually shifting. The harbour, however, is certainly capable of vast improvement; and, from its situation, attention to this object must prove of great national importance. Wexford was formerly possessed of some general traffic, but now it is nearly limited to the corn trade; and the manufacture of malt is so considerable, that this district was some years ago computed to produce one-fourth of the revenue raised on that article in Ireland. The town is surrounded by its ancient wall, still perfect, except at the public entrances, which have been broken down for public convenience. The ruins of churches and abbeys are to be seen, which, even in neglect and decay, exhibit marks of ancient magnificence; and the Protestant church, Roman

Catholic chapel, market-house, and barracks—buildings which are not inferior to those of other places, of equal, or perhaps superior importance. The general appearance of the town is, however, very indifferent, the streets being very narrow, and having but few good houses; yet it is in a state of improvement, and when the quay shall be filled in and well banked, an operation now in progress, it will, in all likelihood, induce people to pay more attention to the art of building, as the situation is inviting. The remarkable wooden bridge built in 1795, over the mouth of the Slaney, leading northward from the town, is undoubtedly a very great curiosity, being fifteen hundred and fifty-nine feet long, with a portcullis, and thirty-four feet wide through its whole extent, with a toll-house at each extremity. On each side are foot-ways, ornamented with Chinese railings supported by strong bars. There are also two recesses, with seats for shelter against sudden showers; for it is the *beau walk* of the town, and thus contributes much to the tolls collected to defray the expense of the building. About two miles up the river, there is also another wooden bridge with a portcullis, at a place called Carrig, where the first square castle built in Ireland was reared by Fitzstephen after the landing of Strongbow. Many other castles are to be seen throughout the county, particularly in the baronies of Forth and Bargy. There do not at present exist any traces of round towers; but there are innumerable Danish forts and raths. Wexford returns one member to the imperial Parliament.

Taghmon is on the road from Wexford to Ross, at the foot of the mountain of Forth. It lies inland, has a market, fairs, and a post-office, also the remains of an old castle, and is surrounded by good lands.

New Ross, sixty-seven miles from Dublin, and

nineteen west of Wexford, is situated on the Barrow, and well stationed for trade, in which it is rapidly improving, as well as in the appearance of the town itself, which has been greatly retarded from the want of proper encouragement. It is built on the side of a hill, commanding a beautiful view of the river, and part of the county of Kilkenny, the passage to which over it, is by a fine wooden bridge, from the upper part of the quay, with a portcullis, foot-ways, Chinese railings, and recesses in the centre. Here are the ruins of abbeys and some churches; part of one of the latter now forms the Protestant church. The old town walls were standing until lately, and their partial destruction was much regretted on the attack of the insurgents in June, 1798. It returns a member to Parliament.

Enniscorthy lies fifty-eight miles from Dublin, fifteen from Ross, eleven from Wexford by land, and fourteen by the windings of the Slaney which waters it, and whose banks are unrivalled in beauty; but it is to be lamented that its navigation has not been attended to, as at a small expense, it could be so improved as to render Enniscorthy a very flourishing town, which also feels the disadvantage of not possessing the fostering care of a resident landlord. It would be a most excellent situation for carrying on any kind of manufacture. When woods were in greater abundance in Ireland, it was remarkable for its iron works, some of which are still existing near it; there now remain the extensive woods of Kilaughram in its neighbourhood. The town now exhibits a melancholy picture of the devastation consequent on civil war, being mostly destroyed during the insurrection in 1798, which, among other effects, has occasioned its not being, what it otherwise would have been, one of the representative towns of Ireland. A fine old castle is still in tolerable repair, and the town is rebuilding very fast.

Gorey or Newborough is forty-two miles from Dublin, nine from Arklow, twenty-two miles north of Wexford, and fifteen from Enniscorthy. It lies inland, has little or no trade, but what arises from fairs and markets, and is a post-town.

Ferns lies six miles from Enniscorthy, and nine from Gorey ; is a Bishop's See, since the Reformation united to Leighlin in the Protestant, but never annexed in the Catholic Church. It was founded by St. Maod'og (pronounced by the inhabitants, and written at this day, St. Mogue), in reverence of whom the primacy of Leinster was transferred to it from Kildare, towards the latter end of the sixth century. Part of the very large old church, now grand even in ruin, dedicated to him as first bishop, constitutes the present cathedral. His sepulchre is even still preserved and in good repair, in part of the parent church, having been rescued from obscurity by one of the late bishops. The episcopal palace is contiguous to the town, and is its principal ornament. Here also stand the ruins of an abbey, and of the memorable castle of Dermod M'Morragh, King of Leinster, whither, as his principal residence, he retired with the beauteous and fatal Dervorgal, daughter of O'Malfechlin, King of Meath, and wife of O'Rorke, Prince of Breifny, now denominated the county of Leitrim, from whom, by every wily contrivance, he is said to have seduced and persuaded her to elope with him, which eventually produced one of the most momentous epochs, as marked with one of the greatest and most serious revolutions, that occurs in the history of Ireland, producing a complete and total change in its laws, customs, government, and proprietors; and, to a great extent, even in its population ; and, finally, in our own days, in its imperial dominion and independence. This libertine and licentious deed introduced the adventuring Anglo-Norman chiefs, at the head of the Welsh or British and English invaders; who, by long and persevering efforts, established a transcendent ascendency in Ireland. For Dermod, odious as notorious for other acts of tyranny and violence, attracted, by this flagitious crime, the aggravated execration and resentment of Roderic O'Connor, the reigning monarch, as well as of all the other chiefs and princes of the land; who, making common cause against the execrable outrage, forced him out of the island, whither he ere long returned, introducing those invaders (from one of whom I am myself descended), who ultimately succeeded in its utter reduction. Hence it cannot be fantastical to deem in similitude, Dermod the Paris, Dervorgal the Helen, Ferns the Troy, and the Anglo-Norman and Welsh adventurers, the Greeks of Ireland; and were there another Homer in existence, he might rejoice in having a second equivalent subject to display anew his powers. At all events, the Irish have to exclaim in sympathy with the Trojans in Virgil, from a similarity of circumstances—

"——— fuimus Troes, fuit Ilium et ingens
Gloria Teucrorum ———."

"For there were Irish—they possessed dominion—they were greatly renowned—but they are now no more!"

The English, when established in the baronies of Forth and Bargy, willing to extend their dominion over the whole county of Wexford, encountered very vigorous resistance. Forced by various oppressions, the natives rose under a youthful hero of the ancient royal blood, Arthur M'Murchad O'Cavanagh, who defeated them in several rencounters, and brought the Pale to the verge of destruction. On this occasion, Richard II. of England hastened to its assistance with forty thousand men; but foiled and defeated by the Leinster chieftain, he was glad to purchase present safety by a dishonourable peace; and, perhaps, this expedition was the cause of his losing both life and crown. The chiefs of the Pale, after repeated and fruitless contests, in which the best English generals were defeated, thought themselves happy in obtaining toleration to remain in Ireland, on condition of paying a yearly tribute to the chieftain of Leinster. This tax is well known under the name of Black Rent, which continued to be paid until the reign of Henry VIII. In fine, the inhabitants of that quarter of Ireland including Wexford, were always remarkable for their bravery; and, in latter times, the Wexfordians had the firmness and courage to resist Cromwell, after the rest of the island was intimidated, partly by the fame, and partly by the experience of his cruelties and victories.

Were it not for these circumstances, Ferns would at present excite little consideration, being otherwise mean and of little importance.

Bunclody, now Newtownbarry, is situated partly in the county of Wexford, and partly in the county of Carlow, forty-nine miles from Dublin, and ten north of Enniscorthy, on the Slaney, where the situation is admirably beautiful; and although Newtownbarry cannot assume the name of a town, in its strictest sense, it is incomparable as a village. Its importance in a military point of view, pronounces it one of the principal keys of the county of Wexford.

Feathard, Bannow, and Clomines, were boroughs, but long since have fallen into decay; the silver and lead mines in their neighbourhood, when worked, made them of some consequence. The high and extensive mountains of Black Stairs and Mount Leinster, already mentioned, separate the county of Carlow from the county of Wexford; as Croghan mountain, with others of inferior note, divide the latter from the county of Wicklow. Within the county itself are the mountains of Forth, between Wexford and Taghmon; as are Camarus, Carrigbyrne, Slieykeltra, and Brie, between Ross, Taghmon, and Enniscorthy; Slieye-buy, which rises conically, and Carrigrew, near Ferns, and Tara Hill, north of Gorey; intermixed with several small hills and eminences, forming an undulative appearance, in such a manner that no part of the county can be termed level, except the baronies of Forth and Bargy, south of the town of Wexford. On the southern coast are two bays, of little note but their superficial appearance—those of Ballytiegue and Bannow, into the latter of which runs the river of that name, which is passable at the point called the Scar, at low water. The Saltee Islands, round which there is a considerable lobster and crab fishery, and which in the times of falconry were famous for producing the most excellent hawks, lie nine miles off the coast, opposite the bay of Ballytiegue. Duncannon fort is a military station on the shore, commanding the entrance of the Barrow, of which and the Slaney there is sufficient mention and observation made already; and surely of *"Bannow's banks"* we have heard enough. On the Barrow are three ferries, between the county of Wexford and those of Kilkenny and Waterford: the two first are, one at Mountgarret, above Ross, and another at Ballinlaw, below Ross, into the county of Kilkenny; the third is below the confluence of the Suir and Barrow, between the trifling villages of Ballyhack, in the county of Wexford, and Passage, in the county of Waterford. The Bann rises in the county of Wicklow, passes by Ferns, and joins the Slaney above Enniscorthy.

Lough Tra, or the Lake of the Ladies' Island, is very singularly circumstanced; it receives into its bosom two or three small rivulets, whose currents, however, are not strong enough to force a passage in opposition to a powerful tide rushing directly against them, and continually drifting quicksand, which accumulates so as to form the southern bank of the lake. This every three or four years occasions an inundation of the adjacent country, obliging the people with vast labour to open a way through the mound for the collected waters to disembogue; but this is soon choked up again by the like agglomeration as before. The lake of Tacumshin is nearly adjoining, but the currents with which it is supplied not being so abundant as the former, the task of letting out the waters does not occur for many years together.

The ruins of several abbeys appear throughout the county; but those that preserve the greatest remains of magnificence are, Dunbrody, Tintern, and one in Wexford, founded by the Earl of Pembroke, Fitzstephen, and De Moresco. From this stock the family of Morres in Ireland claims descent. In Wexford there were two other abbeys also. The rest we take in the order of precedence from the best authorities. Clomines; Dune, on the little river Derry; the abbey of St. Mary's in Ferns; St. Mary's of Glass-carrig, or Green rock, on the sea-coast; Horetown, near Fookes's-mill; one at Enniscorthy, and another at the village of St. John's, not far distant from that town; Kilclogan, on the Barrow, below Dunbrody; and two at Ross, of Minorets and Augustins.

The county of Wexford contains eight baronies—

namely, Gorey, Scarawalsh, Ballaghkeen, Bantry, Shelmaliere, Shelburne, Bargy, and Forth, in which are one hundred and forty-two parishes; and the acreable extent of the whole is computed to be three hundred and forty-two thousand nine hundred, or five hundred and thirty-five square miles. Its population, according to Mr. Bushe's estimate, taking the houses to be twenty-thousand four hundred and forty-eight, is one hundred and thirty-two thousand nine hundred and twelve inhabitants. The town of Wexford itself contains one thousand four hundred and twelve houses, and upwards of nine thousand souls; but I apprehend the population is underrated by Mr. Bushe, as I hope to be enabled to show at a future period.

The county of Wexford has been long remarkable for the peaceable demeanour of its inhabitants; and their good behaviour and industry have been held out as exemplary for other parts of Ireland; so little and so seldom infested with disturbance or riots of any kind, that an execution for a capital crime rarely took place there; and in the calendar of its criminals, it has as few on record as any part either of Great Britain or Ireland. This county bore such reputation, that landed property was considered of higher value in it, than in many other parts of this country; purchasers not hesitating to advance some years' rental more for lands in the county of Wexford, than for the like in most other parts of Ireland. Even at the time that different parts of the nation were disturbed by the riots of Whiteboys, etc., they scarcely made their appearance here, owing to the vigilance and exertions of the gentlemen of the county. These formed an armed association at Enniscorthy, for the preservation of the peace, under the command of Sir Vesey Colclough; and this association afterwards became a corps of Volunteers, the first of the kind in the land; and thus can the county of Wexford boast of having set the example, and of being the first to promote the illustrious institution of the Volunteers of Ireland. Having set so conspicuous a precedent, the Volunteers of the county of Wexford, by their printed resolutions, fully coincided with those of all other parts of the nation; and, in the spirit of the times, adopted the memorable resolutions of the meeting at Dungannon, and sent their deputation to the grand provincial meeting of Leinster, assembled at the guild-hall in the Tholsel of Dublin, on Thursday, the 9th of October, 1783, and afterwards to the general convention of the Volunteers of Ireland, held at the Rotunda on the 10th of November following.

The liberality of the times invited men of all persuasions to the Volunteer ranks—Catholics stood by their Protestant fellow-soldiers in the glorious cause, and proved themselves worthy of the liberal confidence that dictated their admission, which the existing laws did not strictly sanction. Amidst this general spirit of toleration, however, I am sorry to remark that there was no admission for a Catholic among the Volunteers of the county of Wexford—a circumstance the more remarkable, as it was the only county in Ireland that exclusively held up this prejudice. There were, indeed, some Catholic gentlemen of the county of Wexford Volunteers; but they belonged to corps in other counties, and on this account their number was but inconsiderable, as few of them could undergo the expense, or waste the time necessary for attending meetings out of their own county; and thus the great body were prevented from manifesting their sentiments to the extent of their wishes. This exclusion, as unwise as impolitic, must be attributed to that bane of society, the odious prejudice of religious bigotry, so generally inculcated in early youth, and blended with education; which sad experience proves to have been so fatal to the interest of Ireland, the perpetual bar to her otherwise infallible prosperity. If men would but so far divest themselves of prejudice, and indulge sentiments of Christian charity, as not to avoid the society of their fellow-men on account of a difference in religious opinion, the great advantage would be soon perceptible. It would be quickly found, that uncharitable principles could not be cherished by any denomination of people professing the religion of peace and love—the delusion would vanish, and the unhallowed monster of bigotry and prejudice would soon be abhorred and abandoned. Every man of serious and feeling mind must think it a very awful misfortune to be born and reared in a country, where the great majority of the people is an object of hatred and horror to most of the superior order. A person of high rank, entertaining unfavourable sentiments of a community, must prove a horrible scourge to a nation. The balance of justice may be placed in his hands, while his prejudice must inevitably prevent its impartial administration; for it is the nature of prejudice to warp and supersede all other affections, so far even as to pervert the fair dictates of moral truth and of mild and generous humanity. Alas! that Ireland should verify the reflection! But let our regret avert our contemplation, and direct our view to better prospects.

Since the time of volunteering, till of late, nothing very remarkable happened in the county of Wexford. It continued to flourish from the memorable period of 1782 with the same progressive improvement of the nation at large, still holding up its pre-eminence in the value of landed property. The peasantry were certainly more comfortably situated here than in most parts of Ireland south of Dublin, but far from enjoying the happiness experienced by the like class of people in other countries; and although their condition was less wretched than that of the greater portion of their countrymen, yet this amelioration must be attributed more to their own industry, than to any encouragement or indulgence of their landlords. Many gentlemen becoming needy by dissipation and extravagance, feel indispensable necessity to support accustomed luxury by wresting occasional supplies from the hard labour of a wretched and dependent tenantry, whose calamitous appearance (enough to send horror to the soul of humanity) is unnoticed in the general view of misery and distress which Ireland exhibits as a singular and melancholy spectacle to the world. Such are the men who detest the simple hind that cultivates their lands, and who calumniate to other countries the subdued and crawling peasant of their own—whose ears are to be gratified, whose hearts are cheerfully delighted by a defamatory, rancorous, and indiscriminate reviling of their countrymen—calumnies that, if directed against their fellow-natives, would excite horror and indignation in the breasts of the gentry of any other country in Europe, or perhaps on the globe.

In Ireland, a good and kind landlord is a rare blessing; and a traveller, in his passage through the country, must readily distinguish the fostering care and benevolent superintendence of such, wherever to be found. It is easy to gain the affections of the warm-hearted Irish. If a person of rank deigns but to pay them those attentions which are accounted but common care of the lower classes in other countries, he is universally beloved; and on his approach delight beams on the countenance of the neighbourhood around him; so that it is much to be wondered at, that more are not found to purchase at so easy a rate the love and attachment of a generous and ingenuous people. This, however, the generality of landlords forfeit for a rack-rent on their lands; and not unfrequently even some who may feel a better disposition, see their lands occupied by a still more miserable peasantry if possible, and incur equal disgrace with the unrelenting, by parcelling out, to support a false consequence, their estates in freeholds to middle-men—a set of harpies so hardened, as to view with the coldest unconcern the most distressing scenes of misery; who hold it meritorious to wrest the last farthing from the toilsome and laborious industry of starved and naked wretchedness. This evil was most severely felt by the Catholics, who could not, till very lately, become freeholders; and the grievance arose from their being deprived of the right of elective franchise, which constituted the lower Protestants middle-men. By the restoration of this right, however, it is to be hoped that, by degrees, as leases shall fall in to the landlords, they will be induced, even by self-interest, to multiply their freeholders, by setting their lands to the occupiers of the soil; and this will prevent the intercourse of landlord and tenant from being intercepted by the hated interference of the odious tribe of middle-men, and restore some degree of comfort and happiness to the people at large.

Some years ago, the proprietors of land in the baronies of Forth and Bargy determined themselves to farm the soil occupied by their tenants, who were on this account obliged to seek out new situations in other parts of the county of Wexford. Their approved mode of tillage was soon adopted in the several neighbourhoods where they settled, and through them a new spirit of industry was generally diffused, and the face of the country assumed an appearance of much superior advantage to its former state. For although the county of Wexford produces vast quantities of grain, particularly barley, it is obtained more through the industry of the cultivators, than from the fertility of the soil, whose barrenness is overcome by the labour and exertions of the inhabitants. The baronies of Forth and Bargy are occupied by the descendants of an English colony, who came over with Strongbow in the reign of Henry II. They have ever since, in the course of upwards of six hundred years, lived entirely, with little or no admixture, within themselves. Until of late years it was a rare thing to find a man among them that had ever gone farther from home than Wexford. They have even preserved their language, probably without alteration or improvement, as may be presumed, if not absolutely concluded from this fact—that although there was no regular intercourse kept up between these and a sister colony from Wales, who at the same time settled at Fingal in the county of Dublin, and have continued of similar unmixed habits, yet upon the accidental meeting of individuals from both places, they can completely understand each other.

Early in the year 1792, the Catholics of Ireland were invited by a circular letter, inserted in the public papers, signed Edward Byrne, to depute from all the counties and principal towns, delegates, to meet in Dublin to frame a petition to the king for a redress of the grievances under which they laboured. The Catholics of the county of Wexford elected delegates, according to the plan proposed, the July following, and the whole kingdom at the same time made like returns. Resolutions of many grand juries and corporations were published soon after, reprobating this circular letter. Counties were assembled for the purpose of joining in the outcry. The county of Wexford was convened on the 22nd of September, by Mr. Derenzy, the high sheriff, to take into consideration this circular letter of the general committee of the Catholics of Ireland, signed Edward Byrne. The court was opened at one o'clock, when Mr. Maxwell was about to produce resolutions, but the Hon. Francis Hutchinson, having first risen, and being in possession of the chair, after a manly and eloquent speech of some length, proposed resolutions declaratory of the rights of the subject. The first resolution, which asserted the right to petition the throne or either house of Parliament, though for some time attempted to be got rid of by Mr. C. Dawson, and an objection upon a point of order, was at length unanimously adopted; but the other resolutions proposed by Mr. Hutchinson, though equally constitutional and self-evident, were rejected by the party who avowedly came to oppose every measure which might either tend to gratify the feelings or administer a hope of obtaining justice to the Roman Catholics. Mr. Hutchinson, however, most ably supported his motion, and was powerfully assisted by his brother, the Honourable Christopher Hutchinson (the present member for the city of Cork), and Captain Sweetman, who, in the most energetic language, delivered a speech very prophetic of events that have since taken place; but no one argument was adduced by his opponents to controvert the principles which he sought to establish.

On the question, a division took place, when the number of the silent freeholders who opposed a declaration of the inalienable rights of the subject, appeared to be one hundred and ten against forty-five; three or four gentlemen of the respectable and liberal-minded minority possessed more landed property in the county than the whole of the majority, so that the Roman Catholics had the satisfaction to see almost every man of considerable landed property, and of legal and constitutional information, go out on the division with them.

The business being then disposed of, Mr. Maxwell produced his string of resolutions, but declined making any comment on them, alleging, that it was intended they should be presented by another gentleman, whose attendance at the meeting was prevented by family reasons, and that they had only that morning been put into his hands. It was expected, that as the proposer of the resolutions had declined to go into the discussion of them, some other gentleman who acted with him would have undertaken to explain to the freeholders the expedience or necessity of entering into measures which appeared to be calculated for no other purpose but to create animosities between Protestants and Roman Catholics, and to divide the former. The other gentlemen continuing silent on the merits, but confident in their strength of numbers, and loud in their call for the question, though an adjournment was proposed, it being dark night, and several moderate men declared their wish to have a day's time coolly to consider before the county should be committed to an angry measure, it became necessary for the gentlemen on the other side to commence a debate, which continued until past ten o'clock, when, without even attempting to answer one argument of the many that were urged against the resolutions, the same majority, who had rejected the constitutional and conciliatory motion made in the morning by the Honourable Francis Hutchinson, carried their point.*
An address to the county members was then proposed,

* See Appendix, No. I.

of the same purport as the resolutions, but was afterwards withdrawn.

The next public meeting of the county, convened by the magistrates in the absence of the sheriff, was held in Wexford, on Friday the 11th of January, 1793, at which Walter Hore, Esq., presided. The meeting manifested, by public resolutions, their attachment to the constitution in King, Lords, and Commons; the necessity of a reform in the Commons' House of Parliament, including persons of all religious persuasions—an object which they declared they would endeavour to accomplish by every legal and constitutional means in their power. It was further resolved that the people in the county of Wexford were perfectly peaceable and quiet; no kind of seditious practices known; nor the least symptom of or tendency to riot; but that lest such should be intended by any faction, they declared that all attempts to introduce any new form of government into the country, or in any manner to impair or corrupt the three essential parts of the constitution consisting of King, Lords, and Commons, they would resist with all their force and energy. These resolutions were forwarded to the representatives for the county in Parliament, and inserted in the public papers.*

On the same day a society was formed in the town of Wexford, under the denomination of the Friends of the Constitution, Liberty, and Peace. This association was attended by a great many of the most respectable and independent gentlemen of the county; and their number increased considerably at different successive meetings. They from time to time passed and published resolutions, expressive of their sentiments, views, and opinions, similar to those passed and

See Appendix, No. II.

published by societies of the like nature in Dublin, and many other parts of Ireland. But they have long since ceased to exist, and never tended to disturb public tranquillity. They were, indeed, the friends of peace and harmony; but their powers were not proportionate to their wishes, and their benevolent efforts failed of the intended effect.

When, in the spring of the year 1793, the militia regiments were, pursuant to an Act of the Legislature, embodied in Ireland, it occasioned great commotion in different parts of the country, from some silly misconceptions that were dispersed through the populace with regard to the object of the enrolment. It had been rumoured that the people were to be cajoled into the militia regiments, to be torn from their families, and sent on foreign service. But notwithstanding this, the measure was carried into effect in the county of Wexford, perhaps with less ferment than in any other part of Ireland. I had the best possible opportunity of knowing the fact, having been appointed a deputy governor of the county.

In the summer of this year, some tithe-farmers took tithes in the county of Wexford, which had been formerly rented by others. These, unwilling to lose their prey without an effort to retain it, excited the populace to resist the demands of the new undertakers, whom they called innovators and intruders. Soon after, oaths were framed in imitation of similar practices in Munster. From the neighbourhood of Tottenham Green, extending towards Mount Leinster, and to that part of the county of Wexford called the Duffrey, the inhabitants were generally sworn. On Sundays, a great concourse of people attended at the different places of worship—as well Protestant churches as Catholic chapels—and swore the several congregations to resist paying tithes under certain restrictions, with a modification of the fees of the Catholic clergy, and an injunction to swear their neighbouring parishes. Thus about one-eighth of the county was sworn, and, in all probability, the delusion might have generally spread, but for the timely exertions of several of the country gentlemen, who used all their influence to prevent their tenants and neighbours from joining in such unlawful pursuits. Different magistrates also attended, with parties of the military, at several places of worship, and so put a stop to the general diffusion of this symptom of riot.

On Sunday the 7th July, however, a man was taken in a chapel-yard near Enniscorthy, in the act of administering those unlawful oaths, and sent into the town a prisoner. The report of this fact being quickly circulated through the country, excited those that had been already sworn to rise in a body on the Monday immediately following, for this man's liberation. Intelligence of the approach of these people having been received at Enniscorthy, a party of the fifty-sixth regiment, under the direction of Mr. Vero, a magistrate, came up with the rioters at the hill of Scobie. Here Mr. Vero received an anonymous letter, as a message from the populace, requesting he would liberate the prisoner, who was represented to be a silly, insignificant fellow. Mr. Vero, from motives of humanity, it is to be presumed, although he had a military force to act with him, thought it most prudent not to resist the demand. The prisoner was set at liberty; and this so pleased the people, that the air was rent with their shouts of joy; and after a general volley of what fire-arms they had that would go off, they dispersed to their several homes, without committing further outrage, and the military marched back to Enniscorthy.

On the same day, Mr. Maxwell (now Colonel Barry),

at the head of a troop of horse, in the capacity of a
magistrate, set out from Newtownbarry, scoured the
country all along as he passed; found sixteen men
drinking in an ale-house on his way, took them all
and conducted them to Enniscorthy. The sight of so
many prisoners, being a very extraordinary event in
the county of Wexford, alarmed the peaceable inhabitants of the town. Mr. Richards,* the high sheriff,
repaired immediately to Enniscorthy, from whence,
with all possible speed, he dispatched messengers to
convey this alarming intelligence to all the gentlemen
of the neighbourhood; requesting their assistance at
a meeting appointed to be held the next day at
Enniscorthy. Notwithstanding the shortness of the
notice, a great number of gentlemen attended on
Tuesday, the 9th of July, at the Bear inn, in the town
of Enniscorthy. I was one of those present. An
association was then formed for the preservation of
the peace of the county; all the well-disposed were
invited to join, and subscriptions were immediately
entered into, to prosecute the disturbers of the public
peace. In a short time this association was composed
of almost all the resident gentlemen of the county;
and their meetings were afterwards held, from time to
time, at Enniscorthy.

On the first day of meeting, an inquiry into the
case of the sixteen prisoners took place; and various
were the opinions offered on the occasion. I was sorry
to observe in the onset, that an inclination prevailed
to attribute the riots to a spirit of religious bigotry;
but the futility of the prejudiced arguments were so
manifestly contrary to the facts, that this ground was
soon abandoned. The result of the inquiry proved
that the rioters had assembled, the day before, in great

* See his certificate to the Author, Appendix, No. III.

numbers, on Scobie Hill, in a hostile manner, determined to liberate the prisoner by force, if attempted to be detained. The magistrate who attended on the occasion, was deemed to have acted as he did from an idea of mistaken lenity, although his indulgent conduct had so pleased the people, that they dispersed without having committed any act that the laws of the country could punish; for at that time it was necessary to read the Riot Act, to constitute any assemblage an illegal meeting. This measure was not resorted to in the present instance, and if it had, the consequent dispersion of the multitude must have disarmed the law.

It was, however, thought necessary to impress on the minds of the people, that the magistracy would at all times resist the demands of a riotous and armed force with determined firmness; and as among the sixteen prisoners there were two taken with fire-arms, it was judged expedient to commit these to Wexford gaol, and liberate the other fourteen, on giving bail for good behaviour. Accordingly, these two men (whom the law could not punish any more than those who were liberated) were conducted under a military guard from Enniscorthy, through a part of the country that escaped being sworn, to the east of the Slaney, and lodged in the gaol of Wexford.

On the morning of the 11th, great numbers of people assembled from Newtownbarry to the Duffrey, and to Tottenham-green, searching the different houses on their way, on the western side of the river Slaney, making towards Wexford, and forcing every man they met, to come along with them. This concourse of people being observed by many of the country folk, such as could procure boats to convey them to the eastern side of the river, fled on their approach, and thus escaped being compelled to constitute a part of the multitude; but still their numbers were considerably accumulated in the course of their progress.

On this morning, also, an anonymous letter was received in Wexford by a respectable inhabitant of the town, requesting he might apply to the magistrates to liberate the two prisoners—threatening, in case of refusal, that a body of some thousands would come to take them by force. Little notice was taken of this threat, nor did the inhabitants apprehend any alarm, until about three o'clock, a gentleman, who had been forced along by the multitude, was seen galloping into the town, declaring that he had been sent to inform the magistrates that an immense concourse of people, then not more than a quarter of a mile distant, and of apparent determination, were coming to enforce the enlargement of the prisoners. Lieutenant Buckby, of the fifty-sixth, who had been in Wexford that day alone, on regimental business, was, on his return to join his command at Taghmon, seized upon, and forced to come back with the rioters to Wexford. In a few minutes, about fifty soldiers of the fifty-sixth regiment, with three magistrates, headed by the brave Major Vallotton, marched out to meet the rioters, who were all drawn up at the upper end of John-street, on the road leading to Taghmon, in readiness to receive them. The Major, humanely intending to expostulate, advanced a few paces before his party; but on seeing one of his officers a prisoner with the rioters, his benevolent intentions were dissipated; and losing all patience, he made a blow of his sword at the man who had been induced to meet him in expostulation, and wounded him severely. This provoked resistance, and he in return received a desperate wound in the groin, of which he languished for some days. and died.

Thus perished the gallant Vallotton, who had distinguished himself at the siege of Gibraltar, under the immortal Elliot, as first aide-de-camp to that General. Though parleying with rioters may not at all times, perhaps, be advisable; yet, when once entered upon, the dignity of temper should be maintained, and it is much to be lamented, that the Major did not continue his original disposition; for though it should not stand the test of authoritative severity, yet the event might have proved as bloodless as on the previous occasion near Enniscorthy. An attack on both sides immediately took place, the contest was but short. In a few minutes, the rioters gave way in all directions. Those who had been forced along by them, were the first to sheer off, when they found an opportunity, over hedges and ditches, wherever they thought they could best make their escape; numbers not knowing whither they were flying. It may not be unworthy of remark, that Captain Boyd, then of the Wexford militia, had been to Taghmon in the morning, with a party of the fifty-sixth regiment, to escort a prisoner; and was now on his return to Wexford as far as Bettiville, having no other possible intimation of what had happened, but the confused flight of the affrighted rabble. He lay in ambuscade for their approach, and, from behind the ditches, shot numbers of the fugitives. The weather being intensely warm, occasioned the death of a great many of the wounded, who might otherwise recover; but lest their wounds might betray them, they did not apply for medical assistance. Many, too, who were badly wounded, ran as far as they could, and, being exhausted, crawled for concealment into the ditches, where they perished, and whence the first intimation of their fate was conveyed by the putrid exhalation from their bodies. Eleven lay dead on the scene of action in John-street; one

of whom was a poor cobbler of the town, shot by
accident. The others were publicly exposed for some
time, and were at length identified. Among them
there appeared four freeholders, who had been polled
at the preceding election for the county. At that
time, the Catholics of Ireland could not be freeholders
in their native land by the existing laws of which they
were excluded from that privilege. In the hurry and
fright of the action, eight men sought refuge in a hay-
loft, where they were discovered after the conflict, made
prisoners, and committed to gaol. One of them died
of his wounds, two became informers, and five were
brought to trial, condemned at the ensuing assizes, and
executed on the 26th of July following. One of these
men, who had been in town that day to market, was,
on his return home, obliged to come back with the
rioters; and although he was proved a man of most
unexceptionable character, yet such was the idea
entertained of the necessity of public example, that his
character, or the circumstance of innocence, did not
save him.

The inhabitants of Wexford, to prevent such another
surprise, armed and embodied themselves in four
different divisions, officered by several gentlemen who
had served in the army; and all under the command
of Colonel (now General) Nicholls. He gave his orders
every day on parade, and different patrols perambulated
the town and its vicinity every night. Two pieces of
cannon were planted on that part of the barrack-hill
which commands the whole street, and the entrance to
the gaol; and four others were ready to be brought to
any quarter in case of emergency.

During this system of precaution, a soldier of the
fifty-sixth gave the alarm to his comrades in the
barracks, that, as he had been passing through a
church-yard in the town he was attacked by some of

the inhabitants, who threatened him and his regiment with destruction for having fired against the people; and that at last, in the affray, he had been fortunate enough to escape with the loss of some of his fingers. This story, artfully told by the wounded man, roused the fury of the soldiers to such a pitch, that they made preparation, and were actually on the point of sallying forth from their barracks, to take signal vengeance of the towns-people. It required all the exertions and authority of their officers to restrain them; but this they at length happily effected.

The association for preserving the peace of the county assembled always at Enniscorthy (that being the most central situation). The day after this affair had been appointed for one of their meetings. To this meeting a gentleman was dispatched from Wexford, with the foregoing melancholy intelligence; and an express request, that a suitable reward would be offered for the apprehension of the perpetrators of the horrid deed. This would have been immediately carried into effect, and orders sent by that night's post to have the intelligence generally circulated through the medium of the Dublin papers, had it not so happened that there was not a sufficient number of the members of the secret committee of the association present, to order the disbursement of the necessary expenses, they having the command of the funds. But before a competent consenting number of these could be collected, it was discovered that the soldier had been the perpetrator of the horrid deed himself, and had been induced to cut off his fingers to prevent his going abroad with his regiment, then under orders for foreign service. Had it not been for the prudent exertions of the officers, it is more than probable that this imposture would have been attended with dreadful consequences before the real discovery could be made. The peace of the county was attended to with the greatest activity and vigilance by the association; but, in fact, after the affair at Wexford on the 11th of July, 1793, before detailed, no apparent symptom or even a disposition to riot could be traced.

At the meetings of the association, I perceived with regret an insidious spirit, eager and active to attach the entire odium of the disturbances exclusively on the Catholics; although the damning public spectacle, on the exposure of the killed at Wexford, should surely ever have deterred barefaced calumny and prejudiced misrepresentation from future exhibition. Yet, the malignant traducers of their countrymen to foreigners believed, or affected to believe, this vile reproach on mere assertion. In any other part of the world the uttering of such gross detraction would bring down public execration, and perhaps endanger the personal safety of the hated reptile that would dare, in this unqualified manner, to denounce a whole community. Ireland, however, which, by a peculiar providence, is freed from any other, abounds with these monsters in human form, who batten on the ruin of public prosperity.

These groundless insinuations were carried to such lengths, that, even in the House of Lords, in the assemblage of the peers of the realm, Lord Farnham asserted, with confidence, that the riots in the county of Wexford had become seriously alarming; that the people held nightly meetings, and from parish to parish had sworn not to pay rents, tithes, or taxes, and that the lower orders of Catholics had risen in consequence of a disappointed expectation of receiving ten pounds a year, as the consequent advantage of their emancipation, which they had been promised by their delegates. This Lord Farnham alleged in the most solemn manner, on the authority of letters received by himself from a quarter the most respectable, he said, in the county of Wexford.*

My surprise was great, indeed, on finding such allegations thus strongly asserted and become the subject of Parliamentary discussion; knowing, as I did, that the riots had never assumed this serious complexion, nor had in any degree furnished ground for such an exaggerated statement. Being a Catholic delegate for the county, I naturally felt an anxiety to discover whence originated this extraordinary information; and thought the best appeal, at the time, would be to a meeting of the association, composed of almost all the respectable gentlemen of the county. Here I complained that the country was calumniated, and requested to know, if I could be informed who it was that had conveyed such strange and unwarranted intelligence to Lord Farnham? I took the liberty also to declare that, let him be who he may, if the facts existed to his conviction, he should have produced satisfactory evidence of that conviction to the association, the natural and avowed guardians of the peace of the county. I further urged, that not above one-eighth of the county had ever been in a state of disturbance; that the rioters appeared to be a motley multitude of all persuasions, to whom religion appeared to be an object of the least concern.

The result was, after a most minute investigation, that the monstrous charge was deemed a gross and unfounded calumny; and whatever latitude prejudiced conversation might have taken at the festive tables of some gentlemen, not one of them presumed to come forward in support of the principles of bigotry against stubborn truth and undeniable facts. But had not this inquiry been instituted, it is very probable that the

* See Appendix, No. IV.

unrefuted calumnies against the county of Wexford might have led to consequences as fatal and deplorable as happened, from like causes, in the counties of Meath and Louth. These, however, I will not attempt to detail, having limited myself, for the present, to the transactions of my native county, awaiting an opportunity of general information.

The Catholics of the county met at Wexford, on the 30th of July, for the purpose of publicly avowing their sentiments and principles. To this effect they adopted resolutions which were given to the world in all the public papers of the day.*

In the year 1795, when Lord Fitzwilliam's recall from the government of Ireland was made known, the freeholders and other inhabitants of the county of Wexford were summoned to meet on purpose to deliberate on this unexpected event. In the absence of the sheriff, the summons was signed by Cornelius Grogan, Isaac Cornock, Thomas Grogan Knox, Harvey Hay, and John Grogan, magistrates of the county. The meeting, which was held in the county court-house of Wexford, on the 23rd of March, was very numerously attended. Unanimous resolutions were entered into; a petition to the king was voted; and Cornelius Grogan, Edward Hay, and Beauchamp Bagnal Harvey, Esqrs., were appointed delegates to present it to his Majesty.† An address to Lord Fitzwilliam was also voted, and Sir Thomas Esmonde, and Sir Frederick Flood, Baronets, and William Harvey, Esq., were appointed, and they set off instantly for Dublin, to present it to the Lord Lieutenant, who was hourly expected to leave the country. The regret felt on the recall of this nobleman, even whose good intentions produced such cordiality and harmony amongst all ranks and descriptions of people,

* See Appendix, No. V.   † See Appendix, No. VI.

is scarcely credible. From that period may be dated the origin of that dreadful state of calamity and misfortune in which Ireland has been since involved; for it is now evident to all, that had the measures intended to be carried into effect by him been adopted, the nation would have continued its happy career of uncommon, progressive prosperity. It was proposed to his lordship by the British Cabinet to carry the Union, at a time that he had got the Money Bills passed, and was pledged to the country to have the popular measures alluded to brought forward in Parliament. It was even suggested, that these measures might go hand in hand with the other; but he preferred being recalled to giving his support to a business that so strongly met his disapprobation; nor, indeed, is it at all probable that the Irish Legislature and people would have consented at that day to yield up the dignity of independence for any consideration the Ministry could pretend to offer.

The removal of Lord Fitzwilliam must ever be considered as one of the greatest misfortunes that, in the revolution of ages, has befallen this devoted nation. It originated a train of calamitous circumstances, which the disclosing information of every day renders more and more lamentable to the friends of Ireland. The great majority of the people was insulted; public faith was violated; the cup of redress was dashed from the lips of expectation, and it cannot be wondered at that the anger of disappointment should have ensued. Had the healing balm been applied at the critical moment, the fever of commotion had long since passed its crisis. Had the benevolent measures intended by that nobleman as the basis of his administration, been effected, the rankling wounds of division and distraction were for ever closed, nor would the poison of prejudice and party spirit still threaten convulsion and confusion;

but harmony, confidence, and peace would reign throughout the land.

Being one of those who had been chosen to present the petition of the county of Wexford to his Majesty, I proceeded as far as Dublin, on my way to London, with my companions in appointment. Here it was thought most advisable to get individual signatures to the petition, rather than bear it with those of the chairman and secretary, who had signed it by the unanimous order of the county meeting. My brother delegates declined going back, and I undertook the task alone, at the moment I was going into the packet-boat to sail for England; my having sailed was even announced in the public papers. I returned to the county of Wexford, was indefatigable in my exertions, and no greater proof can be adduced of the general public approbation of the measure, and of the unanimity of sentiment prevalent on the occasion, than the account of my success. In the space of one week, I was able to procure twenty-two thousand two hundred and fifty-one signatures, among whom were all the independent and respectable gentlemen of the county. I then proceeded to London, and had the honour of presenting the petition, with all the signatures, to his Majesty, on the 22nd of April, 1795, at the levee at St. James's, along with my brother delegates, and we met with a gracious reception.*

Not many years ago the county of Wexford could boast of independent principles, and the public spirit of its gentry was conspicuous. This, it may be observed, was chiefly owing to the great number of resident landlords, whose properties were so equally divided, that they were comparatively but few overgrown fortunes among them. While this state of easy parity prevailed, so long lasted the peace and prosperity of the county.

* See Appendix, No. VI.

At that time respectable characters voluntarily engaged themselves to preserve and maintain public order, and it is easy to conceive, that the laws of a country will be well and cheerfully obeyed, when the police is undertaken by a body of uninfluenced gentlemen, whose interest and inclinations induce them to watch, with incessant vigilance, over its tranquillity. The unbiassed exertions of such men must always ensure what the Irish have ever yearned after, an impartial administration of justice; without which, laws, even of the best description, are nothing better than instruments of tyranny. But the times have changed, and other men and other measures have succeeded. Of these we shall presently have occasion to make mention.

The principle of volunteering, while it was productive of social and liberal intercourse, appears to have diffused a spirit of conviviality throughout the country; and so far were the pleasures of the table indulged, that the fortunes of many were thereby impaired, and their distresses obliged them to resign their independence. Representatives and their most zealous friends and adherents fell into a dereliction and abandonment of public concerns, at the same time that they neglected their private interests; and hence the county may date the loss of its independent character. Of this a most striking instance can be adduced. At an election, some years back, one of the candidates, who was esteemed by his party a *staunch* patriot, came forward and declared to the people on the hustings, that "no human consideration should ever induce him to accept of a place or a pension, if he became their representative." This declaration, however, as will appear by the sequel, he seems *to have thought no more about than if he had swallowed a poached egg* (a memorable expression of his own on a late occasion). He was chosen a knight of the shire, and at a subsequent meeting he was actually *absolved* from this solemn and voluntary engagement; nay, truly, it was requested *he would accept of some employment;* and he shortly after meekly condescended to gratify their wishes, by accepting of a pension and a place, which he still comfortably retains, and is likely to retain as long as he lives. It must be here observed, by-the-by, that the object of such a *plenary indulgence* must be greatly endeared to such attached and accommodating constituents; the pleasing effect of convivial talents among constant companions who thus constitute their favourite the king of his company; a situation so fascinating to some dispositions, that they will risk all possible hazards for its maintenance. It will not be easily impressed on ingenuous minds, that men who would fain uphold in the highest degree the dignified character of independence, should so far forget themselves as to hold forth to the world, in a *public paper*, such a memorial of total indifference to that character. Yet in the case before us the fact is incontrovertible.

It has been too common a foible with some of our gentry to aim at equal splendour and expense with their superiors in fortune. Such men, before being aware of their situation, have incautiously expended largely above their incomes. A system of such careless dissipation and extravagant squandering must destroy the most ample resources; and men, long in the habit of indulging those propensities, and finding their means abridged, and themselves deeply involved, have still an aching reluctance to give up any share of their ideal consequence. Instead, therefore, of resorting to any rational plan of economy, they endeavour to get within the circle of some lord or great man, supposed to be possessed of extensive patronage. They court his smiles, and if their efforts are crowned with any degree of success, they instantly conclude, that all their misapplied expenditure must be amply reimbursed by this very often empty speculation. They count upon places and employments of great emoluments for themselves and their children; and thus they abandon all idea of the certain pursuits of industry, trade, and honourable profession; they launch into the lottery of patronage, and yield up their spirit of independence, and all their actions (out of the circle of their families) to the utter control and directing will of their adopted patron. It is presumed, that any person acquainted with the state of Ireland must perceive that this system has unfortunately been but too largely pursued, and too much acted upon; and it is also pretty notorious, that the county of Wexford has been for some time past what is not unaptly termed *lord-ridden*. Slaves to their superiors, but tyrants to their inferiors; these needy adventurers become the tools of prevailing power. Justices of the Peace are selected from this class, and these, by this degree of elevation (certainly to them the station is an exalted one), think themselves raised to a level of equality with the most respectable gentlemen in the country. But their ignorance is so preposterous, and their behaviour so assuming, that men of education, talents, and fortune, are induced to withhold themselves from a situation they would otherwise grace, as it might oblige them to confer with fellows with whom they would not by any means hold communion or keep company. Thus are the very men who ought to be the magistrates of the country, and who would cheerfully accept the office, were they to associate with proper companions in duty, deterred from holding Commissions of the Peace; while the justice and police of the community is left to ignorant, presuming, and intemperate upstarts, devoid of all qualification and endowment, except that alone, if it may be termed such, of unconditional submission and obedience to the controlling nod of their boasted patrons. If they faithfully adhere to this, they may go all lengths to raise their consequence, and enhance their estimation with the multitude. These creatures have therefore the effrontery to push themselves forward on every occasion; and after a series of habitual acts of turpitude, whenever an opportunity offers itself, they become the scourges and the firebrands of the country. It is much to be lamented, that there are but too many examples of this melancholy truth, and that in too many instances these wretches have been set on to commit flagrant acts of outrage, to answer the political purposes of their patrons, who shrink from appearing personally concerned in these deeds of shame. On such occasions, from behind the curtain, the hireling crew are sent out to riot on the public stage, and dreadful are the consequences that follow; while the vile under-strappers are utterly ignorant of the cause, and never question the motive of their subornation.

In the beginning of the year 1795, parties of contending rioters, denominated *Peep-o'-Day Boys* and *Defenders*, disturbed different parts of the province of Ulster, by acts of violence and outrage against each other. Some say their animosities originated from electioneering. To these succeeded, in the summer of the same year, a description of public disturbers, calling themselves Orangemen, who now made their first appearance in the county of Armagh. Their object appears to have been, not to suffer a Catholic to remain within the limits of their sphere of action. They posted up on the doors of the Catholics, peremptory notices of departure; specifying the precise time, a *week* at the farthest, pretty nearly in the following words:—"*To hell, or to Connaught with you, you bloody Papists; and if you are not gone by*" (mentioning the day) "*we *will come and destroy yourselves and your properties: we all hate the Papists here."* They generally were as good as their words. The Catholics at first saved themselves by flight; but those who received *notices* at a later period, were able to take some of their properties along with them. It is astonishing to think that such events could take place, where there were any men of intelligence, honesty, or public spirit; and still the facts are indubitable: nay, these enormities seem to have been connived at, or totally overlooked, until many thousands of the Catholics were thus driven from that part of the country, and that it became necessary to find occupiers for the lands they had been obliged to abandon. Even the gentlemen of landed interest in the county did not exhibit, by any public testimony, a disavowal of these horrid atrocities, until the period of setting the forsaken territory roused them from their slumbers. Then they discovered, to their amazement and dismay, that among the few bidders who appeared, not one was found to offer more for any lot than about half what was paid for the same before by the Catholic tenant. Then, indeed, and not till then, did the banishment of the Catholics appear alarming. It was seriously alarming to gentlemen, thus in a moment to lose half their incomes, but until this fatal discovery was made, the number of wretched poor, proscribed, and violently driven from their homes, deprived of their cabins and their all, was a circumstance unworthy of these gentlemen's notice.

To counteract this calamity as much as possible, a numerous meeting of the magistrates of the county of Armagh was held at the special instance of the governor, Lord Viscount Gosford, on the 28th day of December, 1795. To this assemblage, on taking the chair as president, his lordship spoke a pointed address on the occasion; which, together with the proceedings, was published in *The Dublin Journal* of the 5th of January, 1796.*

A circumstantial detail of these occurrences in the North would be inconsistent with my original intention, of confining myself, for the present, to the transactions in the county of Wexford; but I have been led into this, I hope excusable digression, in order to account to the reader, in a great measure, for the dreadful impression made on the minds of the people, at a future period, by the rumours, that Orangemen were sworn for the destruction of the Catholics! Were these rumours to be grounded only on Lord Gosford's statement (too authentic to admit a possibility of denial), and true only to the extent his lordship has allowed them, with what terrible apprehensions must they fill the minds of a simple, oppressed, and degraded people, such as the Irish peasantry are generally known to be for ages past? But when it is considered, that the horrid acts themselves have never been disavowed; and the reports of them have rung in the ears of every individual throughout the nation (perhaps with aggravated circumstances, as it usually happens), the reflecting reader is referred to his own judgment, to estimate how much the woful tale of the forlorn sufferers, by its reverberation from one end of the island to the other, must affect the mind, alarm the imagination, and inflame the resentments of an irritated, insulted, and violated community? What advantage might not be taken of a ferment thus excited by designing men—perhaps, too, by the greatest enemies of the people? For such frequently assume the mask of friendship and condolence, and apparently affect counteracting the sinister designs of their minions, in order to accomplish their private views, through a show of popularity.

* See Appendix, No. VII.

Various, as has been observed, were the descriptions of the disturbers of the public peace in Ulster. Numbers went about in the night, searching houses, and taking away all the arms they could find, without violating any other property. This becoming generally known, the houses were usually opened upon the first summons. This easy mode of admittance was afterwards taken advantage of by common robbers; who at first only assumed the character of disarmers, to come at their prey with less trouble and more certainty. After a continued series of similar circumstances of violence and outrage, arising from a nation's greatest curse, the disunion of its people, but which our limits will not permit us to detail at present, General Lake issued his proclamation for disarming the inhabitants of the North of Ireland, on the 13th of March, 1797; and on the 21st of the same month, Mr. Grattan, after a speech delivered with his usual force of talent and brilliant ability, moved for an inquiry into the causes which produced this proclamation; but his motion was unfortunately rejected. The persecutions in the county of Armagh were so flagrant, and the conduct of many of the magistrates so contrary to law, that applications were made to the Court of King's Bench for attachments against several of them, but a Bill of Indemnity prevented a judicial investigation of their conduct; and thus they were screened from merited punishment. This total disregard of their grievances, and inattention to their complaints, added to the barbarous outrages afterwards committed by the military in the northern counties, very much exasperated the feelings of the suffering party. They resorted for temporary relief to private sorrow and secret lamentation. In this sad state, bordering on despair, every injured person sympathised with his neighbour in affliction; and their united resentments, like a raging flame, suppressed, but not extinguished, were the more likely to burst forth with sudden fury and unexpected violence. It may not be impertinent to remark, that in all cases of popular commotion, an inquiry into the alleged grievances ought to go hand in hand with the measures of rigour and coercion. These two principles are far from being incompatible, and any Government acting upon them, must be certain of conciliating obedience and affection, respect and attachment.

The Earl of Moira, with that dignified humanity which has ever graced his noble character, brought the distresses of Ireland before the British House of Lords, on the 22nd of November, 1797 ; when he gave a heart-rending description, in his native strain of elevation, of the savage cruelties practised by the military against the people ; and offered at the moment, to produce at the bar incontrovertible proof of his assertions. He concluded his able statement by moving an Address to the Sovereign, the principal purport of which was:—
" Humbly hoping that his Majesty might be graciously pleased to take into his paternal consideration the disturbed state of Ireland ; and to adopt such lenient measures, as might appear to his royal wisdom and benignity, best calculated to restore tranquillity and excite affection." But sad to tell, his lordship was not more fortunate in the British House of Lords, than was Mr. Grattan the preceding March in the Irish House of Commons. Both motions had the same unlucky fate of rejection. On the following day (the 23rd of November), Mr. Fox made a similar benevolent and patriotic effort (and who is unacquainted with his powers ?) in the British House of Commons, but with the like success. He concluded a lucid and animated speech with the following pointed and emphatic quotation from Cicero, which I cannot resist inserting :—
" *Carum esse civibus, benè de republicâ mereri,*

laudari, coli, diligi, gloriosum est; metui vero et in odio esse, invidiosum, detestabile, imbecillum, caducum." To be dear to one's countrymen, to deserve well of the commonweal, to be praised, to be respected, to be beloved, is glorious; but to be feared and encompassed with hatred is invidious, is detestable, is tottering, is ruinous.

The appointment of General Sir Ralph Abercromby on the 12th of December, 1797, to the chief command of the forces in Ireland, gave general satisfaction, and afforded a ray of hope to drooping despondency. The subsequent display of his eminent virtues evinced the justice of favourable expectation. Having been quartered in Ireland through most of his gradations of well-merited promotion, he possessed a perfect local knowledge of the country; and he now resolved in person to visit every district, and thus he made a tour of observation through the whole island. After a strict review of every object worthy of his attention, he published on his return to Dublin general orders to the several military commanders, wherein, after having reprobated the irregularities of the soldiery, he directed the necessary restraint for their disorderly conduct. These orders were issued from the Adjutant-General's Office, in Dublin, on the 26th of February, 1797.*

The Earl of Moira, animated by the same generous motives that always influenced his conduct, made his last effort to avert the impending storm. With this benevolent intention, on the 19th of February, 1798, he moved in the Irish House of Lords:—"That an humble Address be presented to his Excellency the Lord Lieutenant, representing, that as Parliament hath confided to his Excellency extraordinary powers for supporting the laws and defeating any traitorous com-

* See Appendix, No. VIII.

binations which may exist in this kingdom, this House feels it, at the same time, its duty, as those powers have not produced the desired effect, to recommend the adoption of such conciliatory measures as may allay the apprehensions and extinguish the discontents unhappily prevalent in this country." This motion was introduced after an affecting speech of uncommon energy, but it was negatived without further investigation—a circumstance that furnishes strong ground for the opinion of many intelligent men, that the door was shut, at that time, against all inquiry, for purposes not then known, or even imagined by the public; but which, however, were foretold, as if from a spirit of inspiration, even in the minutest circumstances, by those elevated geniuses whose comprehensive views in regard to the concerns of their country were unlimited. The great measure was still in reserve, and not to be brought forward until the country should be completely paralysed. This unhappy crisis, it is thought, was long in agitation and deeply premeditated. I crave the reader's permission, while I endeavour to sketch a brief outline of the manner in which it is supposed to have been finally effected.

During the American War, at one time, nearly all the troops on the Irish establishment were drawn off to support that unfortunate contest. The combined fleets of France and Spain were riding triumphant in the Channel, and our shores were every moment threatened with a formidable invasion. In this perilous situation Ireland was advised by the British Ministry to defend herself as well as she could, as she was now left no other resource. The latent spirit of the nation was roused at the approach of danger. Upwards of one hundred thousand heroes instantly appeared, self-clothed, self-armed, perfectly equipped and appointed, ready to oppose with dauntless courage the menacing foe that would rashly venture to insult our coast.

These were the ever memorable and ever glorious Volunteers of Ireland. Our enemies were all at once completely scared; they shrunk into their ports; and our shores, then too commanding for an attempt to land, were left unmolested. Our people were united in harmonious resolution; every breast glowed with patriotic ardour; and the salvation of Ireland, otherwise left to inevitable destruction, was the consequence. The hour of security and social intercourse produced reflection. The saviours of their country quickly discovered that they existed in a state of thraldom to the British Parliament. They demanded a redress of grievances; it could not be refused; and the national legislature was consequently declared independent. This great event took place in 1782, and a rapid increase of national prosperity succeeded; our commerce being less shackled, became more extensive, and the capital of the island improved in splendour and magnificence. But it was with the utmost reluctance, and under circumstances of imperious necessity, that these concessions seemed to be made by the British Cabinet, while the most malignant envy rankled in the bosoms of the enemies of Ireland. But there was no alternative. A diffusion of liberal sentiment and an unity of interests had combined men of all ranks and persuasions in the common cause. The unhallowed monster of religious bigotry could no longer be introduced to foment prejudice and sow baleful division; all was concord and unanimity. But the object of creating disunion and annulling the benefits obtained was never lost sight of; and the happy state of Ireland continued uninterrupted only until the dissolution of the Volunteer associations (and this was contrived as speedily as possible), and till other schemes were put in practice to dissipate the union of sentiment which so happily prevailed. Much time was not lost, therefore, to put

every engine at work for this detested purpose. In
1786 a set of commercial regulations, denominated
propositions, was drawn up in the Irish House of
Commons, and transmitted for the consideration of the
British Parliament. From thence they were returned
so altered, that the Irish Minister of the day found it
expedient not to press them forward. It was asserted
that the propositions so garbled, went the full length of
annihilating by implication the independence so lately
acquired; and this proceeding excited no small degree
of irritation. The same year, among other means of
disturbing the harmony of the people, the Right Rev.
Doctor Woodward, late Bishop of Cloyne, taking advantage of some disturbances, excited by the exactions of
tithe-farmers in Munster, fulminated a pamphlet pro-
nouncing the Church and State in danger. The trump
of discord thus deliberately blown, was resounded by
an intemperate writer, under the assumed name of
"Theophilus." This scurrilous publication (at first
acknowledged, but afterwards denied by its reputed
author), was always with good reason attributed to a
civilian engaged in the service of the Established
Church, and now at the head of its judicial concerns.
This author's publication is notorious for virulent abuse,
for gross and foul invectives against Catholics in public
—though he had a Catholic of the gentler sex the
wedded partner of his existence, and though in private
life endeavouring to maintain habits of intimacy with
many of the Catholic clergy; but what reliance is to be
placed on the declamations of a man whose practice is
so contrary to his professions? But he may well play
the ambidexter, when his pleadings have heaped on him
a multiplicity of profitable situations (which he does not
admit to be places or employments), and in his convivial
moments he is foully belied if he does not mightily
enjoy the joke. These, and such like productions,

dictated by the spirit of discord, were refuted by several able pens of the day, but particularly convicted by the irresistible force of the benevolent O'Leary's dignified ridicule. This divine, professing the true spirit of the Gospel, excited by the purest motives of patriotism and Christian charity, steps forward, and by his exhortations and example, contributed more effectually to quiet the minds of the people and appease the tempest, by bringing them back to a sense of their religion, and without the loss of a life, effected more than an host prompted by prejudiced coercion, or a formidable army. The happy effects of the exertions of this extraordinary man, whose talents were so eminently useful at this critical period, attracted the notice of Majesty, and with becoming gratitude, unsolicited on his part, received a small annuity as a token of royal favour; his talents were considered too conspicuous to lie dormant, and very advantageous offers were made to him to write for a periodical publication that militated against his principles; he had no other property, yet he rejects it with scorn, although he was certain thereby to incur the displeasure of the ruling powers in Ireland, that would do all in their power to injure him, which he preferred to the prostitution of his heavenly talents, and he retires from his native country and repairs to England, where the enviable blessings of the Constitution are experienced infinitely more than in Ireland. Yet all these exertions did not allay the public ferment, and the hateful and melancholy effects of religious dissension were but too general; and hence may be deduced the most lamentable misfortunes to Ireland— *the revival of religious enmity.*

No means were omitted thenceforward by the principal actors on the occasion, of cherishing the animosities thus excited; confident that this procedure alone would best bear them to their end. This may be fairly concluded from what dropped in the debate on the famous propositions. A leading person, then high in confidence and official situation, and who, before the final object was attained, arrived at the chief judicial capacity of the land, pronounced in the moment of exasperated disappointment, that "*the Irish were a besotted people, easily roused, and easily appeased;*" and, in terms unfit for decency to utter, he is said to have threatened to tame their refractory spirits. In truth, he then delivered the sentiments of his party, as well as his own determination, to which he strictly adhered ever after. This man of narrow politics omitted no occasion of accomplishing the humiliation of his native country. Opposing with licentious petulance all rational schemes of reform ; reprobating with plebeian ribaldry the justice of Catholic claims; and provoking public anger by insulting public feeling, he saw with gloomy satisfaction, before his premature dissolution, his ruthless system carried into woful effect. The trampled populace were goaded to resistance ; their smothered resentments burst into a flame that was not very *easily* extinguished ; the nation was distracted ; and the long premeditated measure of incorporating union succeeded, after a spirited but ineffectual resistance; and thus ended the political drama of Ireland. But to return.

Sir Ralph Abercromby, after the publication of his General Orders, and the knowledge he had acquired in his general view of the country, endeavoured in vain to impress the minds of those in power with his own well-founded opinion, that coercive measures, to the extent determined on, were by no means necessary in Ireland. Unwilling, therefore, to tarnish his military fame, or risk the loss of humane and manly character by leading troops to scenes of cold-blood slaughter and civil desolation ; sooner than sanction by his presence proceedings so abhorrent to his nature, he resigned the chief command of the army in Ireland, on the 29th of April, 1798. His departure has, indeed, been a sore misfortune to this unhappy nation; and had any casualty detained him here but one month longer, it would have been providential, for when the Insurrection had actually broken out, he could not so well have resigned the command; and his dignified authority would have restrained the soldiery from the horrid excesses they afterwards committed. He was too good and too great a blessing for this ill-fated land to possess at that time; he did all in his power to prevent the woful calamities that followed; his splendid exploits in Egypt have rendered his fame immortal; and his death, though glorious, has left an aching pang in the bosom of every true lover of this distracted country. May the olive branch which he waved in Ireland be never forgotten among his unfading laurels!

A strong confirmation, if further proof were at all necessary, of the great discrimination of General Abercromby's comprehensive mind, is his marked selection of a dignified character with whom to share his confidence, as second in command when going on the expedition to Egypt. His choice could not have fallen more judiciously than on Lord Hutchinson, whose brilliant achievements and splendid triumphs have since so largely added to Irish fame, and adorned himself with merited honours. This nobleman appears to have rivalled his great friend as well in humanity as glory. Their opinions respecting Ireland strictly coincided. Witness his lordship's well-known sentiment of "I ABOMINATE THE TORTURE," delivered in the winter of 1798, in the Irish Parliament in the debate on the Bill of Indemnity, for screening the violent proceedings of the Sheriff of the county of Tipperary; and it is happy such sentiment did not deprive him of command.

The opposition of the entire Hutchinson family to oppressive measures was conspicuous on this occasion; and their exertions were indefatigable for the maintenance of peace and order throughout the whole of the arduous period of disturbance. They all breathed the same sentiment of benevolence and humanity. The Earl of Donoughmore exerted all his power and influence to throw open the gates of mercy to the wretched people; and his brother, the Hon. Francis Hely Hutchinson, who succeeded Mr. Judkin Fitzgerald as Sheriff of the county of Tipperary, was eminent in support of abhorrence of the torture. In short, the affable demeanour, the kind and conciliating manners of this entire family, fascinated the minds of the people, and thus prevented shocking scenes of dreadful devastation, wherever they possessed influence or had command, particularly in the counties of Tipperary, Cork, and Galway, much more effectually than any measures of violence or coercion could ever accomplish. I hope, at a future period, to be enabled to do more justice to the great merits of this family, by faithfully recording their generous actions in Munster in 1798, a task that must be grateful to every lover of humanity, and of Ireland, and those of other celebrated characters, that the limits of my present publication permits me only to glance at.

Immediately on the departure of General Abercromby, the military were sent out at free quarters in the county of Kildare and parts of the counties of Carlow and Wicklow. What hardships, what calamity, what misery must not the wretched people suffer, on whom were let loose such a body as the soldiery then in Ireland are described to be in the General Orders before alluded to of the 26th of April, 1798! They became masters of every house in the country; the real owners were obliged to procure them every necessary they thought proper to demand; and, as their will was then the only law—and a very imperious and tyrannical law it was—the people dare not, except at the risk of their lives, complain of any outrage or brutality of which their savage disposition prompted them to be guilty. The inevitable consequence was, that such horrid acts were perpetrated, such shocking scenes were exhibited, as must rouse the indignation and provoke the abhorrence of all not dead to humane feeling, or not barbarised by unnatural hatred of their fellow-creatures!

At this period of confusion, the first public intimation of disturbance in the county of Wexford was from a meeting of magistrates held at Gorey, on the 28th of November, 1797. There the proclaiming of sixteen parishes out of one hundred and forty-two, of which the county consists, was voted by a majority, of which my information does not afford me the number; but the measure was strongly opposed by eight of the magistrates present, including Lord Mountnorris, who must be naturally supposed to feel substantial reasons for his opposition to have the part of the county proclaimed wherein his property principally lay; and it is to be fairly presumed (whatever ground may be had by some reflecting people for thinking otherwise), that his lordship was not influenced, on this occasion at least, by motives of opposition to Lord Ely, his successful rival in the patronage of the county. Shortly after this meeting at Gorey, I spent some days at Camolin Park, the seat of Lord Mountnorris, while he was soliciting the people from parish to parish to take the oath of allegiance. His lordship requested I would use what influence I might possess with the priests in my neighbourhood, to induce them and their flocks to join in this general test of loyalty, in order, as he said, to put the Catholic interest in the county of Wexford on the most respectable footing; suggesting, at the same time, that from his "*great consequence and influence, his representation of facts must counteract and outweigh the misrepresentations of others.*" He also showed me the oaths he usually administered on these occasions, and which he stated himself to have improved from time to time by several alterations; he produced one, in particular, which he conceived to be wrought up to the highest perfection of loyalty. Although I agreed with his lordship so far as really to think the county was then in a state of perfect peace and tranquillity (and therefore thought this overweening parade unnecessary), yet I never believed him, notwithstanding all his lordship's strong professions to that effect, a sincere friend to Catholics; I was rather strongly of opinion, that he affected a show of concern for their interests at this critical period in mere opposition to the noble lord his competitor for influence.

I therefore took the most civil means in my power of declining the interference to which his lordship would have directed my exertions. Lord Mountnorris, however, was not singular in courting Catholic popularity at that time, for all the newspapers of the day teemed with addresses from the Catholics throughout the island, published, not at the desire or at the expense of the subscribers, but by the political manœuverers who took the trouble of procuring them, to answer their private purposes, by playing them off against the schemes of other opponents.

Previous to the Spring Assizes of 1798, several prisoners were transmitted from Wexford to abide their trials at Wicklow, on the prosecution of an informer, whose real name was Morgan, and who had been transported some years before for robbery, but had returned to the country under the assumed name of Cooper. This miscreant was encouraged by some magistrates of the county of Wicklow, to swear informations against United Irishmen; and this he did most copiously. On producing him, however, at Wicklow, his character appeared so infamous, that the gentlemen of the bar were unreserved in declaring that the baseness of such a nefarious villain reflected not a little on those magistrates that encouraged him to come forward. All the prisoners were consequently acquitted, and it was therefore not deemed expedient to bring him on to prosecute at Wexford, where there were also some prisoners confined on his information.

At this assizes also, one man of the name of Collins, otherwise M'Quillen, was brought to trial for spreading false news and alarming the country; it was clearly proved, that this man circulated a report of the arrival of the French off Bantry, and that the yeomen or Orangemen (indifferently supposed by the people to be the same) were to march to resist the invasion; and that it was designed by them previously to commit a massacre upon the Catholics of the country. Such implicit belief did the report gain, that every person from Bray to Arklow, between four and five and twenty miles extent, abandoned their habitations and slept in the open fields; and some women were even delivered in that exposed condition. It is worthy of remark, that these people must have from some previous cause been led to form so bad an opinion of their neighbours, when they gave credit with so much facility to these reports.

Several had been confined in Wexford as United Irishmen, to be prosecuted by an informer of a description quite different from that of the Wicklow ruffian. The name of this second informer was Joseph Murphy, a creature of such idiot aspect, that it was impossible, even at first view, not to conclude him destitute of common intellect, so that it appeared strange that any magistrate of the least discrimination could venture to produce him: yet, this was the man chosen craftily to insinuate himself to be sworn an United Irishman, and then to develop this whole scheme of the combination to a magistrate of the county, who had employed him for that purpose, as he afterwards asserted in the most solemn manner; and his testimony on the trial, when he was produced as an informer, sufficiently warrants this confession. Only one trial was ventured on by the Crown Solicitor at the prosecution of this man, and on hearing his evidence the prisoner was instantly acquitted, and the remainder of those against whom he had given information were turned out of the dock, without any trial whatever. I should not dwell upon these apparently trivial circumstances, but that the public can judge of the truth only by a faithful relation of facts; and these facts also tend to prove that the system of the United Irishmen had not diffused itself through the county of Wexford to the extent so confidently affirmed by an author, whose veracity in almost every other instance appears equally questionable. The truth is, that no authentic proof existed at the time to support these arrogant assertions; and subsequent information confirms how little the county of Wexford was concerned in that conspiracy, as no return appears of its being organised, in the discoveries of the secret committees of the Houses of Lords and Commons. It would be as contrary to truth, however, to say there were no United Irishmen in the county of Wexford; but by every statement worthy of credit, that has ever appeared, their numbers were comparatively fewer in this than in any other county in Ireland; and such as were of that description here seem to have been privately sworn in the detached, unconnected manner of the first progress of that business, before it assumed the form of regular organization. According to this system, now so universally known, the United Irishmen of the county of Wexford, considering the means whereby those were urged into the conspiracy, do not appear to come strictly under that denomination; for their first inducement to combine was, to render their party strong enough to resist the Orangemen, whom they actually believed to be associated and sworn for the extermination of the Catholics, and "*to wade ankle deep in their blood!*" What dreadful notions of terror and alarm must not fill the minds of people believing themselves thus devoted to inevitable destruction?—so strongly, indeed, was it endeavoured to impress the horrid belief, that it was frequently reported through the country, that the Orangemen were to rise in the night-time to murder all the Catholics. Reports of an opposite kind also went abroad, as it appears, by a public advertisement, that a reward of one hundred guineas was offered by the Roman Catholic inhabitants of the neighbourhood of Gorey, for the discovery of some wicked and designing persons who had a malevolent and detestable rumour, that all the churches were to be attacked on Sunday the 29th of April, and that a general massacre of the Protestants was to follow. The advertisement was signed by the priests and principal inhabitants of the place, with Sir Thomas Esmonde, Baronet, at their head; and thus did the Catholics do all in their power to satisfy the minds of their Protestant brethren. These reports certainly occasioned a great deal of mischief among the ignorant and uninformed of all descriptions, whose minds were wrought up to such fury and animosity, that the opposite parties united for mutual defence and hostility to their opponents.

. On the 30th of March, 1798, all Ireland was put

under martial law, and officially declared to be in a state of rebellion by a proclamation from the Lord Lieutenant and Privy Council of the realm. In this proclamation the military were directed to use the most summary method of repressing disturbances.

The Orange system made no public appearance in the county of Wexford until the beginning of April, on the arrival there of the North Cork militia, commanded by Lord Kingsborough. In this regiment there were a great number of Orangemen, who were zealous in making proselytes, and displaying their devices; having medals and Orange ribbons triumphantly pendant from their bosoms. It is believed, that previous to this period there were but few actual Orangemen in the county; but soon after, those whose principles inclined that way, finding themselves supported by the military, joined the association, and publicly avowed themselves, by assuming the devices of the fraternity.

It is said, that the North Cork regiment were also the inventors—but they certainly were the introducers of pitch-cap torture into the county of Wexford. Any person having their hair cut short (and therefore called a *Croppy*, by which appellation the soldiery designated an United Irishman), on being pointed out by some loyal neighbour, was immediately seized and brought into a guard-house, where caps, either of coarse linen, or strong brown paper, besmeared inside with pitch, were always kept ready for service. The unfortunate victim had one of these well heated, compressed on his head, and when judged of a proper degree of coolness, so that it could not be easily pulled off, the sufferer was turned out amidst the horrid acclamations of the merciless torturers; and to the view of vast numbers of people, who generally crowded about the guard-house door, attracted by the afflicted cries of the tormented.

Many of those persecuted in this manner experienced additional anguish from the melted pitch trickling into their eyes. This afforded a rare addition of enjoyment to these keen sportsmen, who reiterated their horrid yells of exultation on the repetition of the several accidents to which their game was liable upon being turned out; for in the confusion and hurry of escaping from the ferocious hands of these more than savage barbarians, the blinded victims frequently fell, or inadvertently dashed their heads against the walls in their way. The pain of disengaging this pitched cap from the head must be next to intolerable. The hair was often torn out by the roots, and not unfrequently parts of the skin were so scalded or blistered as to adhere and come off along with it. The terror and dismay that these outrages occasioned are inconceivable. A sergeant of the North Cork, nicknamed *Tom the Devil*, was most ingenious in devising new modes of torture. Moistened gunpowder was frequently rubbed into the hair cut close and then set on fire; some, while shearing for this purpose, had the tips of their ears snipt off; sometimes an entire ear, and often both ears were completely cut off; and many lost part of their noses during the like preparation. But, strange to tell, these atrocities were publicly practised without the least reserve in open day, and no magistrate or officer ever interfered, but shamefully connived at this extraordinary mode of quieting the people! Some of the miserable sufferers on these shocking occasions, or some of their relations or friends, actuated by a principle of retaliation, if not of revenge, cut short the hair of several persons whom they either considered as enemies or suspected of having pointed them out as objects for such desperate treatment. This was done with a view that those active citizens should fall in for a little experience of the like discipline, or to make the fashion of short hair so general that it might no longer be a mark of party distinction. Females were also exposed to the grossest insults from these military ruffians. Many women had their petticoats, handkerchiefs, caps, ribbons, and all parts of their dress that exhibited a shade of green (considered the national colour of Ireland) torn off, and their ears assailed by the most vile and indecent ribaldry. This was a circumstance so unforeseen, and of course so little provided against, that many women of enthusiastic loyalty suffered outrage in this manner. Some of these ladies would not on any account have worn any thing which they could even imagine partook in any degree of *Croppyism*. They were, however, unwarily involved, until undeceived by these gentle hints from these kind guardians of allegiance.

Great as the apprehensions from Orangemen had been before among the people, they were now multiplied tenfold, and aggravated terror led them in numbers to be sworn United Irishmen, in order to counteract the supposed plan of their rumoured exterminators. The fears of the people became so great at length, that they forsook their houses in the night and slept (if under such circumstances they could sleep) in the ditches. These facts were notorious at the time, and had the magistrates and gentlemen of the country been actuated by the feelings that humanity naturally excites on such occasions, they might with very little trouble have convinced the deluded populace of the fallacy of such reports, and they should have promised them public protection. In general, however, the fact was otherwise. The melancholy situation of the people was regarded with the utmost indifference: few individuals felt any concern or gave themselves any trouble about what they thought; and no effort whatever was made to allay their apprehensions, or at all to undeceive them. Their minds were left to the operation of their fears, to dissipate which if any pains had been taken, it is certain that these horrid conceptions entertained of Orangemen could never have taken such strong hold of their scared imaginations, and that violence would have been repressed in its origin. I had the good fortune to succeed so far, in my own neighbourhood, as to induce the people to remain in their houses at night; and the trouble it gave me to effect so much cannot be conceived without actual experience. I was much amazed to find that this notion was so firmly entertained by some people of respectability, that I believe myself to have been the only person that slept in a house wherein I was on a visit. The fears of the family had been so great, that they had formed a plan of escape, in case of any attempt by the Orangemen to murder them in the night, and with this plan I was made acquainted the next morning. I endeavoured to inculcate my own fixed opinion of the impossibility of a Christian harbouring the thought of putting to death an unoffending fellow-creature. The disposition is too shocking for any Christian to cherish against another; but more especially so for a Christian boasting that of all persuasions his own disposes most to liberality. I rejected the odious, infernal thought with abhorrence, and railed at the weakness that would give it a moment's reception in the mind; and I succeeded in dispelling the fears of some of my friends.

The minds of the people being thus greatly irritated, (particularly by the impunity of the acts of outrage already related), and their alarms having made them abandon their houses at night, they collected in great numbers in their lurking-places. Measures of self-defence were naturally suggested in consequence of their apprehensions, and they were readily led to adopt the means that were deemed best calculated to ensure security. The United Irishmen eagerly advanced the arguments most likely to induce the body of the people to embrace their system, and they met with powerful support and co-operation from those of the opposite faction; whose violent conduct and zealous persecutions proved more efficacious in urging on the people, than any allurements whatsoever. Men thus desperately circumstanced uphold and stimulate each other's confidence, and all consideration of the weakness of individual exertion is removed by a reliance on collective force. In this state is man no longer connected in the way of civil society, but finds himself surrounded by one convulsed and half-dissolved, and a fever of the mind ensues that banishes all idea of calm circumspection. A soul thus impressed cannot abide in solitude, and is therefore led by irresistible impulse to adopt any plausible project that holds out additional means of preservation, protection, or defence.

On the 25th day of April, 1798, an assembly of twenty-seven magistrates was held at Gorey, where it was resolved, that the whole county of Wexford should be forthwith proclaimed; and this accordingly took place on the 27th. From this period forward, many magistrates of the county made themselves conspicuous in practising the summary mode of quieting the country, by the infliction of all kinds of torture. They seem, indeed, to have emulated or rather rivalled the conduct of the magistrates of other counties, who had made trial of the *salutary* effects of persecution somewhat sooner. In the several neighbourhoods of Ross, Enniscorthy, and Gorey, the people suffered most, as in each of these towns a magistrate started up, eager for the glorious distinction of outstripping all others, each by his own superior deeds of death, deflagration, and torture! but it is to be observed, that none of these men had ever before possessed either talents or respectability sufficient to entitle him to take a leading part; yet, if burning houses, whipping and half-hanging numbers, hanging some all out, and shooting others, with attendant atrocities, constitute the characteristic of loyal and good magistrates, they must be allowed strong claim to eminence. In the meantime it must be observed also, that such proceedings, however sanctioned, are contrary to the spirit of the Constitution, a principal part of the excellence of which is the exclusion of all torture. In all the riots and disturbances that took place in England, does it appear, in any one instance, that an infliction of torture was ever attempted? Yet have we heard of associations there, as alarming in their tendency as any that can be imputed to United Irishmen, although no one has been found possessed of sufficient hardihood there to try this desperate experiment. Would the most powerful, the richest, or the most violent man in England be hazardous enough to treat the meanest subject with the barbarous severity practised, in numberless instances, on respectable as well as humble individuals in Ireland? The attempt would be too dangerous. I apprehend the result would prove, that the people would rise in a mass in resistance to such oppressive treatment; and it is submitted to the determination of the candid and impartial, if the feelings of the people of England would not yield to such tyranny without meeting it with the most violent opposition, whether it be not natural to suppose, that it must have roused the resentments of the people of Ireland? I am firmly persuaded, that the conduct of the magistrates before alluded to (and of some others not entitled to quite such renown in this cause), supported by the yeomen under their control, together with the co-operation of the military, occasioned or rather forced the rising of the people in the county of Wexford. While I endeavour to establish the truth of this assertion, I beg the reader's attention to the particular dates of the several outrages, and of the respective periods at which different parts of the county joined the insurgents, as it will be necessary to take them in regular order, to form an adequate and impartial opinion. The proclamation of the county of Wexford having given greater scope to the ingenuity of magistrates to devise means of quelling all symptoms of rebellion, as well as of using every exertion to procure discoveries, they soon fell to burning of houses wherein pikes or other offensive weapons were discovered, no matter how brought there; but they did not stop here, for the dwellings of suspected persons, and those 'from which any of the inhabitants were found to be absent at night, were also consumed. This circumstance of absence from the houses very generally prevailed through the country, although there were the strictest orders forbidding it. This was occasioned at first, as was before observed, from apprehension of the Orangemen, but afterwards proceeded from the actual experience of torture, by the people, from the yeomen and magistrates. Some, too, abandoned their homes for fear of being whipped, if, on being apprehended, confessions satisfactory to the magistrates could either be given or extorted, and this infliction many persons seemed to fear more than death itself. Many unfortunate men who were taken in their own houses were strung up as it were to be hanged, but were let down now and then to try if strangulation would oblige them to become informers. After these and the like experiments, several persons languished for some time, and at length perished in consequence of them. Smiths

INSURRECTION OF 1798.

and carpenters, whose assistance was considered indispensable in the fabrication of pikes, were pointed out, on evidence of their trades, as the first and fittest objects of torture. But the sagacity of some magistrates became at length so acute, from habit and exercise, that they *discerned* an United Irishman even at the first glance! and their zeal never suffered any person whom they deigned to honour with such distinction, to pass without convincing proof of their attention. The two following instances are selected from "An Account of the late Rebellion," by Mr. Alexander, a Protestant inhabitant of Ross, who keeps an academy in that town:—

"I now heard of many punishments of suspected persons, both by flogging and strangulation, being put into execution in the barrack-yard (in Ross), to extort confession of guilt. There were two of these victims brought from the barrack to the Court-house to undergo a repetition of former punishments. One of them, of the name of Driscol, was found in Camlin Wood, near Ross, where he said he generally wandered as a hermit. Upon him were found two Roman Catholic prayer-books, with which it is supposed he administered oaths of disloyalty. He had been strangled three times and flogged four times during confinement, but to no purpose! His fellow-sufferer was one Fitzpatrick of Dunganstown, near Sutton's parish. This man had been a Newfoundland sailor, but long utterly disqualified to follow that occupation, by reason of an inveterate scurvy in his legs. He therefore commenced abecedarian, near Sutton's parish. It happened that a magistrate who was a yeoman, and others of his corps, passed by his noisy mansion, which was no other than a little thatched stable, that, like a bee-hive, proclaimed the industry of its inhabitants. The magistrate entered, followed by the other yeomen,

'Here is a man,' says the magistrate, speaking of the master, as I shall call him, though his authority was now for some months to have an end—and a severe vacation it was—' Here is a man who, I presume, can have no objection to take the oath of allegiance. What do you say, Mr. Teacher ?'—'*O dar a leoursa*' (*i.e.*, by this book), 'I will take it, sir, and thank you for bringing it to me.' So saying, he took the book, which the magistrate held forth, and not only took the oath with the most cordial emphasis, but added another expressive of his loyalty at all times. Upon this, the magistrate regarded his companions with a look of dry humour, and observed, that *this must be a loyal man indeed.* 'Well then, my loyal friend, I suppose you will readily swear to all the pikes, and to the owners and possessors of them, of which you have any knowledge ?' The man swore he had no certain knowledge of the kind; and that he never saw a rebel's pike in his life, or a pike of any kind since the rebellion. 'Then,' says the magistrate, 'you shall swear that you will, to the utmost of your future knowledge or information this way, give, in the best manner you can, all such information to a lawful magistrate, or other officer in his Majesty's service.' 'No, sir,' answered Fitzpatrick, 'I will not swear that; I will bring no man's blood on my head ; and if I do inform, who will support and protect me when I have lost all my scholars, and my neighbours turn upon me ?' Upon this he was immediately apprehended and escorted to Ross: he was not strangled, however, but flogged with great severity ; and it was not with dry eyes that I saw the punishment inflicted on this humble pioneer of literature. About a month after the battle, both these men were tried before General Cowley, and matters appearing no farther against them than I have stated, they were liberated from a close and filthy confinement. The General presented both with a small sum of money, expressing a good-natured concern, that he could not then give them any greater pecuniary assistance. He also gave them written protections, expressive of his opinion of their being peaceably disposed. I never once heard an authentic account of any immediate good effect produced by these punishments. However, it is most certain, that the severities in general served to accelerate the rebellion, and thereby, very considerably, to weaken its progress."*

Many innocent men were thus taken up while peaceably engaged in their own private concerns, walking along the road, or passing through the market in the several towns, without any previous accusation, but in consequence of military whim, or the caprice of magisterial loyalty; and those who had been at market, and were passed by unnoticed, had the news of a public exhibition to bring home; for the unfortunate victims thus seized upon, were instantly subjected, at least, to the torture of public whipping. People of timid dispositions, therefore, avoided going to market, fearing that they might be forced to display the like spectacle. Provisions of course became dear, for want of the usual supply in the market towns; and the military, to redress this evil, went out into the country and brought in what they wanted, at what price they pleased; the owners thinking themselves well treated if they got but half the value of their goods; and in case of a second visit, happy if they escaped unhurt, which, however, was not always the case; and thus were the minds of the people brought to admit such powerful impressions of terror, that death itself was sometimes the consequence. The

* See Alexander's Account of the Rebellion, pages 28, 29.

following is a strong instance of this melancholy fact, related by the Rev. Mr. Gordon:—

"Whether an insurrection in the then existing state of the kingdom would have taken place in the county of Wexford, or, in case of its eruption, how far less formidable and sanguinary it would have been, if no acts of severity had been committed by the soldiery, the yeomen, or their supplementary associates, without the direct authority of their superiors, or command of the magistrate, is a question which I am not able positively to answer. In the neighbourhood of Gorey, if I am not mistaken, the terror of the whippings was in particular so great, that the people would have been extremely glad to renounce for ever all notions of opposition to Government, if they could have been assured of permission to remain in a state of quietness. As an instance of this terror, I shall relate the following fact:—On the morning of the 23rd of May, a labouring man, named Denis M'Daniel, came to my house with looks of the utmost consternation and dismay, and confessed to me that he had taken the United Irishman's oath, and had paid for a pike, with which he had not yet been furnished, nineteen-pence halfpenny, to one Kilty, a smith, who had administered the oath to him and many others. While I sent my eldest son, who was a lieutenant of yeomanry, to arrest Kilty, I exhorted M'Daniel to surrender himself to a magistrate, and make his confession; but this he positively refused, saying that he should, in that case, be lashed to make him produce a pike, which he had not, and to confess what he knew not. I then advised him, as the only alternative, to remain quietly at home, promising that if he should be arrested on the information of others, I would represent his case to the magistrates. He took my advice, but the fear of arrest and lashing had so taken possession of his thoughts that he could neither eat nor sleep; and on the morning of the 25th, he fell on his face and expired in a little grove near my house."*

The Reverend Mr. Gordon, from whose history I have quoted the foregoing narrative, is a clergyman of the Established Church, who resided in the neighbourhood of Gorey, as a curate, for twenty-three years; and as he was an eye-witness, his relation of the fact deserves the utmost credit. He had every opportunity of watching the approach of the Insurrection, and I sincerely wish there were many like him possessed of liberal sentiments and benevolent feelings for the delusions and sufferings of the people. With regard to his opinion, that they would remain quiet in the neighbourhood of Gorey, if they were certain of being left in peace at home, I perfectly coincide with him; and I can confidently assert the same of the neighbourhood in which I resided. It was not possible that the convulsed state of the country could escape the observation of any humane or intelligent person; an inquiry into the cause would naturally succeed such notice, and the result must be the consequent conviction of this truth. I have also reason to believe, that such was the disposition throughout the whole country, as I have heard several respectable magistrates and other persons of veracity from various parts of it express the same sentiment; and, as each individual was undoubtedly the best judge in his own neighbourhood of the conduct of the inhabitants, the inference to be collected from these several uniform statements must be conclusive evidence for the establishment of a fact, to which subsequent events afford a strong corroboration.

While the minds of the people were in this state of distraction and alarm, numbers, condemned to trans-

* See Gordon's History of the Irish Rebellion, pp. 87, 88.

portation by the magistrates of other counties, daily passed through the county of Wexford on their way to Duncannon Fort. Groups of from twelve to fifteen car-loads at a time have gone through Ross alone. These terrifying examples added if possible to the apprehensions already entertained, and the precedent was soon after put in practice in the county of Wexford itself.

Great as the atrocities already related may appear (and surely they are very deplorable), enormities still more shocking to humanity remained to be perpetrated. However grating to generous and benevolent feeling the sad detail must prove, imperious truth imposes the irksome necessity of proceeding to facts.

Mr. Hunter Gowan had for many years distinguished himself by his activity in apprehending robbers, for which he was rewarded with a pension of £100 per annum, and it were much to be wished that every one who has obtained a pension had as well deserved it. Now exalted to the rank of magistrate, and promoted to be captain of a corps of yeomen, he was zealous in exertions to inspire the people about Gorey with dutiful submission to the magistracy, and a respectful awe of the yeomanry. On a public day in the week preceding the Insurrection, the town of Gorey beheld the triumphal entry of Mr. Gowan at the head of his corps, with his sword drawn, and a human finger stuck on the point of it.

With this trophy he marched into the town, parading up and down the streets several times, so that there was not a person in Gorey who did not witness this exhibition; while in the meantime the triumphant corps displayed all the devices of Orangemen. After the labour and fatigue of the day, Mr. Gowan and his men retired to a public-house to refresh themselves, and, *like true blades of game*, their punch was stirred about with the finger that had *graced* their ovation, in imitation of keen fox-hunters who *whisk* a bowl of punch with the brush of a fox before their boozing commences. This captain and magistrate afterwards went to the house of Mr. Jones, where his daughters were; and, while taking a snack that was set before him, he bragged of having blooded his corps that day, and that they were as staunch blood-hounds as any in the world. The daughters begged of their father to show them the Croppy finger, which he deliberately took from his pocket and handed to them. Misses dandled it about with senseless exultation, at which a young lady in the room was so shocked that she turned about to a window, holding her hand to her face to avoid the horrid sight. Mr. Gowan perceiving this, took the finger from his daughters, and *archly* dropped it into the disgusted lady's bosom. She instantly fainted, and thus the scene ended !!! Mr. Gowan constantly boasted of this and other *similar heroic actions*, which he repeated in the presence of Brigade-Major Fitzgerald, on whom he had waited officially; but, so far from meeting with his wonted applause, the Major obliged him instantly to leave the company.

Enniscorthy and its neighbourhood were similarly protected by the activity of Archibald Hamilton Jacob, aided by the yeomen cavalry, thoroughly equipped for this kind of service. They scoured the country, having in their train a regular executioner, completely appointed with his implements—a hanging rope and a cat-o'-nine-tails. Many detections and consequent prosecutions of United Irishmen soon followed. A law had been recently enacted, that magistrates upon their own authority could sentence to transportation persons accused and convicted before them. Great numbers were accordingly taken up, prosecuted, and condemned. Some, however, appealed to an adjournment of a

Quarter Session held in Wexford, on the 23rd of May, in the County Court-house; at which three-and-twenty magistrates from different parts of the county attended. Here all the private sentences were confirmed, except that of one man who was brought in on horseback that morning, carrying a pike with a handle of enormous length through Wexford town, on his way to the gaol. This exhibition procured him the reversion of his sentence, at the instance of the very magistrates who had condemned him. In the course of the trials on these appeals in the public Court-house of Wexford, Mr. A. H. Jacob appeared as evidence against the prisoners, and publicly avowed the happy discoveries he had made in consequence of inflicting the torture: many instances of whipping and strangulation he particularly detailed with a degree of self-approbation and complacency, that clearly demonstrated how highly he was pleased to rate the merits of his own *great* and *loyal* services!

From the construction of the new law regarding the discretionary power of magistrates, the ratification of these sentences did not surprise me, except in two instances, at the discussion of which I was actually present. One was that of a Roman Catholic priest of the name of Dixon, taken up shortly before by Captain Boyd, on the information of a gardener, who averred he had been in Wexford on a market-day, in a public-house, where he met with the priest, who spent a considerable time, he said, to induce him to become a United Irishman; very plausibly relating a train of circumstances tending to that effect. In contradiction to this man's testimony, there appeared three credible witnesses, describing the situation of the house and the several companies there assembled at the time specified; by which it was manifest, that the particulars stated by the prosecutor were utterly unfounded, as they could not possibly have taken place without their knowledge. The other was that of a man named William Graham, servant to Lieutenant Joseph Gray, of the Wexford yeomen cavalry. He was taken up for being out of his master's house at eleven o'clock at night, and was supposed to be a United Irishman. His defence was a good character given him by different gentlemen, and that although the general proclamation of the county prohibited all persons from being out of their dwellings at night, yet from the peaceable demeanour of the inhabitants of the town of Wexford, so rigorous and strict an adherence to its literal tenor had not been insisted on in any one instance but against him. However, the alleged necessity of public example was a sufficient excuse with the majority of the magistrates to condemn these men to transportation.

The magistrates after this public discussion retired to the Grand Jury room to deliberate, from whence the following public notice was issued, printed, and distributed through the county:—

"NOTICE.—We, the High Sheriff and Magistrates of the County of Wexford, assembled at Sessions held at the County Court-house in Wexford, this 23rd day of May, 1798, have received the most clear and unequivocal evidence, private as well as public, that the system and plans of those deluded persons who style themselves, and are commonly known by the name of United Irishmen, have been generally adopted by the inhabitants of the several parishes in this county, who have provided themselves with pikes and other arms for the purpose of carrying their plans into execution. And whereas we have received information, that the inhabitants of some parts of this county have, within these few days past, returned to their allegiance, surrendering their arms, and confessing the errors of their past misconduct. Now we, the High Sheriff and Magistrates, assembled as aforesaid, do give this public notice, that if within the space of fourteen days from the date hereof, the inhabitants of the other parts of this county do not come in to some of the magistrates of this county, and surrender their arms and other offensive weapons, concealed or otherwise, and give such proof of their return to their allegiance as shall appear sufficient, an application will be made to Government to send the army, at free quarters, into such parishes as shall fail to comply, to enforce due obedience to this notice.

EDWARD PERCIVAL, Sheriff;
COURTOWN,
JOHN HENRY LYSTER,
JAMES BOYD,
GEORGE LE-HUNTE,
THOMAS HANDCOCK,
JOHN JAMES,
JOHN POUNDEN,
HAWTREY WHITE,
JAMES WHITE,
EBENEZER JACOB,
WILLIAM HORE,
EDWARD D'ARCY,
JOHN HEATLY,
JOHN GROGAN,
ARCHIBALD JACOB,
EDWARD TURNER,
ISAAC CORNOCK,
CORNELIUS GROGAN,
FRANCIS TURNER,
WILLIAM TOOLE,
RICHARD NEWTON KING,
CHARLES VERO."

"Resolved unanimously: That the thanks of this meeting be given to Archibald Jacob, Esq., for his manly, spirited, active, and efficacious exertions as a magistrate for the establishment and preservation of the public peace."

I have heard some of these very magistrates give opinions so totally contrary to what is publicly declared in this resolution of thanks, that it is with the utmost surprise I saw their names annexed to a document, whereby they publicly approved of conduct whereof in private they expressed the strongest detestation. But it often happens that well disposed men are led thus to sanction proceedings they abhor; not possessing sufficient firmness of mind to maintain their own sentiments, and fearing that their humanity should appear to derogate in any degree from their loyalty. It is remarkable, that on this very day the rebellion broke out in the county of Kildare, the news of which, running as it were with the wind, quickly reached the county of Wexford. The people in this county, however, who were possessed of pikes or other arms, were continually crowding in to the different magistrates throughout the whole county, for the purpose of surrendering them, conformable to the notice before mentioned; and following the like example set them by the county of Wicklow, where it appears there had been leaders (afterwards imprisoned) who made discoveries which led the public to believe that all idea of a rising was at that time given up.

As this notice specified that there were fourteen days allowed for the return of the people to their allegiance, it was reasonably concluded the protection of such as would submit within that time was guaranteed by the magistrates who had signed it; and it was also natural to imply, that all measures would cease during that interval which might tend in any degree to subvert the peaceable intentions of the people. Would to God! that even at this period the spirit of this publication had been adhered to; for, in such an event, it is very probable that the county of Wexford would have escaped the dreadful misfortune of open insurrection! In Enniscorthy, Ross, and Gorey, several persons were not only put to the torture in the usual manner, but a greater number of houses were burnt, and measures of the strongest coercion were practised, although the people continued to flock in to the different magistrates for protections. Mr. Perry of Inch, a Protestant gentleman, was seized on and brought a prisoner to Gorey, guarded by the North Cork militia; one of whom—the noted sergeant nicknamed *Tom the Devil*—gave him woful experience of his ingenuity and adroitness at devising torment. As a specimen of his *savoir faire*, he cut off the hair of his head very closely, cut the sign of the cross from the front to the back, and transversely from ear to ear, still closer ; and probably a pitched cap not being in readiness, gunpowder was mixed through the hair, which was then set on fire, and the shocking process repeated, until every atom of hair that remained could be easily pulled out by the roots ; and still a burning candle was continually applied, until the entire was completely singed away, and the head left totally and miserably blistered ! At Carnew things were carried to still greater length ; for, independent of burning, whipping, and torture in all shapes, on Friday, the 25th of May, twenty-eight prisoners were brought out of the place of confinement, and deliberately shot in a ball-alley by the yeomen, and a party of the Antrim militia ; the infernal deed being sanctioned by the presence of their officers ! Many of the men thus inhumanly butchered had been confined on mere suspicion ! ! !

Lord Courtown is said to have been for adopting lenient measures ; and although it might be reasonably thought that his rank and character ought to have had due influence in the neighbourhood of Gorey, yet his benevolent intentions were overpowered by the disposition to severity of most of the magistrates ; and consequently, the measures of the most violent were adopted. The following is the Rev. Mr. Gordon's representation of his lordship's conduct:—" As the Earl of Courtown had performed much in providing a force to obviate or suppress rebellion, so his treatment of the common people, by his affable manners, had been always such as was best adapted to produce content in the lower classes, and prevent a proneness to insurrection. I consider myself as bound in strictness of justice to society, thus far to represent the conduct of this nobleman. Doubtless, the people in the neighbourhood of Gorey were the last and least violent of all in the county of Wexford, in rising against the established authority; and certainly the behaviour of the Stopford family in that neighbourhood has been always remarkably conciliating and humane?"—Page 104.

Can any thing be more convincing than this testimony, to show of what inestimable value it is for any country to possess good men; but especially for Ireland, where it is a prevalent system to treat inferiors with the utmost cruelty and contempt, as if they were a different and odious species of being? If one family could effect so much good by their affable and conciliating manners, is it not painful to reflect on the consequences of a contrary behaviour to a people, who, of all others in the world, are the most generous and open-hearted; and want only the fostering hand of humanity, due encouragement, and a cultivation of their natural talents, to vie in excellence with any race of men on the globe.

Having spent Friday, the 25th of May, with Mr. Turner, a magistrate of the county, at Newfort, he requested of me to attend him next day at Newpark, the seat of Mr. Fitzgerald, where, as the most central place, he had appointed to meet the people of the neighbourhood. I accordingly met him there, on Saturday the 26th, where he continued the whole day administering the oath of allegiance to vast numbers of people: a certificate was given to every person who took the oath, and surrendered any offensive weapon. Many attended who offered to take the oath, and also to depose that they were not United Irishmen, and that they possessed no arms of any kind whatever; and earnestly asked for certificates. But so great was the concourse of these, that considering the trouble of writing them out, it was found impossible to supply them all with such testimonials at that time. Mr. Turner, therefore, continued to receive surrendered arms, desiring such as had none, to wait a more convenient opportunity. Numbers, however, still conceiving that they would not be secure without a written protection, offered ten times their intrinsic value to such as had brought pike blades to surrender; but these, being unwilling to forego the benefit of a written protection for the moment, refused to part with their weapons on any other consideration. Among the great numbers assembled on this occasion were some men from the village of Ballaghkeen, who had the appearance of being more dead than alive, from the apprehensions they were under of having their houses burnt, or themselves whipt, should they return home. These apprehensions had been excited to this degree, because that on the night of Thursday the 24th, the Enniscorthy cavalry, conducted by Mr. Archibald Hamilton Jacob, had come to Ballaghkeen; but on hearing the approaching noise, the inhabitants ran out of their houses, and fled into large brakes of furze on a hill immediately above the village, from whence they could hear the cries of one of their neighbours, who was dragged out of his house, tied up to a thorn-tree, and while one yeoman continued flogging him, another was throwing water on his back. The groans of the unfortunate sufferer, from the stillness of the night, reverberated widely through the appalled neighbourhood; and the spot of execution these men represented to have appeared next morning, "as if a *pig* had been killed there." After this transaction Mr. Jacob went round to all the rest of the houses, and signified, that if he should find the owners out of them, on his next visit, he would burn them. These men, whose countenances exhibited marks of real terror, particularly from apprehension of flogging, which they seemed to dread more than death itself, offered to surrender themselves prisoners to Mr. Turner, who did all in his power to allay their fears, offering to give them all certificates, the production of which to Mr. Jacob, he was sure, would afford them protection; but they still persisted in preferring to remain as prisoners with Mr. Turner, rather than to place any confidence in Mr. Jacob. Mr. Turner then gave them certificates, declaring their absence from home to be by his permission, to be left with their families, and told them they might come to his house if they pleased. Mr. Turner's feelings appeared but too sensibly affected at the recital of these excesses. He lamented that such scenes had been exhibited, and said he had conceived that all coercive measures were to cease, during the fourteen days allowed by the magistrates for the people to surrender their arms; adding, that he greatly feared that very desirable object would be much retarded by such violence, which would prove the more lamentable, on account of the recent news from the county of Kildare. On this very day, too, we had the mortification to be informed that the furniture and effects of a shop-keeper at Enniscorthy were brought out and burned in the public street; and, on the next morning, a man was hanged there, and his body dragged up and down several times through the market place, with shocking inhumanity and inefficient cruelty!

I remained the whole day with Mr. Turner, who did not go home till after ten o'clock. We indulged in the fond hope at parting, that the county of Wexford would remain quiet, from the disposition generally shown by the people, and we separated with the expectation of being able to pay our friendly visits to each other as usual. Indeed all over the county of Wexford, the people had now given up all thought of insurrection, of which nothing can afford a more convincing proof than the general surrender of arms; and I have heard respectable magistrates, to whom they were surrendered, declare their conviction to the same effect. Mr. Richards, of Solborough, captain of the Enniscorthy cavalry; Mr. Beauman, of Hyde Park, captain of the Coolgreny cavalry; Mr. Cornock, captain of the Scarawalsh infantry; and the Rev. Mr. Colclough, of Duffrey Hall, distinguished themselves by their anxiety to satisfy and calm the agitated minds of the populace; and were busily employed in granting certificates to such as surrendered their arms. Many other magistrates attended at different places for the same purpose. Mr. Bagnal Harvey had collected the arms of all his tenantry and neighbourhood, and on this very day (Saturday the 26th of May,) brought them into Wexford. As it was late when he delivered them up, he did not return home that night, but remained in town; and just as he was going to bed, he was arrested by Captain Boyd, and lodged in the gaol. Mr. Percivall, the High Sheriff, and Captain Boyd, with a strong party of the Wexford cavalry, proceeded on the same night to Newpark, the seat of Mr. Fitzgerald, to take him prisoner. I had remained there that night, and was alarmed and roused from my bed by a loud rapping at the door about midnight, which I soon discovered to be the party before mentioned, who came to arrest Mr. Fitzgerald. I requested permission to accompany my friend, which was granted; but as these gentlemen refused taking the pikes and other arms that had been surrendered at the place the day before to Mr. Turner, and had remained there, I despatched a messenger to him with the intelligence of what had happened, before we set out with this escort, which met with no other delay but while they chose to continue rummaging Mr. Fitzgerald's papers, among which, by-the-by, they could discover nothing that could in the remotest degree criminate him. We arrived a little after daylight in Wexford, where Mr. Fitzgerald was lodged in the gaol. The Wexford cavalry then set off to Ballyteigue, ten miles from town, from whence they brought Mr. John Henry Colclough prisoner in the course of the day, and lodged him also in the gaol.

Early on this morning, being Whit Sunday, I saw Mr. Turner on his entrance into Wexford. He brought the first intelligence of the rising of the people, from whom, he said, he could not have been so fortunate as to escape but for my messenger, who had called him up before day; otherwise he would have been at home when his house was attacked by the multitude for arms, as were all the houses throughout the whole neighbourhood at that time. When he had given notice of the fact to the officer commanding in the barracks, I accompanied him to the gaol, and after having seen our friend, set out with him to Castlebridge, where finding the Insurrection much more serious than was at first imagined, all kind of parleying being deemed ineffectual, on consultation with the officers present, I returned to Wexford, as they considered my situation would be too perilous should I accompany them in coloured clothes. The Shilmalier cavalry, commanded by Colonel Le-Hunte, had already assembled, before the arrival of one hundred and ten of the North Cork militia, who took route by the lower road along the sea-side, while the yeomen had taken the upper road by Castlebridge. Both met at Ballifanock, and proceeded together as far as Ballinamonabeg, where Mr. Turner, not finding a man of the name of Darby Kavanagh, who kept a public-house there, at home, and having remembered that he had surrendered a pike the day before, he ordered the house to be set on fire, after getting what spirits and beer it contained to refresh the soldiers, who were much fatigued after their hasty march through heavy sandy roads. A proposal was made to burn the chapel of Ballinamonabeg just adjoining, which was over-ruled, particularly by Armstrong Browne, Esq., who observed it would be a very indifferent compliment to pay the Catholics to burn their place of worship, while a considerable part of the force then assembled were of that persuasion,* which sentiment actually prevented the burning of the chapel.

Having halted here for some time, they proceeded three miles farther, and came in sight of the insurgents collected in great numbers on the hill of Oulart, distant about ten miles from Wexford. Colonel Foote of the North Cork, seeing their position so strong and commanding, thought it advisable not to attack them; but Major Lombard, of the same regiment, being of a contrary opinion, orders were given to burn two houses, situated in a hollow, between the army and the insurgents, and Mr. Turner volunteered his service for that purpose. This was done with a view to stimulate the insurgents to revenge, and thus, if possible, to induce them to abandon the advantage of their situation. This feint, however, not succeeding, and Colonel Foote still persisting in his opinion, Major Lombard instantly addressed the soldiers in terms animating them at once to attack the insurgents, who, he said, would fly at their approach. His words had the effect of making them advance. They descended from the small eminence which they occupied, and crossing the valley between,

* Shilmailer cavalry present, viz., Colonel Le-Hunte, Lieutenant Armstrong Browne, Lieutenant Kavanagh, Colonel Watson, Sergeant Edward Turner, Henry Hatchell, Samuel Maude, Richard Gainfort, Maurice Jones, and Richard Williams, Protestants.—Nicholas Dixon, Ignatius Rosseter, Walter Redmond, James Lambert, Michael Waddick, Richard Kinselagh, Charles Dunn, Patrick Dixon, and —— Murphy, Catholics.

began to ascend the hill of Oulart, while the Shilmalier cavalry took a circuitous route, round the hill to the left, with the intention of preventing a retreat, but in fact they caused numbers to rally, who attempted to run off, on perceiving the approach of a serious engagement. This also contributed to make the insurgents rush in greater number, and with accumulated force, on the North Cork, who were charging up the hill. They had fired but two volleys when they were totally discomfited. This success of the insurgents was much promoted by the address of a servant boy, who, as the military were ascending the hill, advised such of the insurgents as were then about him, to lie down under cover of the ditches, and wait the close approach of the military. By this manœuvre these were suddenly surprised by a force not greatly outnumbering themselves, but the impetuosity of the attack occasioned their total overthrow, while the fact was, at the instant, utterly unknown to the great body of the insurgents, who attended their commanders on the other side of the hill. Of the North Cork party, Major Lombard, the Hon. Captain de Courcy, Lieutenants Williams, Ware, Barry, and Ensign Keogh, were left on the field of battle. In short, none escaped except Colonel Foote, a sergeant who mounted the Major's horse, a drummer, and two privates. It may not be unworthy of remark, that here was a fool who followed the North Cork, and who, when he saw the Major fall, ran to the body and embraced it, then took the Major's sword, and with it dispatched two men before he fell himself. The insurgents had but five men killed, and two wounded. The Shilmalier cavalry, and Colonel Foote, made a precipitate retreat to Wexford. A large party of the Wexford cavalry also, who had no share whatever in the action, were involved in this retreat. Having lodged Mr. Colclough in gaol, they set out on another excursion to Ballimurrin. In their course they shot some straggling men, and burned two houses on finding two men killed near them. They were thus employed in scouring the country when informed of the defeat at Oulart, and this determined them without hesitation to retreat with all speed homewards.

The remainder of the North Cork regiment were instantly under arms in the barracks, when informed of the defeat of that part of their body which had gone out to action. Burning for revenge, they actually marched to the bridge, as if determined to proceed and meet the insurgents; but they were induced to return by some gentlemen, who endeavoured to dissuade them from so headlong and unsafe an undertaking.

The great suspense felt by the inhabitants of Wexford, during the whole of this day, on account of so sudden an insurrection, now grew into serious alarm, such as unexpected news like this must inspire. The lamentations of the unfortunate widows and orphans of the soldiers who had fallen in the encounter, increased the general consternation. These, clapping their hands, ran about the streets quite frantic, mixing their piteous moanings with the plaintive cries of their children, and uttering their bitterest maledictions against the yeomen, whom they charged with having run away, and left their husbands to destruction! Letters were despatched to Duncannon Fort and to Waterford with these disastrous accounts, and requesting reinforcements.

Those of the North Cork militia then in the town vowed vengeance against the prisoners confined in the gaol, particularly against Messrs. Harvey, Fitzgerald, and Colclough, so lately taken up; and so explicitly and without reserve were these intentions manifested, that I myself heard a sergeant and others of the regiment declare that they could not *die easy* if they should not have the satisfaction of putting the prisoners in the gaol of Wexford to death, particularly the three gentlemen last mentioned. Nor was this monstrous design harboured only by the common soldiers: some of the officers declared the same intentions. I communicated all to the gaoler, who informed me that he had himself heard the guards of the gaol express their hostile intentions. He was so alarmed and apprehensive of their putting their threats into execution, that he contrived means to get them out, then locked the door, and determined to defend his charge at the risk of his life. He then, with a humanity and presence of mind, that would have become a better station, communicated his apprehensions to all the prisoners, whom he advised to remain close in their cells, so as to avoid being shot in case of an actual attack. He armed the three gentlemen, and formed so judicious a plan of defence, that in the event of their being overpowered, their lives could not be had at a cheap rate. Of this scene I was myself an eye-witness, having permission from the High Sheriff to pay every attention to my friend and relation, Mr. Fitzgerald. The latter gentleman gave me his watch, pocket-book and every thing valuable about him; and we took leave, as if we expected never to see each other more. Several of the North Cork came to the gaol door, but were refused admittance. At last a party of them came with a woman, or one who feigned a female voice, begging admittance; and the door being opened, the soldiers instantly rushed forward to get in, but were prevented by a half-door that remained still shut. The whole door was then closed, and it jambed in a soldier's arm, who desisted not from his design, until his bayonet, with which he attempted to stab the gaoler several times, was wrested from him. A number of soldiers went round the gaol several times, as if to reconnoitre, and were overheard threatening the prisoners with certain destruction, if they could but get in ; and I verily believe that, had it not been for the indefatigable exertions of the gaoler, the prisoners would have been all massacred; and dreadful it is to think what consequences must have ensued ! The alarms of the three gentlemen already named were so much increased by these circumstances, as well as by other reports, that they made every disposition of their properties, as if on the point of death.

The rising of the people in the county of Wexford took place in the direction from Carnew to Oulart, for fear, as they alleged, of being whipped, burned, or exterminated by the Orangemen ; hearing of the numbers of people that were put to death, unarmed and unoffending, through the country; the deliberate massacre and shooting of eight and twenty prisoners in the ball-alley of Carnew, without trial, and some under sentence of transportation, who stopped there on their way to Geneva,—among these was a Mr. William Young, a Protestant, who was ordered to be transported by a military tribunal. At Dunlavin, thirty-four men were shot without trial, and among them the informer on whose evidence they were arrested. Strange to tell, officers presided to sanction these proceedings ! A man escaped by feigning to be killed ; he was one out of eighteen of the corps of Captain Saunders, of Saunders Grove, Baltinglass. These reports, together with all the dreadful accounts from the county of Kildare, roused their minds to the utmost pitch of alarm, indignation, and fury. They were forming from the evening of the 26th during the whole of the night, in two bodies. One assembled on Kilthomas Hill, against whom marched from Carnew, on the morning of the 27th, a body of yeomen cavalry and infantry, who proceeded boldly up the hill, where

the insurgents possessed a strong and commanding
situation if they knew how to take advantage of it;
but they were panic-struck, and fled at the approach of
the military, who pursued them with great slaughter.
They spared no man they met, and burned at least
one hundred houses in the course of a march of seven
miles.

The Rev. Michael Murphy had been so alarmed on
hearing of the rising of the people, that he fled into
the town of Gorey early on Whit Sunday; on his
arrival, not finding Mr. Kenny, with whom he had
lodged there, he was induced to return for him and his
family, for which purpose, not being able to procure a
driver, he himself led a horse and car, and pursued a
by-road to get, if possible, unobserved into Ballecanow,
by which means he did not meet some yeomen and
others that had gone on the high-road to Gorey, after
they had torn up the altar, broken the windows, and
otherwise damaged the Roman Catholic chapel; uttering the most violent threats against the priest and his
flock, which specimens were very unlikely to remove the
dreadful reports of the intended extermination of the
Catholics. These depredations had so much weight on
the Rev. Michael Murphy as to induce him to alter
his original intentions not to fly to such men for
protection, and he was then led on by the multitude to
Kilthomas Hill; the Rev. John Murphy had from
similar unforeseen occurrences joined the insurgents.
These two clergymen had been remarkable for their
exhortations and exertions against the system of United
Irishmen, until they were thus whirled into this
political vortex, which, from all the information I have
been able to collect, they undertook under the apprehension of extermination.

The Rev. John Murphy was acting coadjutor of the
parish of Monageer; and, impressed with horror at the

desolation around him, took up arms with the people, representing to them that they had better die courageously in the field, than to be butchered in their houses. The insurgents in this quarter now began their career by imitating the example that had been set before them. They commenced burning the houses of those who were most obnoxious to them. Every gentleman's house in the country was summoned to surrender their arms, and where any resistance was offered, the house was attacked, plundered, and burnt, and most of the inhabitants killed in the conflict. The Camolin cavalry were the first that attacked these insurgents: in the action Lieutenant Bookey and some privates lost their lives—the rest retreated to Gorey. On the 27th of May, Captain Hawtrey White led out two troops of horse from Gorey, determined to revenge the death of their companions. They came in sight of the insurgents on the north side of the hill of Oulart; but they appeared in such force that they thought it not prudent to attack them, but returned to Gorey, burning the houses of suspected persons, and putting every straggler to death on their way. Numbers were called to their doors and shot, while many more met the like fate within their house, and some even that were asleep.

Thus it appears that the Insurrection broke out at first in a line from west to east, pretty nearly across the midde of the county, unsupported by the inhabitants either north or south of that direction. These were the tracts whose natives appeared most peaceably inclined, and who thought to avoid joining in the Insurrection. The yeomanry of the north of the county proceeded on the 27th against a quiet and defenceless populace; sallied forth in their neighbourhoods, burned numbers of houses, and put to death hundreds of persons who were unarmed, unoffending, and unresisting, so that those who had taken up arms had the greater chance of escape at that time. I cannot avoid mentioning a circumstance, though not a singular one, that took place amidst these calamities. Mr. William Hore of Harperstown, on his return home from Wexford, was induced to set fire to the house of Miles Redmond of Harvey's Town, a lime burner. This occasioned his subsequent confinement, and afterwards his death on the bridge of Wexford. He had offered to build him a better house, which Mrs. Hore, his widow, notwithstanding her irretrievable loss, has since actually performed.

Such was the state of the northern part of the county, which continued, during the whole of Whit Sunday, ignorant of the state of the south.

On the evening of the 26th, Captain John Grogan, perceiving, from a height near his house, several houses on fire between Enniscorthy and Oulart, assembled as many of his yeomen as he could muster, and proceeded with them to Enniscorthy, whence he accompanied Captain Solomon Richards, of the Enniscorthy cavalry, to meet the insurgents, who were committing great devastation throughout the country, in retaliation, as they alleged, for what they had previously suffered. In fact there seemed to exist between the parties an emulation of enmity, as they endeavoured to outdo each other in mischief, by burning and destroying on both sides those whom they deemed their enemies. The Roman Catholic Chapel of Boolevogue was burnt, as was the house of the Rev. John Murphy, already mentioned; and several houses were set on fire, and some of the inhabitants consumed within them: no man that was seen in coloured clothes escaped the fury of the yeomanry. In and about Ferns, a party of the North Cork militia and some yeomen pursued the like conduct, as well as in the course of their retreat from thence to Enniscorthy, where they arrived on the morning of the 27th. The Shilmailer infantry, commanded by the Right Hon. George Ogle, were then in Enniscorthy also. They took an excursion to Darby Gap, and on their return they marched home. Captain John Grogan escorted Sergeant Stanley as far as Waterford, on his way to Cork as Judge of Assize. The town of Enniscorthy was crowded by great numbers of people who fled into it from the country—Catholics among the rest. Some of the latter were put into confinement in the castle, notwithstanding the deplorable evils of which that impolitic system had been already producive; and although it must be naturally imagined, that a greater proof could not be given of not wishing to join the insurgents than that of flying into the town for refuge.

On Monday morning, the 28th of May, every preparation was made for defence, and every precaution observed in the town. Part of the North Cork militia, commanded by Captain Snowe, Captain Cornock, and Captain Pounden's infantry corps, with their supernumeraries, and the Enniscorthy cavalry, commanded by Captain Richards (the whole military force in the town), were on the alert, and under arms in expectation of an immediate attack. Many of the inhabitants of the town offered their services, and armed themselves as well as they could to contribute to the general defence. Some of the most respectable were permitted to join the troops; but most of those who had offered their assistance were, during the battle, ordered to ground their arms and retire into their houses, out of which they were peremptorily warned not to stir on pain of death. Good God! what miserable policy in such times, to brand them as Catholics with disaffection, when their actions bespoke so much the contrary, and thus to force them into the ranks of the insurgents! After the battle of Oulart the insurgents encamped for the night at Carrigrew, from whence they set out at seven o'clock on Monday morning, the 28th, to Camolin, from thence to Ferns, where meeting with no interruption, or any military force to oppose them, they crossed the Slaney by the bridge at Scarawalsh, halted for some time on the hill of Ballioril, and from thence they proceeded to attack Enniscorthy, where they arrived about one o'clock, driving before them a great number of cattle with a view of overpowering the yeoman infantry that had proceeded to the Duffrey Gate, where the attack commenced. The assailants, posting themselves behind the ditches that enclosed the town parks, kept up a severe but irregular fire of musketry, intermixed with pike-men, who were twice charged by the Enniscorthy cavalry along the two roads leading into the town, with little or no effect. The battle lasted with various success for four hours. Captain Snowe, not considering it prudent to quit his situation on the bridge to support the yeomen at the Duffrey Gate, who then fell down by degrees into the town, leaving the suburbs, composed of thatched houses, unprotected, which then were set on fire to (each party accusing the other for doing so), and, as it turned out, nothing could be more conducive to the success of the insurgents. During the confusion the conflagrations occasioned, from which each party retreated, the military taking their station in the town: had they marched out to meet the insurgents, and given them battle where they might have the advantage of the ditches, their superiority in discipline and fire-arms might have enabled them to break and dissipate the tumultuary body opposed to them, that had every advantage over those placed in a hollow. The insurgents made an attempt to cross the river at the island above the bridge, from whence they were so galled as to oblige them to wade through the Slaney higher up at

Blackstoops; some were proceeding to Vinegar Hill, which, from its commanding situation immediately above the town, gave them every advantage of observation, whilst their numbers afforded a sufficiency to attack the town on all sides. The military were at length overpowered by the impetuosity and intrepidity of the insurgents, many of whom fell in the gallant defence made against them; but the soldiers having no cannon to support them, and the suburbs of the town being on fire in several places, they at last sounded a retreat. Whilst the town was thus circumstanced, a proposal was made to Captain Snowe to put the prisoners to death before the evacuation of the place; but he, like a truly brave man, would not listen to such a diabolical proposal, and rejected it with scorn and abhorrence; notwithstanding which a party went to the castle determined to put all confined therein to death. An ineffectual attempt was made to break open the door, the keeper having forgot to leave the key, with which he had set off towards Wexford; and this circumstance providentially saved the lives of the prisoners, as it became too dangerous for the yeomen to wait any longer to put their threats into execution—threats which they constantly repeated the whole of that morning while they stood guard over their prisoners. Indeed, so assured were the prisoners themselves of being put to death, that they had continued for hours on their knees at prayer in preparation for that awful event, when the victors released them from confinement. Captain John Pounden, of the Enniscorthy supplementary infantry, Lieutenant Hunt, of the Enniscorthy yeomen, and Lieutenant Carden, of the Scarawalsh infantry, with about eighty of the military, and some supplementary men, fell in this action. A regular retreat being sounded, gave the military an opportunity of bringing away their families and friends, together with a great many men, women, and children, who proceeded in the best manner they could to Wexford. The only opinion prevailing in the latter town for some hours was, that Enniscorthy and all its inhabitants were totally destroyed. This was occasioned by the arrival in Wexford of Lieutenant Archibald Hamilton Jacob, and a private of the Enniscorthy cavalry, who had been so fortunate as to effect their escape, and who came in with their horses all in a foam, so as to bespeak the most precipitate flight. At the same time, tremendous clouds of smoke were observed over Enniscorthy, which is distant only eleven miles from Wexford, and no news arriving for several hours, left room for no other conjecture, but seemed to confirm the account given by these fugitives. The military in their retreat were very confused at first; however, self-preservation urged their keeping together, suggested by a private in the yeomanry. Officers had been induced to tear off their epaulets and every other mark that could distinguish them from the privates, considering themselves in more danger if they were recognised as officers. However, not being attacked, there was sufficient leisure to escort those that accompanied them, and who were in such a piteous plight as to excite on their arrival the hearty commiseration of all the inhabitants of Wexford, who invited them indiscriminately to their houses, and supplied them with every comfort and necessary in their power, and of which they stood so much in need. How distressing must be the situation of many ladies who were glad to get up behind or before any person that might be tender enough, in the general consternation, to take them on horseback! Some had their clothes scorched about them, others wanted their shoes and other parts of their dress, which had been lost or torn off; besides, the great heat of the day made it doubly distressing to delicate females, many of whom had the additional charge of the burden and care of their children. It was very deplorable to observe the anguish and misery of these fugitives, so suddenly and violently torn from their homes and family endearments ; while each in melancholy detail dwelt upon the relation of private calamity.

Great as the apprehensions of the inhabitants of Wexford had been before, they were much heightened by the mournful appearances and heart-rending recitals of these unhappy sufferers. All dreaded that their houses, their properties, and themselves, should share the fate of Enniscorthy and its inhabitants. At this critical period, the Shilmalier infantry, commanded by the Right Hon. George Ogle, marched from their homes into Wexford. Every possible preparation was now made for defence. The several avenues leading into the town were barricaded, and cannon were placed at the different entrances. The inhabitants universally manifested a zeal to defend their habitations, their properties, and their families against the insurgents; and numbers offered themselves for the ranks, and to perform military duty. Upwards of two hundred were consequently embodied, there being arms for no more, under the command of gentlemen who had been in the army, and officers of the militia then in the town on leave of absence. These occasional soldiers mounted guard in the same manner with the more regular troops of militia and yeomen ; and every precaution was taken to guard against a nocturnal surprise, which was strongly apprehended. The gentlemen confined in the gaol were visited by numbers of those in town, who entreated Messrs. Harvey and Colclough to write to their tenants and neighbours, to induce them to remain quiet at their homes, and to avoid joining the insurgents from the other side of the Slaney. This the gentlemen readily complied with, in the presence of those who besought them, urging it in the most strenuous and persuasive terms they could; and messengers were accordingly dispatched to every person, who it was suggested to them, possessed influence enough for the purpose, or who was imagined capable of contributing to keep the inhabitants of the baronies of Forth and Bargy from rising.

On the morning of the 29th, the dispositions for the defence of the town were continued with unabated vigour. Two hundred men of the Donegal militia, commanded by Colonel Maxwell, with a six-pounder, marched in at eight o'clock in the morning, and were billeted throughout the town to get refreshment, of which they stood in great need, having marched all night from Duncannon Fort, accompanied by the Healthfield cavalry, commanded by Captain John Grogan. This gentleman, having escorted Sergeant Stanley to Waterford, returned to Duncannon Fort, where he met General Fawcett, whose determination he now announced of coming to the assistance of Wexford with an additional force as soon as possible. With this detachment also arrived Colonel Colville, Captain Young, and Lieutenant Soden, officers of the thirteenth regiment, giving the glad tidings of the approach of their body with General Fawcett, and the Meath militia. A gentleman was, however, dispatched to the General, to urge in the most pressing terms the immediate necessity of the reinforcement. The Taghmon cavalry, under the command of Captain Cox, arrived in town in the course of the day. The apprehensions of the inhabitants increased every moment. Every boat in the harbour was busily employed in the conveyance of women and children, with the most valuable effects, on board ships, which now were in great requisition, occasioned by the vast numbers of people who crowded these vessels, in order to escape from the town, which it was dreaded would be burnt. To guard against such a disastrous event, all the fires in the town were strictly ordered to be put out at different intervals; and during the prohibited time, even the bakers were not allowed to heat their ovens. A further measure of precaution adopted on this occasion was, that of stripping all the thatched houses within the walls of the town, which last, by-the-by, were still standing in full preservation, except the gateways, that had been long broken down for public convenience, but were now strongly barricaded. In short, the utmost activity prevailed for purposes of defence. The guards were augmented, and patrols of cavalry were constantly sent out to reconnoitre. The widows of those of the North Cork militia who had fallen in the action at Oulart, still continued inconsolable about the town, uttering their piteous lamentations. The bodies of the officers who were slain on that occasion were this day brought in by Major Lombard's servant, who had gone out for that purpose; and this contributed not a little to dispirit the military in the town.

Some of my friends then in Wexford intimated to me, that it seemed to be the general wish of all the gentlemen in the place that I should go out to the people, and endeavour to induce them to disperse— my great popularity and family influence, it was suggested, pointing me out as the fittest person to undertake such a mission; which, from these circumstances, it was hoped might prove successful. My answer was, that I would not refuse to do anything that was imagined to be for the general good, although I thought the experiment most hazardous, provided a magistrate whose honour might be depended on would accompany me; besides, that I should have my directions in writing, a copy whereof I would leave with my friends, in order that if I should fall in the enterprise, nothing might be left in the power of misrepresentation to state to my dishonour. No magistrate being found, as I suppose, that would venture on this dangerous service, it was then inquired whether the liberation of Messrs. Harvey, Fitzgerald, and Colclough might not appease the people? On this question I declared myself incompetent to decide. I was then asked, whether if enlarged on bail, but particularly Mr. Fitzgerald, whose residence lay in the country then disturbed, they would undertake to go out to the insurgents and endeavour to prevail on them to disperse? On this inquiry my opinion was, that as the lives of these gentlemen were in danger from the fury of the soldiery while they continued in prison, I thought they would comply with this requisition. The matter now became public, and the prisoners were accordingly visited by the most respectable gentlemen in the town; several requesting of me to accompany them to the prison, for the purpose of introduction. Indeed, so marked was the attention paid to them on this occasion, that an indifferent spectator would be led to consider them rather as the governors of the town, than as prisoners. On the 28th and 29th, I had many conversations on this subject with the officers and gentlemen of the place; and at length I was myself, together with five other gentlemen (two for each of the three prisoners), bound in five hundred pounds severally; and Messrs. Harvey, Fitzgerald, and Colclough themselves individually in one thousand pounds security for their appearance at the next Assizes. It was further conditioned, that although they were all three bailed, two only should be at large at any one time; but that they might take their turns of going abroad interchangeably at their discretion, provided one should always remain in gaol as a guarantee for the return of the rest. This compact was entered into with Captain Boyd particularly. Mr. Harvey was then fixed on to remain, and Messrs. Fitzgerald and Colclough were immediately liberated, and sent out to endeavour to prevail on the people to disperse. They were escorted from the gaol by several gentlemen, who conducted them beyond the outposts; and then a yeoman was sent to attend them till they passed the patrols, and so they set off towards Enniscorthy.

The entire military force at this time in Wexford, consisted of three hundred of the North Cork militia, commanded by Colonel Foote; two hundred of the Donegal militia, under the direction of Colonel Maxwell; five troops of yeomen cavalry, viz., those of Wexford, commanded by Captain Boyd; the Enniscorthy, by Captain Richards; the Taghmon, by Captain Cox; the Healthfield, by Captain John Grogan; and the Shilmalier, by Colonel Le-Hunte; the infantry yeomen were those of Wexford, under Captain Jacob, M.D.; the Enniscorthy, under Captain Pounden; the Scarawalsh, under Captain Cornock; and the Shilmalier, under the Right Hon. George Ogle, with their supplementary men, altogether as many as their original number, and two hundred of the townsmen, amounting on the whole to twelve hundred men under arms; who, as the town-wall was in good condition, might defy as many thousand assailants, not supported by a great superiority of ordnance. It would be difficult to state who held the chief command then in Wexford; but Colonel Watson (formerly lieutenant-colonel in the army), who now filled the rank of sergeant in the Shilmalier cavalry, seemed to take the lead more than any other person in the place in stationing the different posts; and really, from the ability he displayed, seemed the fittest of all present to be entrusted with the direction of affairs, having left nothing undone, as far as the exigency of the moment would allow, to put the town in as complete a state of defence as possible.

The insurgents, after having taken Enniscorthy on the 28th, encamped that evening on Vinegar Hill. Several parties were dispatched from thence during the night, to bring in all the respectable persons remaining in the country, with menaces of death in case of refusal; their recent successes having rendered them altogether imperious. One party was particularly directed to Newcastle for Mr. John Hay, in whose professional talents they placed great confidence, as he had been an officer in the French service. On being summoned out of his bed to come to camp, he endeavoured to expostulate, but all in vain; and, at last, he absolutely refused going, notwithstanding the most violent threats uttered against him. At length, however, menaces proceeded to such extremity, that his house should be set on fire, and he and his family consumed within it; and preparations were instantly making to put their threats in actual execution, when, turning with looks of anguish and despair towards his wife and daughter, whom he loved most passionately, with the tenderest emotions he surrendered his judgment for their safety, and was led to Vinegar Hill, where he met several who had been summoned thither out of their beds as unexpectedly as himself; for as the military had abandoned the whole country, the insurgents, who were now the generality of the people, had every one who remained under uncontrollable command. Mr. John Hay, finding, upon inquiry, that the multitude had no ammunition, no warlike stores, nor any degree of preparation, strongly remonstrated on their defenceless situation, representing that they could not possibly stand against a regularly appointed military force, as any soldiery knowing their duty must cut them to pieces. Various and confused

were the consultations that ensued in this tumultuous
assemblage. It was at once proposed, by different
persons, to attack Ross, Newtownbarry, and Gorey, as
each lay more contiguous to their several homes, for
Wexford was then considered too formidable to be at
all attempted; while others laboured to persuade the
whole body to proceed to their respective neighbourhoods, to protect them from the ravages of the military;
and each party persisted so obstinately in their several
determinations, as not to yield or listen to any reasoning
from another side, in opposition to their favourite
opinions: no kind of concert, no unity of design, no
sort of discipline or organization appearing to influence
their counsels or their conduct; which distraction sufficiently indicates that no pre-concerted or any digested
plan of Insurrection existed in the county, previous to
the rising—for in such case, the populace would have
been rendered, in some degree at least, subordinate to
some constituted authority; whereas they now acted,
even after considerable successes, not obedient to any
control, but with the greatest anarchy, violence, and
confusion. In fine, each individual dreaded the devastation of his house or his property; most of the multitude
was dispersed, and on their way to their several homes,
in all directions, from Vinegar Hill, when some of them
met Messrs. Fitzgerald and Colclough (whose arrests
were publicly known), near the village of St. Johns,
and finding them liberated and sent out to them, they
were immediately welcomed by a general shout, which
communicating from one to another, like electricity,
was re-echoed all the way to Enniscorthy, and so on to
the top of Vinegar Hill, and thence through all the
county round. The reverberation of the shouts thus
wildly diffused, arrested the attention of the astonished
multitude, who instantly returned to discover the cause
of such sudden exultation; so that when the deputed

gentlemen arrived on Vinegar Hill, the camp, so deserted but a moment before, now became as thronged as ever. Were it not sufficiently established by the universal acknowledgment of all the inhabitants of the county of Wexford, officers and men, who bore a part in this Insurrection, that there was no concert between this rising and the plan of a general insurrection in and about Dublin; and that it was no more than a tumultuary and momentary exertion of popular resistance to a state of things, found or considered unsupportable, the sole object of which was an attempt to get rid of oppressions, and to retaliate with equal violence, what they had been for some time experiencing; this inclination of each man, and every body of men, to return home, and apply the general force to the correction of their individual sufferings, would furnish a strong proof of the fact; as otherwise the idea of some general system, however confused, would be floating in their imagination, and it is the confirmed opinion of most impartial people, that I have heard discuss the subject, that the Insurrection in the county of Wexford must have subsided at that period, but for this intelligence extraordinary from the town by the deputation of the prisoners, who of necessity informed the people, that they had been liberated, and sent out for the express purpose of remonstrating with them; for this served only to concentrate their wavering opinions, and to point to some object their previously fluctuating determinations. It was but the resolution of a moment to march in a body to attack Wexford. Mr. Fitzgerald they detained in the camp, and Mr. Colclough they sent back to announce their hostile intentions.

Mr. Colclough arrived in Wexford early in the evening, and waited in the Bull Ring (a small square in the town so denominated), until the officers and other gentlemen in the place had there assembled, when he

G

informed them in a very audible voice, from on horseback, that having gone out, according to their directions, to the insurgents on Vinegar Hill, he found, as he had already suggested before his departure, that he possessed no influence with the people, who had ordered him to return and announce their determination of marching to the attack of Wexford; adding, that they had detained Mr. Fitzgerald. Mr. Colclough then requested to be informed if it was intended to make further trial of his services, or to require his longer attendance, as otherwise they must be sensible how eager he must be to relieve the anxiety of his family by his presence. He was then entreated to endeavour to maintain tranquillity in his own neighbourhood, which having promised to do as much as in his power, he called at the gaol to visit Mr. Harvey, with whom he agreed (according to the compact with Captain Boyd) to return next day and take his place in the gaol, and then set off through the barony of Forth to his own dwelling at Ballyteigue, distant about ten miles from Wexford.

If anything could add to the general consternation in Wexford, it was to learn the determination of the insurgents to come to attack the town. Ships became in greater requisition than ever, and all the vessels in the harbour were stowed with amazing numbers; the streets were quite deserted, and the shops and lower windows of all the houses were shut up. Late in the evening, as two of the Taghmon yeomanry were going home, and had proceeded as far as Areandrish, about four miles from Wexford, they descried the advanced guard of the insurgents; with which intelligence they immediately posted back with all speed to the town, which was already in expectation of being attacked every instant. Every degree of vigilance and precaution was now exerted, and the military kept on the alert all night. The portcullis on the remarkable wooden bridge over the Slaney, was hoisted, whereby the greatest part of it was left defenceless, while one piece of cannon would have perfectly protected the whole; and this mismanagement became the more to be regretted as, about break of day, the toll-house on the country-side on the end of it was discovered to be on fire, and burned with great fury, the materials being of deal; and pitch and tar had been spread over the entrance of the bridge to increase the rapidity of the flames. Some boat-loads of sailors from the harbour were the first that ventured to extinguish the fire, having taken their buckets for the purpose. These found the place deserted, as the business had been executed by a party of about twelve insurgents, who fled at their approach. The sharp smoke from the burning wood, drifted by the wind which blew right along the bridge, retarded much the progress of some yeomen, who at length moved towards the fire; but these, leaving the sailors to their own exertions, made a cut across the bridge at some distance from the conflagration. The fire, however, was soon put out, and none of the oak beams that principally supported the bridge were burnt through; the floor and railings only, which were of deal, being consumed. The cries of the women and children throughout the town were so dismal and alarming as to rouse the military from their beds, when they had scarcely time to have fallen asleep, since they had retired from their several posts, to which they were thus summoned back in a hurry to repel the attack of an enemy which was every moment expected. The insurgents were now encamped on the Three Rocks —the end of the low ridge of the mountain of Forth, about three miles from Wexford—and did not seem so willing to advance as was apprehended in the town.

General Fawcett, having ordered his forces to follow, set out alone from Duncannon Fort on the evening of the 29th, and stopped at Taghmon, where he lay down to rest, until his advanced guard should arrive. Captain Adams of the Meath militia, with seventy men of his regiment, and Lieutenant Birch of the artillery, with two howitzers, arrived from Duncannon Fort in the course of the night, at Taghmon, where, not finding, as they expected, the thirteenth regiment, or Meath militia, and not knowing anything about the General, after a short halt they marched on towards Wexford, apprehending no kind of interruption. They had already ascended the road along the side of the mountain of Forth, when perceived by the outposts of the insurgents, who poured down upon them with such rapidity, that they were in a few minutes cut off, except Ensign Wade and sixteen privates who were taken prisoners. The magazine was blown up in the conflict, which circumstance rendered the howitzers not so great a prize as they otherwise would have been to the victors. General Fawcett, on getting out of bed, having learned the fate of his advanced guard, ordered the thirteenth and the rest of the troops who had by this time come up, to retreat to Duncannon Fort, whither he also set off in great haste himself.

From Wexford, in the course of the morning, vast crowds of people were observed assembling on the high ground over Ferry-bank, at the country-side of the wooden bridge, which contributed not a little to heighten the alarm already prevailing in the town. The different posts on the town wall were guarded with the utmost vigilance, and entrusted to the protection of the yeomen, infantry, supplementaries, and armed inhabitants, while the North Cork militia undertook to defend the barracks. It was expected that General Fawcett, now supposed on his march from Taghmon to Wexford, must fall in with the insurgents, and thus keep them so well employed on that side as to afford a favourable opportunity for a sally from the town to attack them on the other. It was, therefore, resolved to try the success of this manœuvre, and accordingly, Colonel Maxwell, with two hundred of the Donegal militia, and Colonel Watson, with the Wexford, Enniscorthy, Taghmon, Healthfield, and Shilmalier yeomen cavalry, marched out to the encounter. They had advanced as far as Belmont, when Colonel Watson, eager to reconnoitre, proceeded up the hill farther than prudence would permit, and was shot from one of the outposts of the insurgents. The Donegal militia then retreated to Wexford, preceded by the cavalry, who pressed upon them very much along the road. Immediately after this a hasty council of war was held, at which it was determined to evacuate the town.

A general and gloomy consternation now prevailed; every countenance appeared clouded and distrustful, and every person was cautious and circumspect how he spoke or acted, as all confidence was entirely done away, and each individual thought only of his own personal safety. Some yeomen and supplementaries, who during the whole of the morning had been stationed in the street opposite the gaol, were heard continually to threaten to put all the prisoners to death; which so roused the attention of the gaoler to protect his charge, that he barricaded the door; and on hearing of a surrender, to manifest more strongly the sincerity of his intentions, he delivered up the key to Mr. Harvey. This gentleman was, indeed, so apprehensive of violence, that he had climbed up inside a chimney, where he had lain concealed a considerable time, when some gentlemen called upon him, but could not gain admittance until they gave the strongest assurances of their pacific intentions. Upon being admitted at length, they still found him up the chimney, and while so situated, entreated him to go out to the camp of the insurgents and announce to them the surrender of the town, on condition that lives and properties should be spared. Mr. Harvey made answer, that as the insurgents on the Three Rocks were not from his neighbourhood, and as he was not himself at all known to them, he imagined he could have no kind of influence with them, adding that they might possibly consider him even as an enemy. He was then requested to write to them, which he declared himself willing to do in any manner that might be judged most advisable. When he had thus consented, it became a task of no little difficulty to bring him out of his lurking-place, as in the descent his clothes were gathered up about his shoulders, so that it required good assistance to pull him out of the chimney by the heels. When he had arranged his apparel, and adjusted himself so as to put off the appearance of a chimney sweeper, about two hours before the troops retreated from Wexford, Right Hon. George Ogle, captain of the Shilmalier infantry; Cornelius Grogan; John Grogan, captain of the Healthfield cavalry; James Boyd, captain of the Wexford cavalry; Solomon Richards, captain of the Enniscorthy cavalry; Isaac Cornock, captain of the Scarawalsh infantry, and Edward Turner of the Shilmalier cavalry — all magistrates — along with Lieutenant-Colonel Colville of the thirteenth regiment of foot, and Lieutenant-Colonel Foote of the North Cork militia, visited Mr. Harvey in the gaol, and at their express request, he wrote the following notice to the insurgents on the mountain of Forth:—

"I have been treated in prison with all possible humanity, and am now at liberty. I have procured the liberty of all the prisoners. If you pretend to Christian charity, do not commit massacre, or burn the property of the inhabitants, and spare your prisoners' lives. "B. B. HARVEY.

"Wednesday, 30th May, 1798."

This note was undertaken to be forwarded by —— Doyle, a yeoman of the Healthfield cavalry, who offered to volunteer on this hazardous service, when the proposal was made to his corps by Captain John Grogan. He had the precaution to put off his uniform, and to dress himself in coloured clothes: but when ready to set off he was discovered to be a Roman Catholic, and therefore reflected upon, for so the whisper went about *"how could a Papist be trusted?"* The yeoman, finding his zeal meet with a reception so contrary to his expectation, again put on his uniform and retreated with his captain; thus proving himself to the full as loyal as any of those who on the occasion displayed their illiberality; which even common policy, it might be well imagined, should repress at so critical a juncture. Doctor Jacob then proposed the enterprise to his corps, and Counsellor Richards, with his brother Mr. Loftus Richards, were appointed to go out to the Three Rocks on this expedition, to announce the surrender of the town to the insurgents, whose camp they reached in safety, though clad in full uniform. Scarcely had these deputies set out upon their mission, when all the military corps, a part of one only excepted, made the best of their way out of the town. Every individual of them seemed to partake of a general panic, and set off whithersoever they imagined they could find safety, without even acquainting their neighbours on duty of their intentions. The principal inhabitants whose services had been accepted of for the defence of the town were mostly Catholics, and, according to the prevalent system, were subject to the greatest insults and reflections. They were always placed in front of the posts, and cautioned to behave well, or that death should be the consequence. Accordingly, persons were placed behind them to keep them to their duty, and these were so watchful to their charge, that they would not even permit them to turn about their heads; and yet these determined heroes were the very first to run off on the apprehended approach of real danger. Thus were the armed inhabitants left at their posts, abandoned by their officers, and actually ignorant of the flight of the soldiery, until the latter had been miles out of the town, and were therefore left no possible means of retreating. Lieutenant William Hughes of the Wexford infantry, with a few of his corps, was, it seems, the only part of the military left uninformed of the intended retreat, and this was owing to his being detached with these few yeomen to defend a distant part of the town wall, and he and they were apprised of their situation, as were also the armed inhabitants, only by the approach of the insurgents; so that Mr. Hughes and his few yeomen, together with the armed inhabitants, are the only people that can be said not to have abandoned their posts in Wexford on this occasion. The confusion and dismay which prevailed was so great, as no kind of signal for retreat had been given, that officers and privates ran promiscuously through the town, threw off their uniforms, and hid themselves wherever they thought they could be best concealed. Some ran to the different quays, in expectation of finding boats to convey them off, and threw their arms and ammunition into the water. All such as could accomplish it embarked on board the vessels in the harbour, having previously turned their horses loose. Some ran to the gaol to put themselves under the protection of Mr. Harvey. Officers, magistrates, and yeomen of every description thus severally endeavoured to escape popular vengeance; and in the contrivance of changing apparel, as there was not a sufficiency of men's clothes at hand for all those who sought safety by this means, female attire was substituted for the purpose of disguise. In short, it is impossible that a greater appearance of confusion, tumult or panic could be at all exhibited. The North Cork regiment on quitting the barracks set them on fire, which, however, was immediately put out. Lieutenants Bowen and Paye, with Ensign Harman, and some sergeants and privates of this regiment, remained in the town.

It has been already observed, that thousands of people were seen to assemble, during the entire morning, on a hill over Ferry-bank, marching and countermarching in hostile appearance, and seemingly waiting only for the moment that the town would be abandoned by the military, to take possession of it themselves; but their entrance, when this took place, was retarded; until boards were procured to supply the place of the flooring of the wooden bridge where it had been burnt. In the meantime, Messrs. Richards, after having run great risk, arrived at the camp at Three Rocks, and making known that they were deputed to inform the people that the town of Wexford would be surrendered to them on condition of sparing lives and properties; these terms would not be complied with, unless the arms and ammunition of the garrison were also surrendered. Mr. Loftus Richards was therefore detained as a hostage, and Counsellor Richards and Mr. Fitzgerald were sent back to the town, to settle and arrange the articles of capitulation; but these gentlemen, on their arrival, to their great astonishment, found the place abandoned by the military. The bridge being at this time nearly made passable, the vast concourse of people that had collected at the other side of the Slaney was just ready to pour in and take unconditional possession of the town. It was therefore necessary to treat with these (it being yet unknown who they were), in order to prevent the mischiefs likely to ensue from such a tumultuary influx of people. Doctor Jacob, then Mayor of the town and Captain of the Wexford infantry, therefore entreated Mr. Fitzgerald to move towards the bridge, and announce to the people rushing in, that the town was surrendered; and to use every other argument that his prudence might suggest, to make their entry as peaceable as possible. Mr. Fitzgerald complied, and instantly after this communication thousands of people poured into the town over the wooden bridge, shouting and exhibiting all marks of extravagant and victorious exultation. They first proceeded to the gaol, released all the prisoners, and insisted that Mr. Harvey should become their commander. All the houses in town not abandoned by the inhabitants now became decorated with green boughs, or green ornaments of one description or another. The doors were universally thrown open, and the most liberal offers made of spirits and drink of every kind, which, however, were not as freely accepted, until the persons offering had first drank themselves, as a proof that the liquor was not poisoned, a report having prevailed to that effect; and which was productive of this good consequence, that it prevented rapid intoxication, and, of course, in the beginning, lamentable excesses.

The insurgents having now got complete possession of the town of Wexford, many persons who had been yeomen, after having thrown off their uniforms, affected a cordial welcome for them, and endeavoured by an exhibition of all the signs and emblems of the United Irishmen, to convince them of their *sworn* friendship; and it is indeed not a little remarkable, that many of those who, in this change of affairs, boldly marched out as occasion demanded to meet the king's forces, now display themselves as staunch Orangemen of unimpeachable loyalty. Almost every person in the town threw open their doors with offers of refreshment and accommodation to the insurgents; and the few who did not suffered by plunder, their substance being considered as enemy's property. Some of all descriptions indeed suffered in their property by plunder, on deserting their houses and leaving none to protect or take care of them. The house of Captain Boyd was a singular exception. It was, though not deserted, pillaged, and exhibited marks of the hatred and vengeance of the people.

As the station of the insurgents' camp on the Three Rocks, on the eastern end of the mountain of Forth, only three miles from Wexford, commanded a full view of the conflagrations and other excesses committed by the military, it required the utmost exertion and prudential efforts of their chiefs, and of others in whom they placed any confidence, to prevent them from rushing into the town and taking inconsiderate vengeance, being utterly ignorant of its abandonment by the troops, and unacquainted with the fact of its being possessed by a different party. They entered the town, however, in tolerable temper, but all moderation was banished upon discovering that the arms and ammunition had not been surrendered, so that it was with the utmost difficulty the town was preserved from being set on fire and consumed; the inhabitants being charged with treason for not insisting on and seeing this article executed. After various scenes of disorder, hurry, and confusion, naturally attendant on such occasions, parties were dispatched in boats to bring on shore all the men, arms, and ammunition they could find in the ships and other vessels in the harbour, which in the morning had fallen down towards the bar, neither wind nor tide being favourable; two only out of the whole had actually sailed for Wales. By these means all the men, as well yeomen as other inhabitants, were directly brought on shore in the evening, and the vessels with the women and children immediately followed to the quay.

Amidst this scene of tumult and confusion, not easily

conceivable to any one who has not witnessed popular commotion, while all wished to accommodate themselves as much as possible to the exigency of the moment, and to appear the friends of their newly denominated conquerors, it was ludicrous to observe a gorgeous military uniform clandestinely changed for loathsome, tattered rags, with more address and expedition than actors on the dramatic stage assume different dresses and appearances.

Among those brought on shore from the ships was Mr. John Boyd, brother to Captain James Boyd, of the Wexford cavalry. He was immediately recognised; and he and his family being obnoxious to the people, he ran off on landing, was chased, overtaken, piked, and left for dead, but he lived in excruciating agony until the next morning, when he expired. I had been brought out of one of the ships myself, and on landing was proceeding through the general confusion, when arriving near the Bull Ring a man of the name of George Sparrow, a butcher from Enniscorthy, chased by the people through the streets, ran up to me and clasped me round the body, imploring protection—beseeching I might save him. I instantly endeavoured as much as in my power to give him succour, and to defend him by extending my arms and body over him, while swords and pikes were pointed and brandished for his destruction; but my endeavours proving ineffectual and rather dangerous to myself, and the unfortunate man, perceiving I could not afford the protection I intended, burst from me, and while I lay prostrate in the street, occasioned by his effort to get off, he had not ran many yards when he was deprived of existence. Some ladies, who were so situated at the instant as to be spectators of the scene, have since assured me they thought I had been also killed at that moment; and considering the dreadful circumstances, I think it most providential that when thrown down, I was not regarded as the devoted victim by the infuriate populace. To describe my feelings on this occasion would be utterly impossible. Ushered into the town against my will, to witness, in the first onset, such a specimen of popular vengeance, and naturally imagining that acts of the like violence were perpetrating in every quarter of the town, I could have but little expectation of escape, particularly when the dreadful denunciation resounded in my ears that the people would put every one to death who would dare to decline joining them; and, indeed, in consequence of this menacing cry, many gentlemen who boast of loyal acts (the very contrary of truth), I have observed to have gone farther on the opposite side than could be considered, either since or before, consistent with their honour or their safety.

The town of Wexford was not only most shamefully abandoned, but even surrendered, to all intents and purposes, when it might have been easily defended, although no one will now acknowledge having been concerned in so scandalous a transaction; and, notwithstanding that the very persons who ought to have been its most strenuous protectors, from their situation and circumstances, were not only the first to yield it, and fly so clandestinely as to put it utterly out of the power of all others besides themselves to retreat, but left even their own wives and families to the mercy of an irritated and ungovernable multitude. In any other country such a manifest dereliction of duty would be punished in the most exemplary manner—the lives of such craven deserters would be forfeited for the miseries they occasioned; but in ill-fated Ireland, a display of unprincipled enmity and illiberal animosity to the great bulk of its people, constitutes loyalty and desert sufficient to wipe away the blame of misconduct, and even to obliterate the indelible stigma of cowardice. The conduct of the inhabitants of Wexford, in accommodating themselves to the circumstances of the moment, after their abandonment, must be considered as totally blameless, particularly of such as subsequently took the earliest opportunity of returning to their allegiance. Of all laws, that of self-preservation is acknowledged the most imperious, and to attain this in times of civil commotion, compliance with the exigency of the instant is indispensable, and warranted by the irresistible force of necessity; for otherwise, as all moral writers agree, there would be an end of justice and civilization. Allowances have certainly been made for numbers whose conduct, in an abstract point of view, was evidently treasonable, but perfectly excusable, considering the situation in which they were placed, by the fundamental laws of all nations of regulated society. But why an exculpation should hold good for some individuals, and not for all those in a similar predicament, is a paradox not happily explained by arguments derived from the sources of bigotry and religious prejudice. With cordial satisfaction I acknowledge it perfectly just, that Protestants have been generally exculpated of treason, on the ground of the urgency of circumstances, but why Catholics should be excluded from the like charitable consideration, will not be fairly or easily answered by those who would fain exhibit the unfortunate contest of this period—a war of religion, which, upon the whole, had but very little to do in it, till forced into action by the upholders of prejudice.

Those of the military who first retreated from Wexford were part of the North Cork regiment, commanded by Captain Snowe, and the Scarawalsh infantry under Captain Cornock. These in their flight met Mr. Colclough with his lady in a phaeton, coming to release Mr. Harvey, by taking his place in the gaol, according to his promise the preceding evening. On falling in with the troops, Mr. and Mrs. Colclough were ordered to wheel about, and led along, while swords drawn and pistols cocked threatened their lives on either side if the people should attempt to attack the military. Mr. Colclough was frequently ordered to stand up and wave his hat to several groups who were seen collected on the rising grounds, led by curiosity, from the disturbed state of the country, to observe what was going forward. These signals were for the people not to approach, with which they complied, and so the parties got safe to the Scar at Barrystown, where Mr. Colclough and his lady were dismissed without further violence. The next division of the military who made their appearance at the Scar were part of the Wexford cavalry under Captain Boyd, who had himself it seems at first attempted to get off by sea, but notwithstanding that he most pathetically entreated a friend of his, who had just put off in a boat only a few yards from the quay, to return and take him on board, yet so strongly did the motive of self-preservation operate upon the person, that he refused to comply. The captain then seized upon his horse, which he had before turned loose, mounted directly, and overtook Colonel Maxwell on the road, with whom, however, he did not continue, but drove forward with all speed till he arrived at Mr. King's of Barrystown. After getting some refreshment here, he and some favourites of his corps embarked on board a boat, the tide being too high to pass otherwise, and so proceeded in safety to Duncannon Fort. Mr. Colclough met several of these flying gentry at Barrystown, and the impression of their fears was such that they all declared that a revolution must inevitably succeed in the nation, for that as the rising was general (so they then supposed it to be), nothing could withstand the people. They even congratulated Mr. Colclough on the happiness of not being obliged to quit his country, as he had taken no active part against the people, and as his recent confinement, on suspicion of being their friend, was greatly in his favour. They next pathetically, many of them in sobs and tears, lamented the unfortunate necessity under which they lay of quitting their native land, as they feared the people would consider their former exertions so inimical to their interests as to render it unsafe for them to remain in the country, and after this they took a cordial leave of Mr. Colclough. The escape of Archibald Hamilton Jacob was most wonderful, as when he had gone out with the troops that advanced towards the Three Rocks, before any others had thoughts of retreating, he got off under the mountain, and by keeping by-roads he most providentially arrived in Ross, where, considering the state of the country, he did not stop, but hastened to Waterford, and was finally induced to sail for England.

Had the retreaters the presence of mind to wait at the Scar until the tide should have fallen, they would have been able to have proceeded with much greater ease than they did to Duncannon Fort. Their halting there would probably have enabled many of the stragglers (numbers of whom were cut off) to come up with them, and it would have taken much less time than it did by the circuitous route which they adopted; but their panic and trepidation were such that they believed the insurgents were at their heels, which brought them into great hardships, during a confused and precipitate flight, continued even through the night, which occasioned many to lag behind, who thereby became devoted victims of destruction; the cause of which we shall presently have occasion to mention. The last of the military that left Wexford were the Donegal militia, commanded by Colonel Maxwell, accompanied by Colonel Colville, Captain Younge, and Lieutenant Soden, of the thirteenth foot; the remaining part of the North Cork regiment, headed by Colonel Foote, the Shilmalier yeomen infantry, under the Right Hon. George Ogle, and the Enniscorthy infantry, under Captain Pounden, with some of the Wexford infantry, some of the Wexford, Shilmalier, and Enniscorthy cavalry; and the rear was brought up by the Healthfield cavalry, under Captain John Grogan, who covered the retreat. These were followed and overtaken by Captain Boyd and a few of his troop, who pushed forward till they came up with the van of the retreaters as before related.

Great numbers of people, from motives of curiosity, assembled in different groups to view the military in their passage through the country, not imagining that they should be any more molested than they had been by the first parties who passed them quietly by; and had any general orders to this effect been issued to the retreating troops, it is probable they would have been attended to and productive of good effect; but although Colonel Colville did all in his power to prevent the soldiery from firing on the people, yet his humane and wise remonstrances were not successful. The first victims of military fury, however, on the retreat, were two men found with arms in a house in Wexford, near where the Shilmalier yeomen infantry, commanded by the Right Hon. George Ogle, had been stationed in the town. These upon the evacuation were brought away by the corps, and shot at Maglass, where the soldiers, giving a loose to their rage, pursued the unoffending populace, and shot numbers of them, who endeavoured to conceal themselves in the ditches, which were well searched for their discovery. The Roman Catholic chapel of Maglass was set on fire, as were a great many other houses in the course of their march, while others were plundered; and not a countryman that was seen and overtaken could escape being sacrificed to military vengeance; nay, not unfrequently

H

did neither feminine weakness nor helpless infancy afford protection, as they obtained in several instances no mercy from the indiscriminate fury of the retreating troops, who immolated some of the women and children of the affrighted peasantry as they fell in their way. These acts of unprovoked, cold-blooded, and unmanly cruelty were avenged on the poor stragglers who were by any casualty separated from the retreating body, as the exasperated country people, goaded as they had been, considered every person in a military garb as a sanguinary and relentless enemy. Several soldiers, who had been followed by their wives and children, were induced to stay behind to afford them assistance on so distressing a march, which cost many of them their lives; but none of the women or children were intentionally hurt by the people: even some children who were abandoned by or lost their parents on this occasion, are still remaining in the country, cherished and protected by the inhabitants. The tide still continuing too high at the Scar for even the rear of the retreating troops to pass, they took the like circuitous route with the rest and arrived at Duncannon Fort on the morning of the 31st of May, worn out with hardship and fatigue, having lost many of their men, and in the utmost confusion and disorder.

On the night of the 30th, the town of Wexford, considering all that had happened, was remarkably quiet, all finding repose necessary after their various hardships. In the evening, vast numbers went to visit their several dwellings in the country, to be informed of the condition of their families and properties; but very early on the morning of the 31st, the streets were as crowded as before, and the confusion and plunder of the day preceding now recommenced. The people were much discontented with the inhabitants for not detaining for their use the arms and ammunition of the garrison; as the entire of their military stores at this time amounted to no more than three barrels of gunpowder found in the barracks, a few hundred cartridges, with some odd casks and pounds of powder found in shops and gentlemen's houses. Their discontent soon proceeded to threats against different individuals, and amongst the rest against Mr. Fitzgerald, who had gone home the night before, and was not as yet returned. He was at once accused of having betrayed the people; vengeance was vowed against him, and he was threatened with instant death. On his appearance soon after, however, the ferment subsided as instantaneously and unaccountably as it had at first originated. The principal inhabitants of Wexford very naturally wished to get rid of these troublesome intruders, and to effect this desirable object, such of the better sort as had any influence with the multitude, lent their cordial assistance, and they at length succeeded. The insurgents were induced to move out of the town and encamp on the Windmill Hills; where, after much confused consultation, they divided into two bodies, one of which, consisting of those who inhabited the Wexford side of the Slaney, marched to Taghmon. As in such a mixed multitude there must be many of all dispositions, it is not wonderful that there were some who would incite to and practise outrage. Some of this description of persons hunted for Orangemen, whom they denominated their enemies; while others, imitating the conduct of the military on the day before, but in a far less degree, plundered private property, burnt the houses of four respectable farmers, and put one man to death on their way to Taghmon, outside of which town they encamped for that night. The other division of the insurgents, consisting of the inhabitants of that part of the county north of the Slaney, directed their march towards Gorey; and in the course of their progress, burned the houses of some whom they considered as enemies, plundered others, and encamped that night on the Hill of Carrigrew. The encampment on Vinegar Hill, by-the-by, continued a permanent one during the whole period of the Insurrection.

As it is an incontrovertible fact, that, before this period, there were fewer United Irishmen in the county of Wexford than in any other part of Ireland, and these few only sworn, as has been already observed, in a detached manner, unconnected with any organization, it is amazing to think with what success the Insurrection appears to have been attended in its commencement; that a people thus roused all of a sudden, without any previous preparation, should gain such signal advantages. If further proof were at all necessary of the little progress made by the system of the United Irishmen in the county of Wexford, anterior to the rising, in addition to no return of numbers being even stated to have been made from thence by any leaders, that proof would be amply supplied by the vast numbers that eagerly came forward, desiring to be sworn, upon these first successes; for, in the existing state of the country, at this juncture when men's minds were totally unmasked and all disguise thrown away, it may be fairly implied, that all who might have been previously sworn would not fail to come forward and take advantage of such circumstances, by boasting, in the moment of exultation, of prior concern in a system then considered universally prevalent through the island, and of the final success of which the least doubt was not entertained at this period. Besides, at this crisis it is natural to conclude that had any organization heretofore existed, the chosen chiefs would be induced to declare themselves and assume their stations, for had they concurred in their appointment when they ran every risk of legal punishment, before the actual breaking out of the Insurrection, now that it was believed victorious and universal, they must feel every encouragement to act without reserve and with their utmost vigour. But the fact was absolutely otherwise, as most of the leaders throughout the disturbances in Wexford, acted in their several stations from the irresistible force of compulsion and constraint after it had actually existed; whatever representations by surmise or presumption may have appeared to the contrary. Another circumstance of general misrepresentation is, that the Insurrection in the county of Wexford was connected with the disturbances in other parts of the nation, while nothing can be more contrary to truth; as on the arrest of the Leinster delegates, assembled at a provincial meeting in Bridge Street, in Dublin, on the 12th of March, 1798, there was not a delegate or any return of numbers from the county of Wexford, as evidently appears from the reports of the secret committees of both Houses of the Irish Parliament; and, during the whole period of its continuance, this county was beset on all sides with troops, so as to be completely insulated, and therefore no efficient intercourse could exist between it and any other part of Ireland; for scarcely any one could, in passing to or from it, escape detection save in a very few instances, in which, whether by connivance or otherwise, some persons from the adjoining counties passed into it, and some of the natives out of it, but as neither returned to their respective homes during the time specified, such instances cannot effectually militate against the general position here laid down, from incontrovertible facts, in opposition to any unqualified assertion and groundless conjecture. In fact, as there was no preconcerted plan of insurrection in the county of Wexford, there was no similarity of circumstances or occasion between that and the commotion in any other part of Ireland, except in the casual incidents of their happening at the same time, and that perhaps the people of other counties expected like effects from their own conduct with those hoped for by the people of the county of Wexford from their own, to rescue themselves from apprehended extermination, which they thought could not be effected otherwise than by the most determined resistance. These facts are thus stated to disabuse the public, as the direct contrary, on mere surmise, has been roundly asserted and pretty generally believed through exaggerated misrepresentation.

Now, that the Insurrection of the county of Wexford was at its height, there existed no kind of subordination or control; individuals assumed the privilege of indulging their own dispositions, and of gratifying private malice. The unruly populace were furious and ungovernable, and many of this description remained in Wexford after the great body of the insurgents had retired from the town. They seized upon and lodged in the gaol many persons from all parts of the surrounding country, who had fled thither for protection, and were now endeavouring to conceal themselves in the different houses of their friends, to escape popular resentment. Many former piques, however remote or trivial they might have been, were avenged in this manner; so that on the 31st of May the gaol of Wexford became absolutely crowded. On this very day Mr. Harvey, who had been released from confinement by the people, as soon as they took possession of the town, and was by them appointed, whether he would or no, their commander-in-chief, had engaged several gentlemen, among whom there were many apprehensive of popular violence, to an entertainment at his former lodgings, which he had then resumed; and all these he naturally supposed under effectual protection with him, from the nature of his appointment, against all popular outrage.

But he soon had lamentable proof how groundless were his fond expectations. In the evening, soon after dinner, a great mob of country people assembled in the street before the house, some of whom knocked violently at the door and insisted that Mr. Turner, whom they knew to be within, should be delivered up to them *to be put to death,* for having burned some of their houses. I was one of those invited by Mr. Harvey, and, as Mr. Turner was a most particular friend of mine, I instantly went out, and was, as I fondly imagined, so far successful as to prevail on the populace to retire; but to my great mortification they returned shortly after, and insisted with redoubled violence on Mr. Turner's being brought out to them. Mr. Fitzgerald, who had now come to my assistance, and myself urged every argument that friendship could suggest, to dissuade them from their dreadful purpose, and Mr. Harvey also interposed for the same intent, by which means the multitude was once more induced to retire. It was but for a short time, however, as they quickly came back to the house with more violence and fury than before. A shot was now fired at the door, as the first notice of their approach, and they reiterated their demand with the loudest and most desperate vociferations. Some of the gentlemen who on that day dined with Mr. Harvey now came out, and all that their united entreaties and remonstrances could obtain from the enraged multitude was, that Mr. Turner might be lodged in the gaol to abide his trial. But the demagogues denounced that if he was not sent thither directly, Mr. Fitzgerald and Mr. Hay (meaning myself) must forfeit their lives. This roused the friendly feelings of Mr. Turner, who had overheard all that passed, and he accordingly requested he might be brought to gaol, as the only place of safety, in his opinion, when neither the house nor the interference of his friends or the chief commander could ensure him protection; as could not, indeed, the house of any one at this perturbed period, as those of the greatest abettors and reputed favourites and supporters of the people were searched and violated by forcibly taking out of them numbers of people denominated enemies.

These outrages determined many to surrender themselves in order to be sent to gaol, in hopes of greater security, as well as it induced others to remain in confinement from similar expectancy of protection from the resentment of their neighbours. From considerations of this nature Mr. Harvey, constrained as he was to conduct Mr. Turner to the gaol, released from thence every other person not violently accused, and the number was considerable whom he thought to be obnoxious to, but by these means secure from the intemperate vengeance of the people. During the first days of the Insurrection, indeed, any person of previous popular character could release a friend from confinement; but such interference soon became so displeasing to the people, that most of those who had been thus liberated were again re-committed, and destruction threatened to any one that would presume again to enlarge them; which prevented numbers from interposing their good offices in favour of such of their friends as had in any manner incurred popular odium. Private malice was on these occasions but too frequently exerted, and any accusation was sufficient to cause any person to be sent to gaol; which, however, was esteemed by many the safest asylum, as it was expected that when popular fury should have abated, the persons confined might be permitted to return quietly to their homes. The only effectual mode of procuring liberation from prison, however, at this period, was, to procure a certificate in favour of the prisoner from the neighbourhood in which he lived; and in this way many were set at liberty, who, to secure themselves against future crimination, generally joined the insurgents. As to the power of popularity, at all times precarious, so difficult of attainment, and so easily lost, and which no truly wise man ever made the scope of his actions, or final object of pursuit, it could effect little in such troublesome and turbulent times as those we are treating of, when an Insurrection prevailed, excited by oppression, and in which there existed no regular plan of operation or system of action; while the minds of the ungovernable multitude were sore and desperate from recent irritation. Amidst such a dreadful public ferment, popularity to a liberal mind proves a most tyrannical subjugation, as it encumbers the possessor with the oppressive weight of mobbish applause, while it confers not on him the power of relieving a suffering friend, who may have attracted, inadvertently or otherwise, the deadly resentment of an unbridled populace; and, what is still more afflicting to generous feelings, the devoted victim of the moment perhaps imagines the popular friend all-powerful for his preservation, while it is melancholy to reflect that, on such occasions, it is in the power of a villain to counteract the benevolent intentions and humane disposition of the highest respectability, intelligence, and virtue!

After the insurgents, as has been related, moved off in two separate divisions from Wexford, there still remained several of their number in the town, who assumed the office of supplying the camps with necessaries, and this by their own authority they declared must be done from Wexford. These self-created commissaries, having put all necessaries accordingly in requisition, began to search all the houses, and in the course of such survey plundered them of every article they thought proper, asserting that all they took away was for the general service. Great abuses were consequently committed in this arbitrary mode of levying contributions, and so great a waste of property, particularly of provisions, was made, that the town and its neighbourhood were threatened with a famine. The people of Wexford, therefore, desirous to get rid of these troublesome marauders, and to have some regulations adopted for the prevention of plunder, appointed twelve of the principal inhabitants as a committee to regulate the distribution of provisions as well as of all other necessaries in requisition; and the generous individuals who undertook this arduous task (it was, indeed, a herculean labour) were actuated by the most virtuous and disinterested motives in their exertions to protect general as well as individual property. As whiskey and leather were the articles most in demand in the camps, distillers and tanners especially entreated the committee to issue regular orders for the supplies from their stores, to prevent as much as possible the total destruction of their substance and concerns, adding that they were very willing to give up their whole stock for the general service. Yet, strange as it may appear, some of this description of persons were most forward afterward in prosecuting those very men, who, by their humane interference, were instrumental in saving their lives and properties; for certainly the worst consequences were to be apprehended from the indiscriminate plunder, and consequently inordinate consumption of spirituous liquors, by the prevention of which and other disorders, through indefatigable exertions, the committee actually proved the salvation of the country, and, what may not appear unworthy of observation, although chosen by the inhabitants at large from among themselves, there was but one United Irishman among them, which could not be the case had the people been generally sworn.

Captain Keugh was appointed military commander of the town, which was now divided into wards, each of which had a company of men, armed with guns and pikes as they could procure them, and these appointed their own officers. There was a regular parade morning and evening on the Custom-house quay; guards were struck off and relieved, and a pass-word and counter-sign regularly given out. The Insurrection had by this time become so general in all parts of the county forsaken by the military, that even the inhabitants of the baronies of Forth and Bargy thought it incumbent on them to show their disposition, and to appear in Wexford; in short, every person remaining in the county thought it best at this period to come forward and make common cause with the insurgents. The inhabitants of the last-mentioned baronies, however, being a race of men of peaceable and industrious habits, and not having experienced the persecutions practised in other districts, were not easily excited to commit those acts of outrage which took place in other quarters; but they were at length terribly alarmed and roused to resistance by the cruel and merciless conduct of the military in their flight from Wexford; but even then their determination of vengeance appeared solely directed against the body whose unprovoked fury had affected them with injury. These people, on their march to Wexford, halted near Johnstown, the seat of Cornelius Grogan, Esq., for whom a party was dispatched to bring him out and oblige him to join them; and thus this aged gentleman was constrained to accommodate himself to the crazy temper of the times; and being placed on horseback, then ill of the gout, he was conducted along by the multitude, consisting of several thousands on foot, and many hundreds of horsemen. On their entrance into the town, and defiling through the streets, not many pikes could be seen, but vast numbers were equipped with spits, pitchforks, and such like offensive weapons, with which they endeavoured, as much as in their power, to imitate and assume the appearance of pikemen; and after having shouted and paraded for some time through the streets, they retired peaceably to their homes, without committing further outrage. All the forges both in town and country were instantly employed in the fabrication of pike-blades, and timber of every description fit for handles was procured for that purpose wherever to be found; so that in a very short time no person could be seen (so general was the principle or affectation of arming) without a warlike weapon of some kind, a green cockade, a hat-band, sash or other ornament of that colour. Four oyster boats were fitted out in the harbour, and manned with five and twenty men each, to cruise outside the bay; and these from time to time brought in several vessels, mostly bound for Dublin, laden with oats, potatoes, and different other kinds of provisions, which became very seasonable supplies for the town, that must otherwise have suffered great distress, as the markets were deserted by the country people. Three old pieces of cannon were brought down and mounted on the fort of Roslare, situate at the entrance of the harbour, to prevent any sloops of war from passing, such armed vessels only being capable of entering the harbour of Wexford; and four old sloops were ready to be scuttled and sunk in the channel to prevent any such armed vessel, in the event of her passing the fort, from approaching the town.

Money seemed to have vanished during the Insurrection, as no person was willing to admit being possessed of any currency exclusive of bank-notes, which were held in such little estimation, that great quantities of them were inconsiderately destroyed—some in lighting tobacco pipes, and others used as waddings for fire-locks; but whatever little provisions appeared at market sold very cheaply for ready money; for instance, butter sold by the pound for twopence, and butcher's meat, of any kind, for one penny. As to bank-notes any one might starve who had no other means of procuring the prime necessaries for which, when offered for sale, nothing but specie would be accepted as payment. Every endeavour was made to have the markets well supplied and attended; but even at the cheap rate just stated, there were scarcely any purchasers; so unwilling did every one appear to acknowledge the possession of money; but it must be mentioned, that indeed the necessity of purchasing at market was in a great measure superseded, for among the various duties of the committee, one was that of supplying every person in town with provisions. On application to them, every house was furnished with a ticket specifying the number of inhabitants, and all persons, even the wives and families of those considered the greatest enemies of the people, were indiscriminately included; and every person sent with a ticket to the public stores appointed for that purpose, received a proportionate quantity of meat, potatoes, and other necessaries free of any expense. The bread in general was bad, as no good flour could be obtained.

In the country the people formed themselves generally into parish divisions, and each division elected its own officers. All persons capable of carrying arms were to attend the camps, on being furnished with pikes or guns, as either could be best procured; some on foot and others on horseback, as they could best accommodate themselves. Most persons were desirous to wear ornaments of some kind or other, and accordingly decorated themselves in the most fantastical manner with feathers, tippets, handkerchiefs, and all the showy parts of ladies' apparel. Green was the most favourite and predominant colour, but on failure of this, decorations of almost any other colour were substituted; and as to their flags or ensigns they were also generally green or of a greenish hue, but on account of a deficiency in this respect, they displayed banners of all colours except orange, to which the people showed the most unalterable dislike, aversion, and antipathy—even blue, black, red, and yellow were remarked among their banners. Many damsels made an offering of their coloured petticoats for the public service, and to make these gifts the more acceptable, they usually decorated them according to their different fancies, and from the variety thus exhibited there appeared not two similar banners in the whole. Several loyal ladies, too, both in town and country, displayed their taste in richly and fancifully ornamenting ensigns, to ingratiate themselves with the people; but many of them, not having time to perfect their *chef-d'œuvres* before the Insurrection was suppressed, have since thought it prudent, I suppose, to destroy these and the like specimens of elegant accomplishment, at which I had opportunities of observing them earnestly employed, during the short-lived period of popular triumph. But now we must return to events which occurred in other parts of the country.

After the battle of Oulart, which was fought on the 27th of May, as already detailed, the yeomanry distinguished themselves in the northern part of the county, by falling on the defenceless and unoffending populace, of whom they slew some hundreds. It being Whit Sunday, the people were as usual going to their chapels to attend divine service, when many of them were led by curiosity, which is generally excited by the report of fire-arms, to ascend different eminences, from which the dreadful and horrid scenes of devastation by fire and sword, prevailing through the country round, as far as the eye could reach, was presented to their astonished and affrighted view; and as the different groups thus collected were perceived by the yeomanry, these pursued and cut them down. The most inoffensive were most likely to suffer by this mode of quieting disturbances, because, conscious of their innocence, they made no effort to avoid the sudden fate which they had no reason to apprehend. Even many who remained within their houses did not fare better than their more curious or less fearful neighbours, as numbers of them were called out and shot at their own doors; nay, some infirm and decrepid old men were plunged into eternity by these valorous guardians and preservers of the public peace! On every occasion, however, they were not inexorable to the piteous petitions for life, as a sum of money, properly offered and timely presented, saved some, who, after the Insurrection was quelled, came forward with their complaints; and among others who were obliged to disgorge these bloody ransoms, Mr. Hunter Gowan, a magistrate and captain of a yeomanry corps, on a complaint made to Mr. Beauman, Sen., of Hyde Park (from whom I had this account), was obliged to refund the money. These people, on surrendering their pikes and other offensive weapons and arms, fondly imagined that they had secured themselves protection, and were, therefore, not at all apprehensive of attack, but they soon found themselves miserably mistaken. Had their intentions been for violence, they would naturally have assembled in a large body on some commanding hill, as the other insurgents did, where they would have appeared formidable; so that their having collected into numberless small groups is certainly to be deemed rather the effect of curiosity than the effort of Insurrection.

Great numbers of people, taking their families and such of their effects as they could conveniently transport thither along with them, fled for refuge into Gorey, where a general panic, however, prevailed, although, besides the yeomanry of the town, a party of the North Cork militia, under the command of Lieutenant Swayne, together with the Ballaghkeen, Coolgreny, Arklow,

Northshire, and Coolatin corps of yeomen cavalry; the Tinnahely and Wingfield corps of yeomen infantry; and a company of the Antrim militia, commanded by Lieutenant Elliot, were stationed there; but, notwithstanding, on a rumour that the insurgents were approaching, it was determined to abandon the town, and proceed to Arklow; but, previous to its evacuation, eleven men taken out of their beds, within a mile's distance, were brought in and shot in the streets, where they were left for dead; but six of them recovered. By order of Mr. White, however, upwards of one hundred prisoners were released from the gaol and market-house, and many of them received protections, which they placed in their hats, in order to exhibit as conspicuously as possible; but this precaution did not prevent some being shot by other yeomen, whom they fell in with on their way home! The order for evacuation being announced at five o'clock on the morning of the 28th, a distressing scene of trepidation and confusion ensued. Affrighted crowds of people might be seen running in all directions, preparing for flight; while such as could were harnessing their horses and placing their families on cars with the utmost precipitation—all endeavouring to escape from the town as speedily as possible. The road was soon thronged to a great extent with a train of cars, which were loaded with women and children, accompanied by a vast multitude on foot, among whom were many women with their children on their back, and from the continued heat and drought of the weather, the dust excited by this crowded procession distressfully obstructed respiration.

By this abandonment of Gorey the whole of the surrounding country was left entirely exposed, and yet the insurgents did not at all, at this time, approach the town, but remained in their encampment on the hill of Carrigrew; nor did the inhabitants of this quarter then rise or join-in the Insurrection; but strictly observed on their part the promises they had made to the magistrates on surrendering their arms; and yet it is a notorious fact, that there were more United Irishmen in this than in any other part of the county of Wexford, and that it even comprehended the district of sixteen parishes already stated to have been proclaimed in November, 1797. While Gorey was thus abandoned by the military, and by such as were allowed, or for whom it would be safe to accompany them, it was filled with the property and effects of the fugitives, yet no plunder was committed, and no disturbance took place; so that on their return they found all belonging to them in perfect security, having been protected by those that remained in the town. The only instance of spoliation supposed to have taken place on this occasion is, that a yeoman got some money belonging to Mr. William Sparrow, by whose desire he came for it on the 30th, and which the owner never received. A party of yeomen returned on the 29th, and brought away provisions, but as these were galloping into the town, one of the shoes of a yeoman's horse struck fire against the pavement; haply on the very spot where a quantity of gunpowder had remained, after a small cask of that dangerous combustible which, previous to the flight, had fallen from a car into the street and was burst. An explosion instantly ensued, by which the horse and horseman were blown up, and narrowly escaped with life; the horse's hair was desperately singed, and the yeoman himself was terribly scorched. On the 31st the military returned to Gorey. On which, although left utterly defenceless since the morning of the 28th, not the smallest attempt was made by the insurgents to take possession; and on the disposition to peace and order manifested by the inhabitants who remained in the town after the abandonment,

I

their laudable conduct is the best comment. Different parties of yeomen went out from the town, ransacked the houses through the country, brought away as much as they could carry, driving off numbers of cattle, some belonging to Lord Mountnorris, and put them into Mr. Ram's demesne. Indeed, they were not very exact or scrupulous as to individual property, for they brought off all the cattle they could collect in the country, and took up bacon, cheese, butter, and provisions of all kinds wherever they found them; and to crown all, they took a great number of men prisoners, to supply the place of those that were liberated in the commencement of the flight; so that this must be acknowledged, if not valorous, at least very active service.

On the morning of the 1st of June, an independent, or self-constituted body of insurgents, unknown to any of the three general encampments of Vinegar Hill, Taghmon, and Carrigrew, proceeded on a secret expedition to Newtownbarry (anciently called Bunclody), garrisoned by the King's County militia, commanded by Colonel Lestrange, and the corps of yeomen cavalry and infantry belonging to the place. These insurgents having divided into two parties, made their attack on both sides of the Slaney, on the western bank whereof lies the town, and of this they were soon left in possession by the retreat of the military; but they instantly proceeded to plunder, particularly whiskey, of which they drank very freely, and being thus regardless of the advantage obtained, they afforded the military, whom they did not attempt to pursue, time to rally and return upon them while in this disorderly state, so as to oblige them to fly with some loss and precipitation.

On this day also, a party of insurgents from Vinegar Hill proceeded to join those encamped at Carrigrew, whose numbers were greatly lessened by desertions for home. They were now, however, mustering pretty strongly all over the country, intending to assemble their collective force on the hill of Ballymenane; but, while moving forward in a detached and disorderly manner, they were met by a force from Gorey, under the command of Lieutenant Elliot, consisting of parties of the Antrim and North Cork militia, above fifty yeomen infantry, and three troops of yeomen cavalry. These, by preserving their order, had great advantage in this unexpected rencounter over the insurgents, who retreated with some loss and in disorder; leaving behind a great number of horses which were brought into Gorey, together with the plunder of many houses, which were burnt after despoiling; among the rest that of Mr. Kenny, a tanner and shopkeeper, confidently asserted to be a loyal man. His character, however, did not protect him, for he was shot in his own garden, and so fell a victim to the angry indiscriminating spirit of the times, like many other innocent persons. This is very strongly exemplified by a transaction mentioned by the Rev. Mr. Gordon as follows:—"A small occurrence after the battle, of which a son of mine was a witness, may help to illustrate the state of the country at that time:—Two yeomen coming to a brake or clump of bushes, and observing a small motion as if some persons were hiding there, one of them fired into it, and the shot was answered by a most piteous and loud screech of a child. The other yeoman was then urged by his companion to fire; but he, being a gentleman, and less ferocious, instead of firing, commanded the concealed persons to appear, when a poor woman and eight children almost naked, one of whom was severely wounded, came trembling from the brake, where they had secreted themselves for safety."*

* See Gordon's History, page 113.

Indeed, the settled practice was, to shoot all men that were met; and by this desperate system, the most innocent and peaceable were generally the most likely to suffer; for being unwilling to join the insurgents, the ungenerous suspicions generally thrown out, however unjustly, against the Catholics, who constituted a vast majority of the people at large, precluded the possibility of their joining the army or yeomen, who professed the rankest and most inveterate distrust of the people, for any of whom it was extremely unsafe to venture into their presence on any occasion whatsoever, as numbers had fallen a sacrifice to a confidence in their own peaceable intentions and innocent demeanour; and this kind of conduct had finally the effect of determining multitudes to join the insurgents, considering it, at length, the only means of self-preservation. The mind of the impartial reader must be strongly impressed with the barbarous impolicy of thus cherishing these odious and unnatural prejudices, as well as with the desperate situation in which the country was placed through these means; and what a dreadful misfortune it must prove to be an inhabitant where not only such sentiments were very strenuously inculcated, but where even the most shocking scenes of foulest outrage were permitted, and perpetrated with the basest and most criminal connivance.

From the inactivity of the insurgents encamped at Carrickbyrne, occasioned in a great degree from their want of an ostensible commander, constant sallies were made out of Ross, and great havoc and devastation committed throughout the country. These occurrences produced a general meeting of the principal inhabitants on the 1st of June, wherein Mr. Harvey was called on to act as commander-in-chief, and various other appointments and regulations took place for the maintenance and supply of the country. The day after, Mr. Harvey took the command in person at Carrickbyrne, where, on his arrival, several fugitives appeared giving dreadful accounts of their suffering from the yeomanry, and at the time several houses were on fire about Old Ross. The Commander-in-chief instantly ordered Mr. Thomas Cloney, with all the horsemen that could be collected, to proceed against the depredators, who fled on their approach, and were chased in full speed to Ross. At this critical period, the Protestant church of Old Ross was burned, by no means with the knowledge or consent of Mr. Cloney or his party; and the result of every inquiry at the time was, that the church was set on fire in revenge and retaliation by individual sufferers, as many houses were burned, and several unresisting persons were shot immediately preceding this conflagration. I should wish to be able to give a more circumstantial account of this occurrence, as it was the only one of the kind that took place during the Insurrection, but have not been able to procure further information; however, a witness on the trial of Mr. Cloney by court-martial at Wexford in 1799, mentioned the circumstance, but in such a manner as only to attract the notice of an enthusiastic maniac. By having reference to the trial, it will also appear, that Mr. Cloney's humanity and exertions for those in any kind of distress, was as conspicuous as his courage in the field, after he had been forced from his house when the military had fled, and left the insurgents in uncontrollable possession of the country.

On the 2nd of June, as one of the armed oyster-boats, already noticed, was cruising outside the harbour of Wexford, she fell in with a boat from Arklow, which, upon being hailed, came to and was taken. On board this vessel were three officers of the North Cork militia, Lord Kingsborough, the Colonel, Captain O'Hea, and Lieutenant Bourke, who were accordingly made prisoners. This nobleman and these his officers were in Dublin when informed of the defeat of part of their regiment at Oulart, as before stated, and immediately purposed to join it; for which purpose, proceeding by land as far as Arklow, and finding the Insurrection more formidable than they could be brought before to imagine, they there hired a boat to carry them to Wexford, not conceiving it possible that it had been abandoned, and then in the hands of the insurgents. They were taken, therefore, at their entrance into the harbour, and conducted without any person in town being previously informed of the fact, to the house of Captain Keugh, then the acknowledged military commander of the town. Here his lordship and the two officers made prisoners with him were entertained for some days before the people expressed any dissatisfaction or apprehension that they might be enabled to escape; but these manifestations of popular distrust being made known, they were conveyed to a house in the Bull Ring, near the mainguard-house, where sentinels were posted inside and outside; and there they continued, under these measures of precaution, until the subsequent surrender of the town to his lordship himself as an officer in the king's service.

The people of the barony of Forth, having by this time sufficiently equipped themselves with pikes, joined the encampment now formed on the hill of Carrickbyrne, whither, it must be observed, the insurgents of the camp near Taghmon had shifted on the 1st of June. A small party from Wexford also, denominated the Faith corps, joined the encampment on Carrigrew.

The committee of general regulation appointed in Wexford, and already noticed, waited on Mr. Harvey, Commander-in-chief of the insurgents, expressing their hopes that the service in the Protestant church, which had been hitherto interrupted, might be no longer discontinued; as they wished to do all in their power to dissipate religious animosities, by inculcating the absurdity of fear on this account alone, and to undeceive the numbers of sudden converts who were applying to the Catholic priests to be baptized, beseeching in the most earnest manner to be thus received into the bosom of the Catholic church, from an idea that it was then the only plan of safety. Nay, so persevering were the generality in their piteous entreaties, that the Catholic clergy found themselves very distressingly circumstanced; for should they refuse to comply with the wishes and earnest solicitations of such Protestants as offered themselves in this way, they perceived that they would be subject to the most violent animadversions for any fatal accident that might befall any of them; and, on the other hand, knowing that imagined necessity alone was the motive of apparent conversion, they must have considered it improper to accept their conformity without serious and solemn probation. On this occasion, however, the humanity of many superseded the dictates of duty, so far as to induce them to risk the profanation of a sacrament for the preservation of lives, and to dispel the dreadful apprehensions from Orangemen; the greatest assurance of not belonging to that combination being that of conversion to the Catholic communion, which was considered to render any person inadmissible into an association which the majority of the people absolutely believed to be instituted for their destruction. Their alarms, however, worked so strongly on the minds of the affected converts, that all arguments exerted to dispel their fears generally proved ineffectual, as they would still persist in most earnest solicitation for admission. Some clergymen, however, in this dilemna positively refused baptizing Protestant converts, but then they took a far better and consistent mode of quieting alarms. They gave the strongest assurances to such as applied to them, that the Catholic Church does not deem it necessary to re-baptize any denomination of Christians otherwise than conditionally, as the existence of any previous baptism whatever, and attendance on duties and divine service, was sufficient conformity.

A curious circumstance, however, occurred in Wexford at this time, which eventually produced a great number of conditional baptisms. A young lady, who on first application failed of persuading a Catholic priest to confer on her the favour of baptism, had the diligence and address afterwards to discover that the Protestant minister who had undertaken to perform that ceremony in her infancy, had only filliped or sprinkled the water at her with his finger, and so it was within the limits of probability that a drop might not have reached her head so as to form an ablution. Being very ingenious and persevering in her arguments, so as to appear capable of puzzling the nicest casuist, she at last made out her own a doubtful case, and was accordingly quieted by conditional baptism. When the particulars of this transaction got abroad, the solicitations to the Catholic clergy for the boon of conditional baptism became considerably more frequent, the applicants quoting this recent precedent, and adducing the hearsay evidence and far-fetched recollection of grandmothers, grand-aunts, and other grave and venerated relatives, with a long train of minute circumstances, to prove a similarity of cases, and claiming on this account an equal consideration. Notwithstanding the earnest exertions of the committee and many of the principal Catholics to dispel the fears of their Protestant brethren, whom they offered to protect even at the risk of their own lives, all endeavours to have service performed in the Protestant church proved ineffectual. It must be remarked, however, that the place itself suffered not the smallest indignity during the whole period of the Insurrection, except in the instance of the abandonment of their usual place of worship by the Protestants, of whom great numbers flocked in the most public and conspicuous manner to the Catholic chapel, where they affected the greatest piety and devotion. The epithet of *craw-thumpers*, opprobriously applied to Catholics for contritely striking their breasts at their devotions, was never more strongly exemplified than by *these converts*. Catholics strike their breasts gently on certain occasions, and with the right hand alone, but Protestants who attended at Mass in these times generally continued to strike themselves vehemently with both hands almost during the whole service. I had the good fortune to prevent all such as consulted me on the occasion as to the expediency of conforming, by persuading them to avoid the disgrace of such a mockery; and I had the satisfaction afterwards to hear those applauded who did not appear to change their religion, while those who turned with the times were reprobated—some as hypocrites, and others as cowards. And in good truth, what favourable opinion could be entertained of such as did not continue faithful even to their God according to the dictates of their conscience?

The Rev. Mr. Dixon, a Roman Catholic clergyman, who had been condemned before a magistrate and sentenced to transportation, was sent off to Duncannon Fort the day preceding the Insurrection; and this was on the testimony of a man named Francis Murphy, whose evidence was positively contradicted by three other witnesses. These facts, together with the public odium incurred by the man himself, induced Thomas Dixon, a sea-faring captain and master of a vessel, who also kept a porter-house in Wexford, to take a summary mode of avenging the fate of the clergyman, who was his relation. For this purpose he brought the man out of gaol, upon his own sole authority, and conducted him down to the Bull Ring, where he obliged three Revenue officers, who were then prisoners, and whom he brought out along with him, to shoot him, and afterwards bear his body to the quay and throw it into the water. This execution took place, with all its shocking circumstances, while most of the town's-people were at prayers, and was utterly unknown to the principal inhabitants; but at all events Dixon could the more readily accomplish his vengeance, without fear of being prevented, on account of the public execration generally prevalent against informers.

The military stationed at Gorey made constant sallies, in the course of which through the country they plundered and burnt many houses, and shot several stragglers who happened to fall in their way. This provoked the insurgents to vie with their opponents in this mode of warfare, and retaliation has, on this as well as on every other occasion, produced many woful scenes. Enormities in fact were committed on both sides, which, among their many lamentable consequences, tended to exasperate the party-animosities already too powerfully destructive of the peace and happiness of the country. At this time reinforcements were every day crowding into Gorey. On the 3rd of June, General Loftus arrived there with fifteen hundred men under his command, as did also Colonel Walpole from Carnew, whence he had several times gone out to reconnoitre the camp at Carrigrew. A determination was formed to attack this on the 4th, with the force then in Gorey, with which the troops from Carnew and Newtownbarry were to co-operate, so as to engage the insurgents on all sides; and from these arrangements, and considering the force that was to act against them, little doubt was entertained of their total and speedy defeat. The army from Gorey marched out at the appointed time and formed into two divisions—the one under General Loftus took route towards Ballycanew; while the other, commanded by Colonel Walpole, proceeded by the Camolin road directly to commence the concerted attack on Carrigrew. The insurgents had, however, quitted this post, and were in full march towards Gorey, when they suddenly and unawares fell in with this military body under Colonel Walpole, at a place called Tubberneering. The meeting was equally unexpected on both sides, and this circumstance, no less true than extraordinary,—neither party having any scouts—produced an instantaneous and confused action, in which Colonel Walpole was killed in a few minutes after its commencement, and his troops immediately gave way and fled in the utmost precipitation and disorder, leaving the victors in possession of three pieces of cannon, two six-pounders, and another of inferior size. The fate of this action was so quickly decided, as to allow General Loftus not the smallest opportunity of affording the troops under Colonel Walpole any assistance. The loss of the military in killed and wounded was considerable, besides Captain M'Manus, Lieutenant Hogg, and Ensign Barry, of the Antrim militia, with many privates, taken prisoners. The rest, in the greatest possible haste, being pursued by the insurgents, reached Gorey, which they as quickly passed through; but would in revenge put the prisoners in the town to death, had they not feared that the delay it would occasion might cost them too dearly. This account I have from a captain of yeomanry, who opposed with all his might the perpetration of such a cruel and barbarous deed, and who, to his honour, was incapable of countenancing such an atrocity under any circumstances. The retreat was thence very precipitate to Arklow, where a council of war was hastily held, at which it was as hastily determined to abandon that town, and this was accordingly put into execution. Some were so panic-struck that they did not stop till they reached Dublin; but others stopped at different distances when their horses or themselves were not able to proceed farther. General Loftus, on hearing the report of the cannon and other fire-arms in the engagement, not being able to go across the country, proceeded round by the road to the scene of action, where he found the bodies of many slain, and did not learn the fate of Colonel Walpole till he saw him stretched on the field of battle. He then moved towards Gorey, but thought it most prudent to alter his line of direction upon being saluted by the insurgents with the cannon they had just taken, and which they had drawn up to the summit of the hill of Gorey, which is immediately over the town, commanding it in every quarter. The General then marched to Carnew, and from that to Tullow. The troops that had proceeded from Carnew in the morning to co-operate in the intended general attack on the insurgents at Carrigrew did not return thither upon hearing of the defeat, but made Newtownbarry with those who had come out from thence on the same expedition.

The insurgents were now in possession of the whole of the county of Wexford, except the fort of Duncannon, the towns of Ross and Newtownbarry; and were at perfect liberty, if they pursued their advantages, to seize upon Carnew, and also to enter Arklow, situated in the county of Wicklow, and what consequences might have ensued are now incalculable.

On the evening of the 4th of June, the insurgents stationed on the hill of Carrickbyrne, whither the Taghmon encampment, as has been observed, was transferred on the 1st, now proceeded to Corbet Hill, within a mile of the town of Ross, the garrison of which had lately received great reinforcements, by the arrival there of the Donegal, Clare, and Meath regiments of militia, a detachment of English and Irish artillery, the fifth dragoons, the Mid-Lothian fencibles; and on this very evening the county of Dublin regiment of militia considerably added to its force, which upon the whole amounted to twelve hundred men, exclusive of the yeomen, all under the command of Major-General Johnson, who expected an attack during the night, and consequently the troops remained under arms without being allowed to take any repose. The insurgents, led by their Commander-in-chief, Mr. Beauchamp Bagnal Harvey, a little after their arrival on Corbet Hill, were saluted with a few cannon-shot and bomb-shells from the town, without producing any other effect than that of increasing their vigilance. Mr. Harvey and his principal officers took up their quarters in the house of Corbet Hill, where, being regaled with an excellent supper and exquisite wines, they were so well pleased with their cheer, and so far forgot their prudence as commanders, that they had scarcely time to fall asleep since the moment of their retirement, until they were roused, by the orders they had given in their sober moments, to commence the attack at break of day. Mr. Furlong was immediately dispatched with a flag of truce, and the following summons to the commanding officer in Ross :—

"SIR—As a friend to humanity, I request you will surrender the town of Ross to the Wexford forces now assembled against that town. Your resistance will but provoke rapine and plunder to the ruin of the most innocent. Flushed with victory, the Wexford forces, now innumerable and irresistible, will not be controlled if they meet with any resistance: to prevent, therefore, the total ruin of all property in the town, I urge you to a speedy surrender, which you will be forced to do in a few hours, with loss and bloodshed, as you are surrounded on all sides. Your answer is required in four hours. Mr. Furlong carries this letter, and will bring the answer.

"I am, sir, &c., &c.,

"B. B. HARVEY.

"Camp at Corbet Hill, half-past three o'clock morning, June 5th, 1798."

Mr. Furlong was shot the moment he approached the outposts, which so exasperated the people that they could not be restrained from instantly rushing on to attack the Three-bullet gate, being the part of the town next to them; and this it was that principally prevented the concerted plan of assault from being carried into execution; as three divisions of their forces were to have begun their operations against different parts of the town at the same time. This particular division, therefore, not waiting till the other two should have reached their several stations of action, the latter not only did not proceed, but were seized with such a panic that they dispersed all over the country, flying in all directions to their several homes, and bearing as they went along the tidings of a total defeat; and this *derout* was in a great degree occasioned by the example of one of the divisional commanders, who, without the least effort to answer the intent of his appointment, turned away from the action, and rode hastily homeward. Even in the town of Wexford, nineteen miles distant from Ross, the news of a defeat was announced, at an early hour of the day, by many fugitives who had taken that direction, relating various and strange adventures to account for their own precipitate flight. One-fourth of the numbers that encamped on Corbet Hill the evening before did not stand in the morning of the day of action, so that even the division that commenced, and afterwards continued the assault, was by no means complete, numbers of those who constituted it having also abandoned their stations, which were far from being adequately supplied by such of the two panic-struck divisions as had the courage and resolution to join in the battle then going forward and in its greatest heat. From this statement, however, it must appear that no plan was pursued in the attack by the insurgents, but that whatever they accomplished in the onset, must have been from individual courage and intrepidity. They first dislodged the army from behind the walls and ditches where they were very advantageously posted, and on this occasion the cavalry in their charges were repulsed with considerable loss, Cornet Dodwell and twenty-seven men of the fifth dragoons having fallen in the first onset. The military then retreated into the town through the Three-bullet gate, pursued hot foot by the insurgents, who obliged them to move from one situation to another, until they at last drove them over the wooden bridge on the Barrow into the county of Kilkenny. The main guard at the market-house, however, consisting of a sergeant and fifteen men, not only maintained their situation, but even defended it with uncommon bravery and resolution, having two swivels to support them. Major Vandeleur, of the Clare militia, also continued the whole of the day with a strong detachment of his regiment at his post at Irishtown, where he stood pretty severe duty, but not altogether so violent as it would be had the place been generally attacked, according to Mr. Harvey's original plan, this being the principal entrance. When the insurgents had thus got possession of the town, they fell to plundering and drinking, on which they became so intent, that they could not be brought to follow up their advantage. In the meantime the army rallied on

the county of Kilkenny side of the bridge; and
although a retreat was before determined on, yet they
were induced to return upon perceiving that there was
no pursuit, and besides they were powerfully instigated
to this by the spirited exhortations of Messrs. M'Cormick
and Devereux, two yeomen not possessed of any command, but the display of whose active courage and
intrepidity contributed in a great degree to turn the
fate of the day, and to whose real merit every praise is
justly due on this occasion, wherein few officers distinguished themselves, as may be fairly concluded from
the official returns of the killed and wounded, these
casualties in regard to the officers not bearing due
proportion to those of the private men, which could
hardly be the case had the former maintained their
stations with becoming firmness. The county of Dublin
militia, on hearing of the death of their favourite
Colonel, Lord Mountjoy, were the first to renew the
attack under the command of Major Vesey. Their
example was followed by the rest of the troops, and
their united efforts shortly compelled such of the
insurgents as were not too drunk, to fly out of the
town, of which they had been by this time some hours
in possession. Having respired a little, however, from
their hasty retreat, which in a great degree made them
sober, they again returned to the charge, and the
contest which now ensued was maintained on both sides
with great obstinacy, both parties being induced, by
experience of the former encounter, not to relax their
exertions. The intrepidity of the insurgents was truly
remarkable, as, notwithstanding the dreadful havoc
made in their ranks by the artillery, they rushed up to
the very mouths of the cannon, regardless of the
numbers that were falling on all sides of them, and
pushed forward with such impetuosity, that they
obliged the army to retire once more and leave the

town to themselves. But even after this they soon fell into the same misconduct as before, crowning their bravery with drunkenness. Of this the proper advantage was quickly taken by the army, who again renewed the attack, by which they finally became perfect masters of the town. Several houses were set on fire, and consumed in the course of this and the former attack, but one of these deserves particular notice: this was a slated house, four stories high, on the summit of the main street near the church, in which seventy-five persons were burnt to ashes; none having escaped but one man, who, in running away, was fortunate enough to get clear of the fire of the soldiery. On the evening of the preceding Wednesday, Mr. Cullimore, a Quaker, wishing to visit his family at his country-house, a short distance from the town, was taken prisoner as he attempted to pass the patrols, brought in, and confined in the market-house, from which he was not released on the day of battle, as if it were by the special interference of Providence, for some of the military, when they imagined the day going against them, had resolved to put all the prisoners in the town to death; but when a party of those on guard entered the place of confinement for the nefarious purpose, Mr. Cullimore addressed them with such an authoritative and impressive tone, saying—*"You shall not shoot the prisoners; there are some men here as loyal as you are."* This address and manner of a man better than Marius, awed and overcame the sanguinary slaves, so that they retired without perpetrating the horrid crime of their bloody intent! Some officers and privates of the king's troops, in the various success of the day, were induced from time to time to attempt a retreat to Waterford, through the county of Kilkenny. Some of these succeeded in their efforts; and from their unfavourable accounts of the battle, the Ros-

K

common militia, who were in full march towards Ross, turned about for Waterford; and even Captain Dillon, with some of the county of Dublin militia, were intercepted and put to death in their progress by the country people, who, on sight of the fugitives, and on the report of the success of the county of Wexford insurgents, were making every preparation, and nearly in readiness, to join them. The insurgents, being upbraided by their chiefs for sullying their bravery by drunkenness, made a third attempt to regain the town, and in this they displayed equal valour with what they exhibited in the earlier part of the day. But by this time the army had acquired a greater degree of confidence in their own strength, while several houses blazed in tremendous conflagration; and the insurgents received an irreparable loss, when their intrepid leader, John Kelly, of Killan, whose dauntless valour on this day was but too conspicuous, received a wound in the leg, which put an end to his career of victory! Paralysed by the loss of such a man's exertions, and no longer able to withstand the violence of the flying artillery, the insurgents sounded a regular retreat, bringing away with them a piece of cannon taken from the army in the course of the action, having lost one which they brought with them, together with some swivels and small pieces which had been drawn on for mere show, and which could not be of much use to either party. The insurgents after their defeat returned to their former station, having encamped this night at Carrickbyrne.

The loss of the army on this day, by official statement, is allowed to be two hundred and thirty, in killed, wounded, and missing; but that of the insurgents has been variously reported even by different eye-witnesses, some making it but five hundred, while others state it at two thousand. Indeed, it is impossible to ascertain their loss during the battle itself, as the number of dead are said to be doubly accumulated by those who were killed unarmed and unresisting after it was all over. Many men had become so intoxicated in the course of the day that they were incapable of flying out of the town in the retreat of their associates, and several of the inhabitants, whose houses were burnt, and having therefore no place to retire to, fell victims alike as straggling insurgents to the undistinguishing fury of the irritated soldiery, from which no person could escape who was not clad in military attire of one kind or other. The following day also the few thatched houses that remained unburnt, being the only places that a common person could get into, were closely searched, and not a man discovered in them left alive. Some houses were set on fire even so thronged that the corpses of the suffocated within them could not fall to the ground, but continued crowded together in an upright posture, until they were taken out to be interred. I cannot suppose that these horrid massacres and conflagrations were committed in revenge for the infernal abomination perpetrated at Scullabogue, of which I shall have occasion presently to make mention, as no intelligence of that lamentable event could have reached Ross at the time; but be that as it may, officers were not only present, but even promoted and encouraged those deeds of dreadful enormity, of which every breast not dead to humane feeling must shudder at the recital.

In the evening after the action, when the troops were assembled on parade, General Johnson singled out Lieutenant Egan of the Royal Irish Artillery (now captain of the Royal Artillery), to whom he returned his public thanks for his gallant and spirited conduct during the action; and, indeed, every praise is due to this officer, who, with a part of the Donegal militia, was principally instrumental in contributing to the fate of the battle. Several proposals were made to the General to abandon the town and retreat to Kilkenny, but he was determined to stand as long as he had a man to support him; however, had the troops been attacked that night, the prevalent opinion is, they would have fled. In the dispatches published, thanks were returned to all commanding officers. The uncommon bravery and exertions of Mr. Edward Devereux appeared so meritorious to General Johnson that he was offered a commission in the army, which his mercantile avocations prevented him from accepting of.

It is an invariable maxim that cowardice and cruelty are very closely allied. This was most strongly exemplified by the barbarous conduct of the runaway murderers who fled from the battle of Ross to Scullabogue, where a number of prisoners were confined in a barn, to which these savage miscreants (having overpowered the guards, who resisted them as long as they could) set fire, and made every person within its walls, nearly eighty in number, perish in the flames. One hundred and eighty-four are confidently asserted to have been victims on this melancholy occasion, besides thirty-seven shot and piked. But then the same account states that the barn was in dimensions only thirty-four feet long, and fifteen feet wide; and it is not, therefore, within the limit of reasonable probability that there were so many, as they would have been so closely crammed in that the cruelty of such confinement could not escape notice; indeed in such case they could scarcely stand together and respire. I am, therefore, led to believe that the asserters of these statements have been imposed upon, as eighty persons would rather crowd such a space too much for the purposes of maintaining life and health; and I am consequently induced the more readily to think the information more correct with which I have been favoured by respectable and disinterested authority from the neighbourhood in which the nefarious transaction took place; and surely it must prove grateful to every mind to be so agreeably undeceived respecting the fewer number of victims. Wickedness is seldom exhibited only in single acts of depravity; it scarcely ever omits exerting every possible action of baseness. Such of the victims at Scullabogue as had anything about them worth taking were plundered before being consigned to their horrible fate. It is alleged on the part of the sanguinary ruffians concerned in this most detestable transaction, that it was in retaliation for like deeds of desperate cruelty practised against themselves, and irritated as they were from recent experience of persecutions and tortures of every kind— whippings, strangulations, and hangings without trial, which some of the party had narrowly escaped a few days before in Ross, where these measures were very prevalent; but no incentive, no persecution, no experience of cruelty can palliate, much less excuse, such unnatural and detestable atrocity. It is but justice, however, to observe, that in this horrid transaction, no person of superior condition—none above the mere *canaille*, or lowest description of men—was at all concerned, however confidently the contrary has been asserted; but infamy of this indelible nature should never so much as glance but at its proper objects. Were the fact otherwise than as here stated, it must have been notoriously manifested in the course of the several trials since had in consequence of the very enormity, and for which some miscreants have been justly doomed to execution. But truth imposes the task of mentioning also that it has appeared from solemn evidence given on those trials, that in consequence of the insurgents being disappointed in their expectation of taking quiet possession of Ross, their flag of truce being shot, and after the attack the fugitives from the town communicating accounts of the tortures practised there,

and that no quarter would be given to the people, an
infuriated multitude of men and women rushed to
Scullabogue vociferating revenge, forced the guards (who
did all in their power to protect their charge), and set
fire to the prison, which was a thatched house; and for
this transaction General Johnson has not escaped animadversion, as it is said he was repeatedly warned to
spare the people or they would resort to retaliation, by
executing all the prisoners in their hands! and if giving
quarter would have prevented the fatality at Scullabogue, humanity excites a wish it had been given. It
is material to observe also that these trials have dis-
closed information manifesting a very strong feature
characteristic of popular commotion, which is, that the
unbridled multitude are as precipitate as indiscriminate
in their deeds of outrage, putting them into execution
as soon as conceived, to prevent the possibility of counteraction. This is, in fact, so true, that very often the
greatest favourites cannot escape the instantaneous
violence of popular fury. Although this cannot be considered as an excuse, nothing being capable of palliat-
ing, much less excusing, the crime at Scullabogue, yet
its guilt would be greatly aggravated did it appear a
deliberate or premeditated action, in which any one
above the meanest vulgar was concerned. Scullabogue
is situated at the foot of the eminence of Carrickbyrne,
whither the insurgents defeated at Ross retreated, as
has been observed, and upon being made acquainted
with the enormity, which all brave men must reprobate,
they universally and loudly expressed their horror and
detestation of the barbarous deed! Surely it is easy
to conceive that the men who had so lately displayed
such a dauntless spirit of courage and consummate
bravery, could not be destitute of its general concomitant—humanity. To counteract the reports of religious
intolerance it must be stated that fifteen or sixteen

Catholics shared in the sorrowful catastrophe of Scullabogue, whence only two Protestants and one Catholic providentially escaped.

It must be universally allowed that robbers and murderers entertain no reverence, as they feel no awe of religion, in the commission of their nefarious acts; and I am confident from all I can learn from the melancholy horrors of Scullabogue, that nothing less than the signal interference of Providence can be considered capable of having saved any person who was within the ill-fated barn on the dreadful day of its conflagration! An investigation of this horrid transaction had been firmly determined on, which subsequent events prevented from being carried into execution. It were much to be wished such an inquiry had taken place, as it would afford no room for misrepresentation. On the day following a proclamation, in the form of resolutions by the whole insurgent army, was published by the Commander-in-chief, signed by himself, and countersigned by the Adjutant-General, with intention to curb all excesses against life and property, and encouraging by every possible means union and harmony among all descriptions of the people. I deem it necessary to insert it, and here accordingly it follows:—

"At a meeting of the general and several officers of the united army of the county of Wexford, the following resolutions were agreed upon:—

"Resolved—That the commander-in-chief shall send guards to certain baronies, for the purpose of bringing in all men they shall find loitering and delaying at home or elsewhere; and if any resistance be given to those guards, so to be sent by the commanding officer's orders, it is our desire and orders that such persons so giving resistance shall be liable to be put to death by the guards, who are to bear a commission for that purpose; and all such persons found to be so loitering and delaying at home, when brought in by the guards, shall be tried by a court-martial appointed and chosen from among the commanders of all the different corps, and be punished with death.

"Resolved—That all officers shall immediately repair to their respective quarters, and remain with their different corps, and not depart therefrom under pain of death, unless authorized to quit by written orders from the commander-in-chief for that purpose.

"It is also ordered, that a guard shall be kept in rear of the different armies, with orders to shoot all persons who shall fly or desert from any engagement; and that these orders shall be taken notice of by all officers commanding in such engagement.

"All men refusing to obey their superior officers, to be tried by a court-martial and punished according to their sentence.

"It is also ordered, that all men who shall attempt to leave their respective quarters when they have been halted by the commander-in-chief, shall suffer death, unless they shall have leave from their officers for so doing.

"It is ordered by the commander-in-chief, that all persons who have stolen or taken away any horse or horses, shall immediately bring in all such horses to the camp, at head-quarters; otherwise for any horse that shall be seen or found in the possession of any person to whom he does not belong, that person shall, on being convicted thereof, suffer death.

"And any goods that shall have been plundered from any house, if not brought into head-quarters, or returned immediately to the houses or owners, that all persons so plundering as aforesaid, shall, on being convicted thereof, suffer death.

"It is also resolved, that any person or persons who

shall take upon them to kill or murder any person or prisoner, burn any house, or commit any plunder, without special written orders from the commander-in-chief, shall suffer death.

"By Order of
"B. B. HARVEY, Commander-in-chief.
FRANCIS BREEN, Sec. and Adj.

"Head-quarters, Carrickbyrne Camp, June 6th, 1798."

A proclamation of similar tendency was issued at Wexford on the 7th, addressed to the insurgent armies by General Edward Roche, conceived in the following words:—

"TO THE PEOPLE OF IRELAND.

"Countrymen and fellow soldiers! Your patriotic exertions in the cause of your country have hitherto exceeded our most sanguine expectations, and in a short time must ultimately be crowned with success. Liberty has raised her drooping head: thousands daily flock to her standard: the voice of her children everywhere prevails. Let us then, in the moment of triumph, return thanks to the Almighty Ruler of the universe, that a total stop has been put to those sanguinary measures which of late were but too often resorted to by the creatures of government, to keep the people in slavery.

"Nothing now, my countrymen, appears necessary to secure the conquests you have already won, but an implicit obedience to the commands of your chiefs; for through a want of proper subordination and discipline, all may be endangered.

"At this eventful period, all Europe must admire, and posterity will read with astonishment, the heroic acts achieved by people strangers to military tactics, and having few professional commanders—but what power can resist men fighting for liberty!

"In the moment of triumph, my countrymen, let not your victories be tarnished with any wanton act of cruelty; many of those unfortunate men now in prison were not your enemies from principle; most of them, compelled by necessity, were obliged to oppose you: neither let a difference in religious sentiments cause a difference among the people. Recur to the debates in the Irish House of Lords on the 19th of February last; you will there see a patriotic and enlightened Protestant Bishop (Down), and many of the lay lords, with manly eloquence pleading for Catholic Emancipation and Parliamentary Reform, in opposition to the haughty arguments of the Lord Chancellor, and the powerful opposition of his fellow-courtiers.

"To promote a union of brotherhood and affection among our countrymen of all religious persuasions, has been our principal object: we have sworn in the most solemn manner—have associated for this laudable purpose, and no power on earth shall shake our resolution.

"To my Protestant soldiers I feel much indebted for their gallant behaviour in the field, where they exhibited signal proofs of bravery in the cause.

"EDWARD ROCHE.

"Wexford, June 7, 1798."

I should have mentioned before this, that in the evening of the day on which the insurgents obtained possession of Enniscorthy, a drummer of the North Cork militia, who had some time before refused to beat his drum, when some tune, obnoxious to the people, was called for, or to whip some of the prisoners, was found hanging in the lodgings of Mr. Handcock, a clergyman and magistrate, who resided in that town! When this fact became generally known, it is impossible to conceive the indignation and fury it excited in the minds of the people, already flushed with victory and heated by intoxication. They considered the murdered soldier as a victim immolated to their cause; they conceived he had met that fate to which they were all doomed unless they had risen against extermination. The more violent were those who themselves or their friends had suffered most severely, previous to the Insurrection, and they instantly took advantage of the ferment occasioned by this circumstance, to wreak their vengeance on those they considered their enemies, who still remained in the town after it had been evacuated by the military. Many were put to death in consequence, notwithstanding that the more sensible and humane part endeavoured to protect the unhappy sufferers, but the voices of those were drowned in the general cry of "They would not let one of us escape if we were in their power—we would be all served like the drummer." I have heard many who were present when this horrid scene took place affirm that this incident produced an effect more violent and instantaneous, and excited a degree of frenzy superior to anything they had witnessed during the Insurrection. It is evident from every day's experience, that causes, insignificant in themselves, do sometimes produce effects the most lamentable; and that artful men take advantage of such incidents in all tumultuary proceedings; and considering the state of mind of the populace at this moment, the knowledge of such a fact must have had a powerful operation. It is remarkable that Mr. N. Hinton's house, in which the drummer was found hanging, received no injury from the people, as they considered him innocent of this abomination.

While the insurgents kept possession of the town of Enniscorthy, another circumstance occurred, which produced much mischief. The cavalry of Newtown-barry made an inroad towards the insurgents' camp, as far as the bridge of Scarawalsh, which is three miles from Enniscorthy, and at this place killed a boy who was an idiot; he happened to be the nephew of a Catholic priest in the neighbourhood; and the killing of this creature, who never could have made use of hostile weapons, produced a violent ferment, which was not appeased until the people sacrificed (as if to his *manes*) twelve or fourteen of their prisoners. These facts, if any are wanting, show the impolicy and wickedness of shedding blood unnecessarily, even in the fury of war. The principle of retaliation is strongly implanted in the human heart, and, therefore, all unnecessary irritation should be sedulously avoided.

A Guinea cutter, having struck against the banks of Blackwater, unshipped her rudder outside the Bay of Wexford, where she cast anchor; and the captain, on entering the harbour to get it repaired, was met by one of the cruising boats, and the vessel was accordingly seized and brought in as a prize. Her burthen was forty-five tons, she was copper-bottomed, had six small cannon, and her crew were eight men. She was an attendant on a Guinea-man, sailed from Liverpool a few days before, had not yet received her small arms on board, but had three barrels of gunpowder, without which the insurgents would have been totally destitute of that article, as the three barrels they found in Wexford barracks, with a few hundred cartridges, some small casks and odd pounds found in different shops and gentlemen's houses, constituted their whole original stock, which by this time was entirely expended. It is, indeed, an extraordinary fact, that the insurgents did not possess, in the whole course of the Insurrection, as much powder as would be deemed necessary by any military man for the supply of one battle, and that their gunsmen, so little used to warfare, never retired until they had fired their last charge, exhibiting on all occasions amazing intrepidity; but it was impossible to furnish fire-arms for the numbers offering their services. In their different encampments they were mostly armed with pikes, and there was scarcely any kind of regularity or order observed, every individual absenting at his own discretion, so that at night the camps were almost totally deserted, but were in the day as crowded as ever. Although most of the people of Ireland can but seldom indulge in the luxury of eating meat, yet, as the vast numbers of the insurgents were now to be supplied with this article, it became an absolute necessary. Such immense consumption always in time of war, even with the strictest economy, being double of the quantity that would supply the like numbers in time of peace, must of itself have soon deprived the country of all its cattle; and yet this provision was made use of with profusion. Corn and potatoes were put in requisition throughout the country; and Wexford was obliged, at the risk of being burnt, to furnish almost all the other supplies, such as spirits, beer, tobacco, salt, and leather. Several self-appointed commissaries, framing different excuses as it were for the advantage of the public service, while their principle was for plunder and private emolument, absented themselves from camp and became horrible public nuisances. These were the cowards who fled in time of action, and generally became murderers and robbers; while those who courageously fought as brave men in the field, always remained at their post, never absenting without leave, and, although suffering many privations, were remarkable for correct behaviour and regular conduct, the true test of brave men; but the *poltroon* cravens, who deserted the camps on various pretences, were guilty of the most desperate deeds of outrage, though vauntingly boastful of actions of valour,—a fact which not only confirms the general position already laid down, that cowardice and cruelty are constantly united, but also that the vicious frequently affect the praises of virtue. While the brave and the virtuous were otherwise engaged, so as not to have it in their power to counteract the depravity of the knaves and cowards, a sad catalogue of victims suffered at the permanent camp on Vinegar Hill. Being declared enemies of the people, on the accusation of one or more persons, for different alleged acts of cruelty or opposition to their interests—and, on these occasions, it was almost impossible to stem the torrent of popular fury—so that the conductors and accusers of the summary trials, thus proceeded upon, were in very many instances but too successful in their schemes of murder; notwithstanding the strenuous endeavours, and the earnest entreaties and remonstrances to the contrary of every humane and respectable person permitted to appear in their assemblage. Of these there were many willing enough to return to their homes, who were, however, prevented from apprehension of being sacrificed themselves, if they dared to act in any manner contrary to the will of the populace. It has been confidently asserted, and too strongly inculcated, that the insurgents were resolved to sacrifice all Protestants. Of this the best refutation is, that had this been their principle or intention, the accomplishment was in their power, and the avoiding its perpetration at the angry and exasperated moment must be considered conclusive in the opposite argument. Indeed, it is too evident that this falsehood has been industriously impressed for the purpose of fostering prejudice, and of continuing baleful division among the several descriptions of the people, by political adventurers, who shamefully encourage and foment those animosities, which have brought so much calamity and ruin on the country; of which, if any Irishman requires further proof, the eventful history of his country since the period of 1798 is abundantly convincing; and I fondly hope the charitable discrimination of all Irishmen will induce them to abandon their prejudices, and cultivate a friendly intercourse with each other, and I am confident they will find this line of conduct connected and congenial with their interests and happiness, as it will prevent their being cajoled or worked up at any future period to mutual rancour, to answer the ends of political seducers, as the destruction of their country must be the consequence.

All Protestants who had the good-will of their neighbours, and who had not adventured in the hanging, burning, flogging, shooting, and exterminating system that immediately preceded the Insurrection, were in general as safe as any other description of men in the country on joining the people, for as to this there was no alternative; but it must be acknowledged, indeed, that many gentlemen who had been formerly much liked, were considered as unpardonable if concerned in any exertion against the people of the description just cited, particular instances of which alleged against them occasioned the imprisonment and death of individuals.

It is asserted, that no Catholic was put to death. Surely the indiscriminate destruction at Scullabogue, where fifteen or sixteen Catholics perished with the rest in the flames, sufficiently refutes this barefaced assertion; but as the public mind has been so misled, I deem it absolutely necessary to state other facts that give the lie to surmise, which, among the general excesses of the day, would not otherwise deserve historical notice. Two Catholics were put to death by the people in Wexford—Francis Murphy on the 3rd and Joseph Murphy on the 14th of June, both for being informers. Certainly if any Catholics had launched forward in the prevalent mode of suppressing Insurrection—namely, violation, flagellation, conflagration, deliberate murder and extermination, they would have incurred equal odium with any Protestant, or even infidel, guilty of the like deeds. Catholics, however, not being of the privileged class (not even one Catholic Justice of Peace in the county), and, therefore, not having the power if they had the inclination, could not be generally involved with the people, on the score of authority or oppression, and this may satisfactorily account why so few Catholics, comparatively with Protestants, were sacrificed to popular frenzy and irritation. In all the proclamations and other documents published during the Insurrection, there does not appear the smallest symptom of religious bigotry; the very contrary is even manifest. But should it be any longer insisted on, that the conduct and expressions of solitary individuals unequivocally discountenanced by the great majority, were the sentiments of the whole people, it must be stated in opposition that the argument would be just as fair that the Protestants had resolved on the extermination of the Catholics, as some individuals of them have expressed themselves favourable to such a measure, and have lamented the arrival of Lord Cornwallis in Ireland, as in their mind it prevented the extirpation of the whole of the insurgents, by them denominated *Catholics*. These sentiments have been so notorious as to find *utterance even in Parliament.*

During the whole period of the Insurrection in the county of Wexford, it is a fact no less surprising than true that the fair sex was respected even by those who did not hesitate to rob or murder; no one instance existing of a female being injured or violated, including the wives, sisters, and daughters of those denominated the greatest enemies of the people, in whose conduct appears another very striking feature. With respect to the king they were silent—his Majesty's name was not mentioned with disrespect, nor was he considered as the cause of their misfortunes; but, indeed, they preserved no such delicacy with respect to the characters of those whom they considered the promoters and supporters of their persecutions. They reviled them in the strongest terms of reprobation, and did not spare many of their lives or properties.

In case of plunder I believe no person was spared that was not at home to prevent it, or who was not fortunate enough to have a confidential person to welcome the marauders, who pleaded the public service in excuse of robbery and outrage; but meat and drink if freely offered and supplied generally preserved a house from otherwise inevitable plunder. On these occasions Catholics and Protestants were alike subject to depredation. I possessed, perhaps, as much popularity as any person in the county of Wexford, and notwithstanding this and my being a Catholic, I was plundered by the insurgents at the very outset. I lost all that could possibly be taken from me; my doors and windows were broken open to get at my guns and pistols; my desks and trunks were searched and rifled; my horses and mules were all rode off; and for this and the like robberies the depredators would plead the public service. Several persons, who had been much disliked by the populace, had the good fortune to possess faithful servants, who by a free offer of what was wanted in the house saved all the rest; while many others who were much beloved by the people, suffered considerably in their houses and properties in consequence of the dishonesty of those who were left in care of them, as they countenanced and encouraged pillage in hopes thereby to screen their own villainy, in appropriating to themselves the best and most valuable part of the plunder.

Great numbers crowded into Wexford from the different camps and other parts of the country demanding supplies of salt, tobacco, spirits and leather; threatening to set fire to the town in case of resistance or want of immediate compliance. The mode adopted in managing the supplies was, that the committee issued orders to those possessing any of the articles in demand to furnish the same in a specified quantity; but the frequency of application so multiplied their employment that it was not possible for them to attend to all the various business that accumulated upon them; and finding themselves unequal to the task they were obliged to call for assistance, and a separate committee for each article in demand was consequently appointed. To please the lower classes, who had expressed dissatisfaction, some of them were now associated with those of higher rank, in this discharge of public duty, the trouble and vexation of which they had no conception of until they shared in the labour whereby those originally appointed were greatly relieved, and the common people henceforward proved less troublesome to them, as their compeers and companions were more successful in their arguments to persuade them of the great difficulty of supplying them in as large quantities as before, and so reconciling them to accept of less. Various plunder took place on the insurgents taking possession of the town, great part of which was afterwards restored, as orders were issued that all kinds of property not belonging to those in whose possession it might be found should be returned on pain of severe punishment. The court-house in Wexford was the depository for such property, which the owners recovered on making their claim.

The peace and quietness existing in the town of Wexford during the Insurrection, except the little disturbance now and again occasioned by the vociferous commissaries from the camps, was very remarkable. At night particularly the most solemn silence continually prevailed, as all the inhabitants retired early to rest, and the utmost regularity of conduct and peaceable behaviour was observed. The weather was remarkably warm and serene, and the physicians in town apprehended a contagious gaol fever from the numbers in confinement. Among the several expedients to remedy this evil, it was suggested to make the church a lodgment for prisoners, being considered a healthy and eligible situation, and then deserted by the Protestants as their place of worship; but this scheme was warmly and effectually opposed by the principal Catholics, as it might be deemed disrespectful to the seat of the Protestant worship, while those of the latter persuasion were eager and urgent to have it so occupied, in order, as they said, to thin the crowds confined in the common prison. As a substitute for this disappointment, the assembly-room was then resorted to, and fifty of the prisoners were confined there, while twenty-four of the principal gentlemen were sent on board a sloop in the harbour, which had been fitted out for that purpose. Another sloop had been also intended for like occupancy, but soon condemned as unfit for that service.

To endeavour to please the people, who were very vociferous against all those they considered as occasioning the cruelties practised against them, the following proclamation was issued:—

PROCLAMATION OF THE PEOPLE OF THE COUNTY OF WEXFORD.

"Whereas it stands manifestly notorious that James Boyd, Hawtrey White, Hunter Gowan, and Archibald Hamilton Jacob, late magistrates of this county, have committed the most horrid acts of cruelty, violence, and oppression against our peaceable and well-disposed countrymen: now we, the people associated and united for the purpose of procuring our just rights, and being determined to protect the persons and properties of those of all religious persuasions, who have not oppressed us, and are willing to join with heart and hand our glorious cause, as well as to show our marked disapprobation and horror of the crimes of the above delinquents, do call on our countrymen at large to use every exertion in their power to apprehend the bodies of the aforesaid James Boyd, Hawtrey White, Hunter Gowan, and Archibald Hamilton Jacob, and to secure and convey them to the gaol of Wexford, to be brought before the tribunal of the people. Done at Wexford this 9th day of June, 1798.

"God save the people."

The camp, which had been stationed at Carrickbyrne, removed to Slieye-kielter, where the encampment continued for a few days, while nothing remarkable happened, except some ineffectual attacks that were made on the gun-boats, going up the Barrow from Passage to Ross; and a mail was taken, going from Ross to Waterford by water, and sent to Wexford.

The country was so guarded in every quarter as to have a party stationed at every cross-road, and this service was allotted to the old and infirm, or such as were incapable of bearing the fatigue of marching; but they were also attended by many others, who absented themselves from the camps on various pretences. Some women and children were likewise to be seen at these several posts; and the vigilance was such, that no person could pass unknown, nor was it possible to be at liberty and be considered neuter; notwithstanding all the boastful vauntings to the contrary of some who think to recommend themselves by these impositions. I am confident such assertions are utterly unfounded, for certainly no person could remain at liberty who was not considered friendly to the people; yet still I am far from being of opinion, that every person who joined the insurgents acted from cordial motives, however professing great zeal and alacrity in the cause. But the imperious necessity of the times was such, as to induce numbers to humour the people so far, as not to say or do anything that might in any degree be construed as opposition to them; and any impartial person must be convinced, on a fair inquiry into the nature of popular commotion, that it would be impossible to control the actions of a multitude, under such circumstances as then existed in the county of Wexford. An irritated populace, becoming masters of a country, are ever ungovernable; and, indeed, those who vaunt most at present of not having yielded to them, were more than any others profuse in their professions, and have gone farther than those whom they now revile in the most unjustifiable manner. Some also who were thus involved, having fled the country early, now pretend to ask, why an escape was not effected by such as were not well inclined to the cause of the insurgents, if not in confinement? Although it may not have been altogether impossible, yet it was not very probable, that any one could get out of the country without the consent of the people, which must have been obtained by imposing on them by the pretence of friendship, to whom the person must shortly after have appeared a traitor (a character not very enviable, under the most favourable circumstances), which conduct would have endangered the safety of his family and friends, if he had any, as well as that of his property; so that I think it reasonable to suppose, that those who urge this argument would not have attempted an escape, were they in the place of those whose conduct they scrutinize.

A pitched cap being found in the barrack of Wexford, and an Orange commission or warrant appointing a sergeant of the North Cork militia to found an Orange lodge in the town, roused the people from the utmost tranquillity to the highest pitch of fury. This quickly drew together great numbers in the barrack-yard, and their horror of the Orange system was so excited, that in those emblems they imagined they possessed the most convincing proof of their intended extermination. After a variety of confused exclamations against the promoters, it was resolved to clap the pitched cap on the head of the Orange lord, who, they said, had been the introducer of that system in the county of Wexford. They accordingly proceeded from the barrack, exhibiting the pitched cap on the top of a pike, displaying at the same time the Orange commission or warrant, and were in direct march, with violent shouts of exultation, to Lord Kingsborough's lodging. I was in the act of bathing at the time, and hearing the tumultuous noise, I dressed quickly and arrived at the house along with them. I went up to Lord Kingsborough's room and sought to appease the multitude by addressing them from the window. But this was not effected till many of the principal inhabitants were brought to the scene of tumult; when one of them, on pretence of looking at the pitched cap, took and threw it over the quay, and the hated emblem being no longer in view, the fury of the people abated, the Orange commission or warrant was taken from them, and they dispersed. Nor was there anything more heard of the affair until the next morning, when the captain of the guard for the day (having every thing previously arranged and ready, after parade, when all others had retired to breakfast, and on his own mere authority,) took down Lord Kingsborough and his two officers to the quay, and conducted them on board the ship that had been fitted out, but condemned, where he provided them with abundance of fresh straw, and placed a detachment of his guard over them. All this was executed with such haste and precaution, that it was not for some time known to the principal inhabitants. These, however, on hearing of the affair, assembled and appealed to the people, then collected to know what was the matter. They represented to them, that as these officers had surrendered on condition of being treated as prisoners of war, they ought not to be confined on board a condemned ship; and the consequence was, that two boat-loads of butchers were sent on board to examine and inspect the state of the vessel, on whose report that she was not fit for a *pig* to be confined in, Lord Kingsborough and his officers were brought back to their former situation, where they remained until the surrender of the town. The vessel was then hauled into the harbour, where she sunk within a foot of her deck.

From the great heat and violence of the people against Lord Kingsborough, in consequence of reports of his cruelty and exertions in flogging, and the other modes previously practised for quieting the people, different parties, from town and country, frequently proceeded to the house where he was confined, with an intention of putting him to death; but the guards always refused to give him out to them without an order, and during the delay thus occasioned, providentially for his lordship, one or other of the principal inhabitants usually came up, and by representing the conditions which had been promised him on surrendering, they prevailed on the people to depart. Considering the great fury of the people against Lord Kingsborough for his previous violent exertions, being reported very cruel and sanguinary, his escape must be considered really wonderful, if not truly astonishing; and I can account for it in no other manner, than that the county of Wexford, not having been his scene of action, and there existing no kind of communication with any other quarter, there could not possibly be any positive proof adduced of his actions, except in a solitary instance, which was easily got over. His lordship had been, previous to his imprisonment, but a very short time in Wexford, as he left that town in two or three days after he had marched into it with his regiment. But some of his officers had observed a lady at a window, viewing the troops as they came in, who attracted their particular notice. After dinner, at which the bottle had pretty freely circulated, the recollection of the sight of this lady had so far worked on the minds of some of the lads, that they proposed to sally forth and endeavour to obtain a nearer view of her; and Lord Kingsborough, being a young man himself, humoured the frolic, and accompanied them. Not gaining admittance, however, as they expected, they, in the military style, resolved to storm the premises; and his lordship, being a tall, athletic man, raised one of the officers on his shoulders, who was thereby enabled, as the house was low, to get in through a window in the second story. The lady's husband was absent, and herself quite alone in the house, but on perceiving their intentions she got out by a back-window, and thus eluded their design, as well as put an end to any further progress in this adventure. When his lordship afterwards became a prisoner, this was quoted as an unfavourable circumstance, but it was obviated with little difficulty by an argument (not at all intending to throw the least reflection on the lady's character), which was, that her husband was himself a prisoner with the people, against whom, therefore, the offence could never have been intended, as no attempt of the kind had been made on any of their wives or families;

but was an insult offered by one whom they called an enemy, to another whom they thought deserving of the same appellation. This point being thus settled, and all other accusations against his lordship being general, they were the more easily overcome; but had they been particular, the event might have been quite otherwise, as the injured person or persons, for the most part, would not listen to any kind of reasoning, but obstinately hold out and persevere in their accusations and complaints, which they so feelingly impressed on the assemblage of people appealed to on such occasions, that they usually gained over their sympathetic approbation of the measures they proposed, and would thus succeed against all intercession.

Of this truth I had most sensible experience; for, although I proved on several occasions providentially instrumental in saving lives, I was utterly incapable in other instances; particularly I found it totally out of my power, notwithstanding the many means I sought, to rescue my ever-to-be-regretted, dear, and valuable friend, Mr. Turner, from the fury of the people, by whom he had been previously very much beloved; but all his former popularity was eclipsed by his having been unfortunately worked up to set fire to some houses; and this being well known to the people of the country, his safety became an impossibility. Taking the cases of Mr. Turner and Lord Kingsborough in any point of view, and considering my frequent success in preserving the man with whom his misfortune alone made me acquainted, while my most earnest and anxious endeavours to protect the friend of my bosom were fatally ineffectual, local circumstances alone can explain the consequences. But how variously will prejudice and misrepresentation detail and expatiate on such intricate facts, according to the feeling, inclination, or judgment of the narrator, who, if he be not a sensible or unbiassed eye-witness, discriminating and dauntless during the period of danger, or discerning in selection of report, will afterward display the thoughts of latent bigotry, wilful perversion of truth, or the flimsy tissue of hearsay information, varied and altered into different shapes of falsehood, according to the several dispositions of the circulators; but ocular evidence must ever supersede the accounts of rumour, even of ever such boasted authenticity, when discrimination may be overpowered by terror.

The insurgents in the different camps being in great want of gunpowder, without which they could not proceed, remained stationary for several days, as the powder in Wexford was considered too little for its defence, and different reports were circulated, that it was to be attacked from the southern quarter. The demand for gunpowder, however, from the camp on Gorey Hill was so pressing, that a barrel of it was sent thither from Wexford to enable the insurgents to proceed to Arklow, which, on the defeat of Colonel Walpole, had been deserted by the military; but the inhabitants of which, on being left to themselves, remained quietly at home, imitating the example that had been set them at Gorey, before the battle of Tubberneering, when they were forced and overwhelmed into the system of the Insurrection. The Cavan militia was ordered from Dublin to join Colonel Walpole's division, then under General Needham, and they marched into Arklow on the 6th of June. Different other parties of the military arrived there on the 7th and 8th, and on the 9th the garrison was considerably reinforced by the Durham fencibles, who suffered no fatigue in their way from Dublin, as they had been conveyed in carriages and jaunting cars pressed for that purpose. The whole force in Arklow amounted altogether to sixteen hundred men. The insurgents had marched from Gorey Hill to Coolgreny, where, arranging their mode of attack, they proceeded in two great columns—one toward the fishery on the sea-side, and the other toward the upper end of the town, the attack being to be made on both ends of the town at once. The military, having full notice of the approach, were very advantageously posted, without which they could not have resisted the impetuous attack made upon them; however, they were obliged to retire somewhat from their original positions. In a violent effort to gain the upper end of the town, the Rev. Michael Murphy, who led on the insurgents on that side, fell, and this stopped the progress, and prevented the success of the attempt.

Variously did the fortune of the day seem to incline. It is necessary, however, to mention that rumours of a retreat of the troops were circulated, and that orders were given, and seeming preparations made for that purpose; but this still appears a disputed point, and as the proverb has it, "all is well that ends well." The insurgents, after having displayed singular bravery, courage, and intrepidity as long as their ammunition lasted, retreated, when that was expended, to their former position at Gorey; and thus ended the battle, at the very moment it was alleged the army had intended to retreat; and most undoubtedly my information warrants me to mention that some of the military had already retreated; and I cannot possibly say that they might not have good authority for their conduct. Although the Rev. Mr. Gordon had documents from under the hand of a distinguished officer, Colonel Bainbridge, that sufficiently warrants the assertion, it was, however, generally circulated by many that were in the action; and as, upon the whole, I would not readily admit hearsay evidence, but on the clearest conviction of the truth, yet I think my account would be deficient if I omitted to mention an important fact, and upon which so much stress is laid, as related by Mr. Gordon.

"Many instances might be given of men, who, at the hazard of their own lives, concealed and maintained loyalists until the storm passed away; on the other hand, many might be given of cruelties committed by persons not natives of Ireland; I shall mention only one act, not of what I shall call cruelty, since no pain was inflicted, but ferocity not calculated to soften the rancour of the insurgents. Some soldiers of the ancient British regiment cut open the dead body of Father Michael Murphy, after the battle of Arklow, took out his heart, roasted his body, and oiled their boots with the grease which dripped from it. Mr. George Taylor, in his Historical Account of the Wexford Rebellion (page 136), says—'Lord Mountnorris and some of his troop, in viewing the scene of action, found the body of the perfidious priest, Murphy, who so much deceived him and the country. Being exasperated, his lordship ordered the head to be struck off, and his body to be thrown into a house that was burning, exclaiming, *Let his body go where his soul is.*' I hope that the writer was misinformed, and that the noble Earl, remarkable for his liberality to Romanists, was not the author of this act."*

The only time I was ever in company with the priest just mentioned, certainly was at Lord Mountnorris's house, in 1797, when his lordship was engaged in the plan of procuring signatures of loyalty from the Catholics; and I understand that this priest greatly contributed to the success of that undertaking, which was afterwards much reflected on, and from the aspersions that were thrown out, it was probably that

* See Gordon's History of the Rebellion, pages 212, 213.

his lordship was induced, by this *coup de main*, to prove to the world that he had not, though he was supposed to have been, a friend to Catholics. Such transactions as took place on this occasion, it must be observed, are the more lamentable, not only as they of themselves serve to keep up animosity, but much more so when they are, not to say connived at, but even encouraged by persons of the highest rank; while all persons of humanity, but even a degree above the lowest vulgar, and even the humane of these (for they are far from being in general destitute of the principle in Ireland), and especially all who have received any degree of education, should set their faces against such pitiful acts of ferocious cruelty, as would disgrace the vilest savages.

While I am on the subject of the Rev. Michael Murphy's death, I must beg leave to express the opinion I have adopted, in conjunction with the most sensible and rational men that I have conversed with on the subject, respecting the priests who were active in the Insurrection. When clergymen so far forget their duty as to take up arms, so contrary to the spirit of the Gospel, they become most dangerous men; and the sooner such are cut off by any fatal catastrophe the better. The duty of a clergyman is to preach peace and charity towards all mankind. When his conduct deviates from this, he acts inconsistent with the profession he has entered into. Why throw off the meek garb of peace for the horrid habiliments of war? Under no possible circumstances ought a clergyman to be instrumental to the death of any person, except in the most urgent necessity of self-defence. Whenever else he takes up arms he becomes a traitor to the Gospel of Christ; and although treason may, on particular occasions, be considered useful, yet a traitor to any cause never can be regarded, even by those for whom he exerts himself.

Besides, the interference of clergymen encouraging any kind of strife, but particularly warfare, must be considered highly culpable, and deserving of a fatal end. Not one of the priests who took up arms in the county of Wexford escaped a violent and sudden death, clearly indicating a providential fate; and although they were not all at the time under suspension or ecclesiastical censure, yet under one so nearly allied to it as to prevent any of them from having arrived to the situation of a parish priest. It is but common justice that those alone should bear the disgrace of reprobation who actually deserved it, and that the great body of the Catholic clergy should be rescued from censure, as they were free from blame. The misconduct of a few individuals should not involve the good character of the many, and it must be recollected that, even among the twelve apostles, there was a traitor. The conduct of the Roman Catholic clergy of the county of Wexford, however unjustly reviled, was, during the Insurrection there, guided by the true dictates and principles of Christianity, really exemplary and meritorious. They comforted the afflicted with all the zeal and warmth of Christian charity, and, in the most trying and critical period, practised every deed that must be considered benevolent by every liberal and enlightened man, whatever brawlers of loyalty may assert to the contrary, endeavouring, with indiscriminating abuse, to brand their conduct in general with the stain of infamy. They by every possible means sought to afford every assistance and protection in their power, to those who stood in need of it, but their influence was greatly diminished by not following the example of the militant priests, who strove to attain an elevation and superiority over their brethren in this way, which they could not otherwise accomplish. If I may be allowed the expression, the conduct of the fighting priests was truly amphibious. For while they cast off the character of priests, and took up that of soldiers, they still wished to maintain an ascendency, even in their new stations, by re-assuming the priest whenever it answered the purpose of superiority, the passion for which was greatly augmented by indulgence in drinking; and notwithstanding all this, they were conspicuous for courage and humanity.

The encampment at Slieye-kielter was transferred from thence to Lacken Hill, within a mile of the town of Ross; and although Mr. Harvey had manifested courage, and had formed an excellent plan for the attack of that town—which failed of success only by not following his directions—yet no consideration prevented his conduct from being found fault with; and he, therefore, leaving the command to the Reverend Philip Roche, whose boisterous conduct pleased the multitude better, returned to Wexford.

The soldiery stationed at Newtownbarry made several excursions, and in the course of their progress some miles from the town, they shot every man they met, however unarmed and unoffending, and plundered and burned several houses. The insurgents on Vinegar Hill, irritated by these excesses, followed the example, and day after day made excursions from their camp to counteract the military; but, however, it so happened that they did not fall in with each other, as they proceeded on different sides of the Slaney, which prevented their meeting, although their depredations were in sight of each other; and while the one party was burning and destroying what they considered the enemy's property in one quarter, the other, actuated by revenge, was committing like devastation in another; and it would seem, as if by preconcertion, that both moved in different directions on every particular day of excursion; so that the only warfare between them was an apparent strife who should cause the greatest desolation, or who should appear the most eager to destroy what was spared by the other; so that the state of the country was truly lamentable.

There were but few gunsmen belonging to the stationary camp at Vinegar Hill, and an attack on that post being apprehended, one hundred and thirty gunsmen were sent thither from Wexford, under the command of Captain Murphy. These men had not experienced any of the persecutions practised previous to the Insurrection, and were consequently untainted with the rancorous spirit of revenge which they produced in other quarters. In short, they were remarkable for regularity of conduct, and they prevented a continuation of the cruel acts that had been hitherto perpetrated there; for being shocked on the morning of the 10th of June, which was the next after their arrival, by seeing a man put to death, the Wexford men would not witness such another scene, and they declared they would not permit another instance of the kind while they remained; and their humane example shamed the most refractory, whom they awed into order, so that not another person suffered on Vinegar Hill thenceforward until the 20th; and, therefore, this important truth completely contradicts the greatly exaggerated accounts of daily victims, and the aggravated statements erroneously propagated of wicked atrocities committed there; and however lamentable it is that many persons were sacrificed to popular fury, yet it is somewhat consoling to be undeceived that half the numbers stated could not have suffered. I do not by any means intend to exculpate the atrocities committed on Vinegar Hill, as a sad catalogue of sufferers could be enumerated; but such misrepresentation has taken place, that I should consider myself deficient in the task I have undertaken, did I not take every opportunity of declaring facts as they occurred, however I lament the existence of the dreadful effects of popular fury. Any deviation from truth in stating such egregious enormities can take place only with a view to keep alive those prejudices, which it is so much the interest of every true lover of his country to suppress; and to learn the real state of occurrences will be the best possible means of inducing contending parties to forgive and forget the past, and to cherish harmony in future.

I must observe respecting those lists, denominated authentic, of persons said to be put to death in particular places, that it is necessary to be intimately and perfectly acquainted with the country and its inhabitants to be able to discover that several individuals are multiplied in the account of their deaths, as the same person is mentioned particularly and generally, in one place by one, and in quite a different situation by another; and thus are narrators imposed on, not being so circumstanced as to be able to select truth from falsehood; for it by no means comes within the province of learning to sift and unravel the many confused stories of several persons, each varying the account of the same deed; which though in fact but one occurrence, yet might be mistaken for separate transactions, as no feature of coincidence is so discernible in the several relations of the same thing as to exhibit the real and uniform picture.

I have undertaken this narrative, with many facts of which I am unfortunately but too well acquainted, from no other idea but a wish to reconcile my countrymen, and not to let misrepresentation or falsehood pass to posterity; which must otherwise, perhaps, be as much imposed on as those who have hitherto written on the subject, when it would be utterly impossible to obviate misrepresentation; and I write as much for the information of those who have been already led astray, as for the public at large; and shall be happy to elucidate any particular that may not appear sufficiently explained

M

to convince them that I advance nothing for which I have not undeniable authority, independent of my personal and local knowledge of the principal events; and if they feel the candour they profess, I trust they will do me credit for wishing to set them right, when they appeal to the public for information and correction of any errors that might possibly have crept into their works.

On the 10th of June an attack was made by some gunboats on Fethard; where, after destroying all the boats mostly belonging to poor fishermen, the crews set fire to and burned many houses. This occurrence, with several ships, seemingly of war, being seen off the coast, renewed the former opinion that a landing and attack were intended in the southern part of the county. Small camps of observation were therefore instituted at Carne and Rastoonstown, to be attended by all the married men of the neighbourhood, they being supposed to prove more watchful for the protection of their wives and families, by obviating sudden emergency; while all the bachelors fit for actual service were ordered to attend at Lacken Hill. In Wexford, attempts were made to manufacture gunpowder to supply the scarcity of that article, which, however, did not succeed, for though it would explode, yet it was with little or no force. The weather continued remarkably fine and serene, a circumstance very favourable to the insurgents' mode of warfare, as they had scarcely any covering but a few booths or tents, not sufficient to contain even their officers; so that the camps were not much encumbered with equipage, and only requiring the choice of a field, and should one not prove ample enough for their numbers, the adjoining enclosures were occupied in sufficient extent to contain them in the open air.

Sir Thomas Esmonde, Bart., and Mr. Laurence Doyle,

officers in the Castletown yeomen cavalry, could not escape the general suspicion entertained against Catholics, and although they were known to have performed their duty at the battle of Arklow, yet this did not protect them from a most contumelious and public arrest on the 12th of June, at Arklow, whence they were conducted under a guard to Dublin, where they continued some days in confinement, and were then liberated without the shadow of a charge being brought against them. The impolicy of this and the like transactions in such critical times, is so flagrant, that it is astonishing to think they should be permitted to be practised; thus exasperating the feelings of any religious description, without more cogent reason than suspicion, was the occasion of many loyal Catholics not joining the army, as they were apprehensive that death might be the consequence of their being suspected.

As the insurgents had not a sufficiency of gunpowder to undertake any new attack, they remained inactive in their several encampments for some days; but in order to obtain a supply of that article, it was resolved to make an attack on Borris, the seat of Mr. Kavanagh, in the county of Carlow, where, it was supposed, lay a great quantity of arms and ammunition. A detachment accordingly proceeded from the camp on Vinegar Hill, to that on Lacken Hill, where receiving reinforcement, the united party moved forward to the attack of Borris, where they arrived after a night's march, early on the morning of the 12th. The cavalry stationed there fled on the approach of the insurgents, but a party of the Donegal militia, who had taken up their quarters in the house, defended it with great bravery, keeping up a constant fire from the upper windows, and losing but one man in the course of the contest. The cannon the insurgents had brought with them was too small to have any effect on the castle, as the only ball, discharged by one of them, rebounded from the wall, and an attack by musketry was of course considered ineffectual. As no hopes then remained of taking the mansion by assault or battery, considering the strength and thickness of the walls, and that the lower windows were also lately built up with strong mason-work, the assailants set the outer offices on fire, in hopes of forcing the garrison to dislodge themselves for their protection; but this manœuvre proving ineffectual, and the insurgents having expended all their ammunition in useless efforts, and having burnt some houses in the village, returned to the several encampments from which they had been detached in the county of Wexford.

The encampment on Gorey Hill had by this time removed to Limerick Hill, and the army, which was now daily reinforced, made frequent sallies from their several stations and committed the most violent excesses, putting to death every man who came in their way, whether by accident or otherwise. Nor were the insurgents backward in retaliation; so that the situation of such as were placed between the contending parties was truly pitiable; being uncertain for an instant of the safety of their lives or properties, and equally subject to military and popular violence and devastation. Several strong reports had now prevailed throughout the county of Wexford, that the most desperate atrocities had been committed by the soldiery in their different quarters, and this roused the already irritated passions of the people to revenge, so as to be productive of many lamentable acts of outrage, ever attendant on civil commotion, and keeping alive those melancholy discords which never occur in modern times between separate and independent nations at war; and which all enlightened and humane people so strongly detest and reprobate. Reports of these enormities very much alarmed the minds of the prisoners in Wexford, as they strongly apprehended it might produce an alteration in the conduct of the inhabitants towards them. A petition to Government, from those confined in the gaol, was accordingly drawn up, expressive of the danger of their situation should the people be prompted to retaliation upon them, by the conduct of the troops towards such of the populace or their friends as might fall into their hands; and on this occasion, the officers who were prisoners in Wexford appeared more alarmed than the others there in confinement. They accordingly communicated to me their apprehensions and wishes, and proposed striking out some mode of putting a stop to the violences, which they very naturally feared might soon involve their inevitable destruction.

Lord Kingsborough was for proposing an exchange of prisoners as the best method of allaying the prevailing alarms, and of suppressing the heat and violence of the people, now roused to the highest pitch of fury, and breathing nothing but revenge. Indeed, from the critical state of the country, and the people in general abiding no control, it was difficult to devise what could be best attempted to avert the fate that seemed to impend over every person of any distinction having the misfortune of being then in the county of Wexford, while all the chiefs throughout the several encampments most feelingly lamented the great disorders prevailing, and in conjunction with every individual of the least respectability, most strongly reprobated the cruelties and excesses that were perpetrated. So violent was the spirit of retaliation and vengeance, which seemed to actuate the whole mass of the people, that every danger was to be apprehended from it, unless some means were taken to allay the existing ferment.

On the 13th of June, several persons from the different encampments, led by the most benevolent motives, as if by preconcerted agreement, waited on the Commander-in-chief, in Wexford, to consult on the best mode of keeping the unruly rabble in some order, over whom they declared they had not (as indeed they never had) any kind of control; and they now expressed their fears, that the best disposed of the men, who had been hitherto distinguished for good conduct and humanity, might be induced by the prevailing rage, to commit acts of which they had yet been so far from guilty, that they gave them the most strenuous opposition. The abomination of Scullabogue had excited such general horror, that it became a material object of consideration on this occasion, when it was resolved to institute an inquiry for the purpose of punishing in the most exemplary manner, the perpetrators of this infernal transaction!!! The existing state of the country prevented the accomplishment of so desirable an object. A favourable circumstance occurred at this time, which led to a hope that conciliation might be attempted with some probability of success. A message was sent to a prison-ship in the harbour of Dublin, offering liberty to any one who would undertake to go to Wexford with letters for Lord Kingsborough. Accordingly, a man of the name of John Tunks undertook the task, and, being provided with all the necessary passes, he arrived safe at Limerick Hill camp, whence he was sent with some principal persons to the Commander-in-chief in Wexford. He immediately assembled those he thought best able to advise him how to proceed, and it was considered fortunate that many respectable persons from the country were then in the town, all of whom approved of endeavouring to forward the sentiments of the prisoners along with Lord Kingsborough's answer, but how to reconcile the people to the measure, without which nothing effectual could be done, was the difficulty.

The committees in Wexford, as various business and orders had been pressed on them from time to time, not at all within the scope of their intentions, upon undertaking that arduous duty, were not considered likely, in the present instance, to act with effect, particularly as their numbers had been increased on the augmentation of business, and this, too, by the accession of low persons who might procrastinate the proceedings for immediate remedy. Accordingly, those who had been in consultation with the Commander-in-chief proceeded along with him to the house wherein the different committees usually met, and here eight persons, considered the most capable of applying a speedy and effectual remedy to the existing evil, were appointed, and the body so selected denominated "The Council appointed to manage the affairs of the people of the County of Wexford," of which Mr. Harvey was chosen president. This plan was to be communicated to the different camps, and such of the persons as might not be approved of by the people, were to be removed and replaced by others. This arrangement met with the heartfelt approbation of all the prisoners, especially as the Council immediately proceeded to forward the very plan they themselves had previously intended to put in operation. It was thought necessary also to confine the messenger Tunks in the gaol, as he was very talkative, particularly with respect to Lord Kingsborough's conduct in Dublin, to some parts of which, he said, he had been an eye-witness. His manner and stories, if left at liberty, might inflame the minds of the people, whom, at the time, it was so necessary not to provoke, but by every possible means to conciliate.

Captain M'Manus, being deputed by the prisoners

in the gaol, was conducted to consult with Lord Kingsborough, who accordingly wrote a letter to the Lord Lieutenant, in the name of all the prisoners (among whom there were thirteen officers, besides several yeomanry officers and principal gentlemen of the county), intimating their great danger, but that they had hitherto been well treated, and, in every respect, as prisoners of war; and, therefore, hoping that the prisoners taken by the army might meet the like good treatment with them, for that otherwise they feared reprisals might be made, and their destruction prove inevitable. This letter, along with any others that the officers chose to send to their friends, was to be forwarded to the next commanding officer of the army, and the messenger was to return with an answer with all convenient speed. Lieutenant Bourke of the North Cork militia was appointed to carry the remainder of this scheme into execution, and accordingly, on the evening of the 14th day of June, he set out from Wexford, accompanied by Mr. Carty to Enniscorthy, and part of the way by Captain Dixon, who, at Wexford, seemingly acquiesced in the business. Yet such was his duplicity, that he galloped on before the others to Enniscorthy, where, by mischievous representations and deceitful contrivances, he so wrought upon the people as to induce them not to suffer the letters to be forwarded; and such was his influence, that not only Lieutenant Bourke was in imminent danger, but even Mr. Carty ran great risk in opposing his villainous machinations. But after being baffled in their laudable intentions, they were, after great hazard, permitted to return in safety, the next day, to Wexford.

As it was now found that no negotiation could be entered into without the express concurrence of the people; with a view of making conciliation more attainable, it was deemed expedient to bind them, as much as possible, to abide the control of their commanders; and as numbers of them had never been sworn United Irishmen, the principles of brotherhood contained in their oath were considered by many of the principal prisoners excellent means of restraint. It was, therefore, thought a prudent measure to adopt it generally, and thereby impress on the minds of the people the orderly and social intercourse that should subsist between all those sworn in the same cause, and the moral obligation of obeying their commanders; and it was imagined the oath itself would curb many from acting licentiously. The measure was accordingly adopted, and oaths were also formed, with the same benevolent intentions, and equally approved of, to be taken by all officers and privates, and by all the people in the most solemn manner, and copies of them were printed and circulated through the county.*

Considering the defenceless state of the country, and the existing circumstances of the day, the situation of the newly appointed Council was far from enviable. It became their duty to endeavour to avert the tremendously impending fate, which threatened the country with inevitable destruction, and to exert themselves to the utmost of their power to concert such measures as would appear most likely to prove effectual. At such a critical period, their undertaking the arduous task must be considered as dictated by the purest sentiments of philanthropy; as what other possible motive could induce any one of them to place himself in such a perilous situation, at a time that it was well known to every man of rational observation, that the efforts of the insurgents would not be attended with final success? They had, indeed, undertaken a most

* See Appendix, No. IX.

difficult task, although they have not escaped the censure of partizans of all sides, who, while they venture to express prejudiced opinions, have no conception of the then existing general state of the county of Wexford. In short, the Council were placed in as embarrassing a predicament as can well be imagined, seemingly at the head of a refractory, outrageous populace, whom they anxiously sought to rescue from destruction, while these mostly counteracted their best and most benevolent intentions. However, when called on, at this dangerous juncture, as considered capable of applying a remedy to the enormous evil, all petty considerations vanished, and they undertook to meet the difficulty with firmness and resolution; and when such urgent necessity existed, any man should be deemed an enemy to the human race, who would refuse to contribute all his might toward the salvation of his countrymen. According to the nature of the existing evil, so should be that of the counteracting measures. From this consideration the Council did not think it right, for the preservation of the people, to declare, or even in the smallest degree to allow their defenceless state. On the contrary, it was considered necessary, along with the endeavour to encourage general union and harmony, to appear to be, as much as possible, able and determined to adopt the most firm and decisive measures, with the view of obtaining the more favourable conditions for the people.

The critical situation of the Council, as far as it regarded the management of the people themselves, may be well exemplified by the following occurrence: The town of Wexford, being in a state of the utmost tranquillity, was all at once thrown into the most violent confusion and alarm by a great cavalcade coming into it over the bridge, preceded by Captain Dixon and his wife, who rode through the streets, while he, with gesture and expression the most outrageous, exhibited a fire-screen, ornamented with various emblematical figures representing some heathen gods, and with orange bordering, fringe, and tassels, which he represented as the insignia of an Orange lodge, and the figures he tremendously announced as the representations of the tortures which the Catholics were to suffer from Orangemen; calling on the people to take signal vengeance, as he produced to them, he said, the discovery of the whole plot, found at Attramont, the seat of Colonel Le-Hunte.

It is impossible to describe the fury of the people on this occasion, roused to the most violent pitch in an instant, and only to be accounted for on the principle of their supposition, or rather persuasion of their intended extermination, which the sight of anything Orange awakened in the most sensitive manner, similarly to what has been before related concerning the Orange Warrant or Commission and pitched cap discovered in the barracks of Wexford. When Captain Dixon had, by this infernal and tumultuous conduct, assembled almost all the inhabitants of the town (whose frenzy, on seeing the Orange ornaments, and hearing his assertions most desperately vociferated, it is impossible to describe), he proceeded directly to the house wherein Colonel Le-Hunte lodged, dragged him out, and marched him down to the gaol, amidst a furious and enraged mob, by whom it was wonderful that his life was spared at the instant.

The principal inhabitants immediately assembled, and very narrowly escaped being all put to death; for as they met in the committee-house, opposite which the mob had collected, a common ruffian had the audacity to come in and fire a shot amidst them all, and actually arrested one of the Council, which so provoked a gentleman present, who happened to have his pstols about him, that he cocked one of them and was ready to shoot the fellow, but was fortunately prevented; for I verily believe, had the ruffian been shot, the destruction of every one in the house would have been the inevitable consequence. The populace at length permitted some gentlemen to address them from the windows, and it was a considerable time before they were able to persuade them that all their fury and madness had proceeded from the exhibition of a fire-screen, on which were represented some heathen gods, and which formed part of the ornaments of a room furnished three years before, with orange borderings and trimmings, then considered the most fashionable colour.

On the 16th the insurgents set out from their encampment at Limerick Hill to Carnew, where, meeting with no force to interrupt their career, they proceeded as far as Tinehaly. Here they had smart skirmishing with the army, from whom they took a great number of cattle, which they drove on before them, and encamped that night at Mountpleasant. On their quitting Limerick Hill in the morning, the prisoners who were confined in Gorey were thence brought to Vinegar Hill, from which they were conveyed under a strong escort, and lodged in the gaol of Wexford. The disposition of the inhabitants of this town, in not permitting any of the prisoners there confined to be brought out of the gaol, where they were considered in perfect safety, was well known, as many refusals had been made to demands of this kind from the country, when it was apprehended the intention was not to set them at liberty, but to put them to death. In the present instance, therefore, the strong escort, which consisted of Enniscorthy men, gave no intimation of any design until they got possession of the gaol, while delivering the prisoners they had brought with them; but then overpowering the guards, they forced away with them four men, who had been very obnoxious to the people, and with them quitted the town immediately, in order to afford no time to rescue the unfortunate victims from them. The four devoted men were taken to the camp on Vinegar Hill, where they were the next morning put to death, the Wexford gunsmen having returned home on the evening before; for during their stay in the camp only one man suffered, soon after their arrival, and they would by no means allow the repetition of such another deed, as has been before observed.

On the 16th several people from the neighbourhood of Gorey formed a small encampment on Ask Hill, between Gorey and Arklow, from which last-mentioned town, since the battle fought there, the troops issued with peculiar caution. On this day, however, a troop of yeomen cavalry had the fortitude to advance toward the little camp of the insurgents. This was, at the time, very inconsiderable as to numbers, having no more than about one hundred men equipped or fit for action, the rest having either dispersed or proceeded to Vinegar Hill; and even half the remaining number precipitately fled at the approach of the cavalry; while the other half, armed with pikes only, stripped to their shirts, to be unencumbered in exertion, and ran in full speed to meet the yeomen; but these avoided the encounter and expeditiously retreated to Arklow. The insurgents then retired from Ask Hill, and moved into the country between Oulart and Wexford, and were distributed through the different houses in that neighbourhood.

On Sunday, the 17th of June, a detachment of four hundred men, sent out from the camp on Vinegar Hill, halted in Ferns until the break of day, when, thus early on Monday, the 18th, they marched forward with an intention of storming Newtownbarry; but meeting at Camolin the insurgents who had now quitted their station at Mountpleasant, they altered their route and returned to Vinegar Hill, while the main body of the others proceeded to Carrigrew, whence they also moved on the next day to Vinegar Hill.

Early on the 19th the encampment on Lacken Hill was surprised by a military force that came out from Ross; and the insurgents, provided with little or no ammunition, and not apprehending an attack, were nearly surrounded before they were aware of their situation. They were also but few in number, for although vast multitudes appeared in their encampments in the day-time, yet they were almost deserted during the night, as all persons took the liberty of going and coming as they pleased. But notwithstanding this and the sudden emergency, they effected a good retreat to the Three Rocks without the loss of a man.

This was contrived in a masterly manner by the address of their commander, the Rev. Philip Roche, who, being roused from his bed by the general alarm, ordered the foot directly to retreat, and having collected immediately round him the few horsemen that could be got together caused them to seize on several banners and keep waving them at different distances, as it were in defiance, so as to intimidate the troops from making a sudden onset; and when he knew that his foot were at a safe distance, he and his few horsemen galloped after them, so that by this contrivance—that might do honour to an experienced General—he completely baffled the military, brought off his whole force entire, and was himself the last in quitting the hill.

General dispositions were now made to attack the insurgents on all sides, and the several divisions of the army had orders from Lieutenant-General Lake to proceed in different directions for that purpose. They were all to move toward the important post of Vinegar Hill, occupied by the permanent encampment of the insurgents, since the 28th of May, on the taking of Enniscorthy. Pursuant to the plan of a general assault, Lieutenant-General Dundas proceeded on the 18th of June from Baltinglass to Hacketstown whence he was to proceed, in conjunction with Major-General Loftus, who was to join him from Tullow, with the forces under his command, to move forward to attack the insurgents posted on Mountpleasant. These seemed willing enough to engage, but the troops were prevented from coming to action here, by other orders from Lieutenant-General Lake, who thought it more prudent to wait the assistance and co-operation of his whole force combined than to risk a partial engagement which might thwart or impede his general plan of operations.

Major-General Needham, who commanded in Arklow, moved on the 19th to Gorey, and on the next day encamped on Oulart Hill, whence he was to proceed to Enniscorthy. Greater devastation was perceivable from Arklow to Oulart than in any other part of the country. On the 19th Major-Generals Johnston and Eustace, after obliging the insurgents posted on Lacken Hill hastily to abandon their situation, proceeded to Bloomfield, where they encamped on the evening of the 20th, while Brigadier-General Moore reached his appointed station at Fook's-mill on the same evening, and Major-General Sir James Duff, who had marched from Newtownbarry, took his station with Major-General Loftus at Scarawalsh. In the course of the progressive march of these several divisions of the army, great devastation took place; numbers of houses were burned, and corn and various kinds of property were plundered and destroyed, mostly at the instance of the yeomen returning to their different neighbourhoods.

It is astonishing that landlords of all descriptions could so far forget their own interests as to join in the destruction of houses on their lands, however they might be induced to hunt out their lessees, and to sacrifice them, and so put an end at once to their leases. Yet many instances of this kind are related throughout the country.

According to the preconcerted and comprehensive plan of operations, all the Generals arrived, with their several divisions, at the different stations to which they had been ordered on the 20th, of which they severally apprised Lieutenant-General Lake, who was himself, with his staff and Lieutenant-General Dundas, posted at Solsborough. The insurgents of the northern part of the county of Wexford had now concentrated their force on their station of Vinegar Hill, and at a consultation of their chiefs it was proposed to make a general assault on the post of Solsborough during the night, but to this the people could not be prevailed upon to agree, who chose rather to depend upon their very scanty provision of powder, and wait for open daylight to engage.

It is very surprising that, considering the great courage and intrepidity displayed by them in so many engagements, the insurgents could never be brought to make a nocturnal attack, wherein they must have inevitably proved successful, as the confusion into which the regular troops would have been thrown by such a proceeding, would reduce them to a level with irregular bodies, whose superiority of numbers must necessarily have given them every advantage.

On the 19th, General Edward Roche, and such of the insurgents of his neighbourhood as were at Vinegar Hill, were sent home to collect the whole mass of the people for general defence. By the march of the army in all directions, towards Vinegar Hill and Wexford, a general flight of such of the inhabitants as could get off took place; and, as the greater part of the county was now occupied by the troops, the whole population was compressed into a very narrow space; and at this time there was not an encampment of insurgents in the northern part of the county, except at Vinegar Hill; while in the southern quarter the small camps of Carne and Rastoonstown were concentrated at the Three Rocks.

The alarm was now general throughout the whole country. All men were called to attend the camps; and Wexford became the universal rendezvous of the fugitives, who reported, with various circumstances of horror, the progress of the different armies approaching in every direction, marking their movements with terrible devastation. Ships of war were also seen off the coast, and several gun-boats blocked up the entrance of the harbour, which precluded the possibility of any vessel getting out; so that Wexford was now on the brink of destruction, and the inhabitants without the smallest hope of escape. It is dreadful to conceive, and impossible to describe, the horrors felt by all who had the misfortune of being in the town on this most critical occasion. The melancholy scenes of devastation perpetrated by the army in the country about Carrickbyrne exhibited a melancholy picture; and from the commanding situation of the camp at the Three Rocks, on the mountain of Forth, the general conflagration, which was as progressive as the march of the troops, was clearly perceivable. On the approach of the army, great numbers of countrymen, with their wives and children, and any little baggage they could hastily pack up, fled toward Wexford, as to an asylum or place of refuge; and the number of these was increased every instant by the arrival of new fugitives, who described, in melancholy strain of lamentation, how their houses were plundered and destroyed, and how they themselves had narrowly escaped with life from the fury of the soldiery, who, when thus let loose and encouraged to range over and ravage a country, become the greatest curse that can befall it!

I must, however, observe that General Moore did all in his power to prevent these atrocities, and got some plunderers immediately put to death; but his humane and benevolent intentions were not so successful from the representations and excitements of the refugees returning home. It is much to be regretted that he was not afterward left in command in the county of Wexford, as he was ordered to Wicklow, where his conciliatory conduct and humanity were conspicuous, and will ever be remembered with gratitude by the people, who flocked to his standard for protection. Did Ireland enjoy the blessings of such rulers, it would never have been involved in such a dreadful situation.

The Reverend Philip Roche, after having settled the encampment at the Three Rocks, came into Wexford and demanded all kind of supplies for his forces; and as the inhabitants (except the gunsmen, who attended for some time on Vinegar Hill) had never quit their homes or assisted at any battle, they were looked upon in a very invidious point of view by the rest of the people; who accordingly vowed the destruction of the town if all its armed men would not appear at the camp on the Three Rocks early the next morning, and join in general defence. The Reverend General Roche, on coming into Wexford, was greatly exhausted from his diligent and unremitting exertions in covering the retreat from Lacken Hill, and not having taken a morsel of food during the whole day, less drink than usual exhibited him in the course of the evening very much intoxicated. Of this man it is, however, necessary to say that, however apparently violent and boisterous, he was remarkable for humanity. He never suffered a man to be put to death on Lacken Hill; and the following, recorded by the Rev. Mr. Gordon, is a most powerful instance of his benevolence. After stating that although "Philip Roche was in appearance fierce and sanguinary, yet several persons now living owe their lives to his boisterous interference," he proceeds to state that "two Protestants in a respectable situation in life, brothers, of the name of Robinson, inhabitants of the parish of Killegny, being seized and carried to Vinegar Hill, some Roman Catholic tenants, anxious for their safety, galloped at full speed to Roche's quarters at Lacken, and begged his assistance. He immediately sent an express with orders to bring the two Robinsons to Lacken, pretending to have charges of a criminal nature against them, for which they should be tried.

The miscreants on Vinegar Hill, who were preparing to butcher these men, though they were advanced in years, and unimpeachable with any other crime than that of Protestantism, on receipt of Roche's orders, relinquished their fury, not doubting that death awaited them at Lacken. But Roche, whose object was to snatch these innocent men from the jaws of the bloodhounds, immediately on their arrival at his quarters gave them written protections, and sent them to their homes, where they were soon after in danger of being hanged by the king's troops, who were too ready to pronounce disloyal all such as had been spared by rebel parties."* But to put the question for ever at rest, whether the Insurrection of this period was a war of religion, it is only necessary to observe, that this was utterly impossible, notwithstanding the fanatic deeds of some base and barbarous individuals, since the militia regiments, who fought with such determined animosity against the insurgents, were mostly composed of Catho-

* See Gordon's History, page 140.

lics. Had there been any possible grounds to establish the rebellion a religious one, it could not have escaped its effect here, as enthusiastic bigots have, however, ventured to utter among them their envenomed sentiments. The late Earl of Clare, who cannot be suspected of being a friend to Catholics, could not have given his opinion in the Imperial Parliament that "religion was not the cause of the rebellion," had he not every opportunity from his official situation of being perfectly possessed of more information than could fall to the lot of the public at large.

While the principal inhabitants of Wexford were in consultation, to which they were now summoned, upon the best mode of self-preservation and defence, the order for all the armed men to appear in camp by break of day became imperative; and the outcry was so loud against the backwardness of the Wexford men that several set off immediately. The six small cannon on board the Guinea cutter were brought on shore, and their carriages being too small for land service, they were tied on cars and taken, thus mounted, by the sailors to the camp at the Three Rocks, where the scarcity of ammunition was so great that not a charge remained for any other cannon. On this evening it was that the Wexford gunsmen had returned home from Vinegar Hill; and about seventy men from the northern side of the Slaney came into town during the night, and were lodged in the barrack by Captain Dixon, who had been remarkably active in spreading alarm through the country north of the town, through which he had rode several miles to induce the people to come into Wexford, as it were for general defence. Early on the morning of the 20th the drum beat to arms, and all the armed inhabitants marched out to camp, leaving none in the town but the guards that had been on duty since the day before.

Some time after, I met Captain Dixon in the street, booted and spurred, and to all appearance thoroughly equipped and accoutred to go out to battle: his horse also stood waiting at his door fully caparisoned. On inquiry, however, I found he had no real intention of quitting the town. I then informed him, that I was sent by the Commander-in-chief to request his immediate attendance at the Three Rocks; but this he declined obeying, and was at the time in the act of sending whiskey to the countrymen who were in the barrack; and on my expressing surprise that these men should remain in the town, contrary to general orders, he replied, that his intention was to keep these men in Wexford to replace the guards, who, he said, had never been in any battle, and must now go out, as it was but fair they should share hardship in their turn, and allow some repose to those men who had been in every engagement.

On this intelligence I immediately got on horseback and rode up to the barracks, where I endeavoured by every means in my power to induce the men to leave the town; and they at length seemed willing to consent. But on the arrival of Captain Dixon with the reinforcement of whiskey, they so far altered their opinions and inclinations, that I was threatened for my interference. From the specimen of Captain Dixon's disposition displayed by his conduct to Colonel Le-Hunte, no confidence could be placed in him; and seeing his influence over these men, who now at his instance absolutely refused to quit the town, measures of precaution naturally suggested themselves.

After recommending to the guards to be vigilant on their station, which they were to quit upon no account, I galloped off to the camp at Three Rocks, to request a reinforcement of the Wexford men to be sent back with me, but which I had the greatest difficulty in obtaining, notwithstanding all my remonstrances, and was at last granted, rather to get rid of my importunity than from any other reason or motive; as no idea of a massacre was at all entertained. I was, however, allowed to take my choice of the Wexford corps, but on no condition should they be permitted to quit the camp, until the whole remaining force should have marched off, as it was apprehended that if they were seen going they might be followed by others. Fearing the men might be countermanded if I should leave them before the main body should have moved off, I waited for that event, which took up a considerable time; during which I also procured a letter from the Commander-in-chief, Mr. Harvey, directed to Captain Dixon, ordering him to come out to camp, as I felt earnest wishes to induce him to leave the town, for which purpose I left no means untried, but all without effect.

On consulting with some gentlemen in the Selsker corps, which was that I had chosen to return with me, as it contained more respectable persons and Protestants, since in different yeomanry corps, than any other in Wexford, I proposed that they should all take an oath not to drink spirits until further orders, as I perceived some drunken men among them, who could not be depended upon. This plan was generally approved of, and all were accordingly sworn, except four or five who were immediately sent off with the main body. This corps consisted of one hundred and twenty-five pike-men (no guns-man being allowed to return), and with these, having secured their sobriety, along with the guards that had remained in Wexford, I thought to be completely able to keep Captain Dixon and his drunken crew of about seventy in awe, should they show an inclination to be refractory.

When I judged all danger of a countermand was over, I set off at full speed toward Wexford, to announce this reinforcement to the guards there on duty. But about half way I met four Protestant gentlemen, with pikes, marching out to camp; and as I had seen them before in the morning, when they declared no intention of this kind, I expressed my surprise at their leaving the town, and insisted on their returning thither with me. But this at first they refused, alleging that, on my quitting the town, Captain Dixon had gone about the streets threatening death and destruction to all who would not immediately go out to camp, which had induced them to set off accordingly. However, I altered their resolution by calming their fears, and by showing the letter from the Commander-in-chief to Captain Dixon, suggesting that they would still be on the best duty by joining the men that were on their return. Upon which they promised to come back and give me their advice and assistance toward the protection of the prisoners; in whose defence I declared I would take up arms, which I had not yet done, and should I fall, I thought it would be a noble death to die on such an occasion. On this information I hastened with all speed to Wexford, from which I had been now absent about four hours, on account of all the delays I unavoidably experienced, the Three Rocks being three miles distant from the town. But how great was my surprise and astonishment on finding the latter taken possession of by a vast multitude of people, consisting of several thousands, many of whom were well armed, and in such force as to banish all hope that the small number of Wexford men remaining in, and returning to the town, could in case of need give them any effectual resistance.

General Edward Roche had, as has been before mentioned, returned home, at a very late hour on the 19th, from the camp on Vinegar Hill, to collect and lead thither all the men in his neighbourhood. The number of these was now immensely increased by the vast crowds of fugitives driven, by the approach of the army, from about Gorey into the part of the country called Shilmalier.

Through this quarter Captain Dixon had made an excursion on the same day, diffusing dread and alarm, and calling on the people to assemble for general defence at Wexford; and unfortunately he was so successful in his efforts, that on the morning of the 20th, when the people were assembled, and that General Edward Roche thought to lead them towards Enniscorthy, they peremptorily refused to proceed, representing Wexford, from the suggestions of Captain Dixon, as more vulnerable; wherefore the General himself thought it more advisable to continue with this body of the people, now consisting chiefly of the fugitives from the northern parts of the county. These were continually relating their misfortunes, the cruelties they suffered, and the hardships they endured, to those with whom they took refuge; which roused and irritated the populace to such a pitch of fury as admits not of description, and of which none but an eye-witness can have an adequate idea.

All entreaties or remonstrances to soothe or calm the exasperated multitude were in vain. However, continuing still on horseback, I endeavoured to address, explain, excuse, and expostulate, and in the course of these attempts many pikes were raised against me, and several guns and pistols cocked and pointed at me, and vengeance vowed against me as an *Orangeman;* for they vociferated that I had distinguished myself by no other feat, but activity in protecting their enemies the *Orangemen;* that I had never attended their camps, or I would be a judge of their miseries by the view of general desolation. One man would roar out, that I had not been flogged as he had been; another pathetically related, that his house had been burned, and he had been driven to beggary with his whole family, and he would have the death of the person that injured him; a third lamented the death of his father, another that of his brother, others of their children; and the appeal was made to me to decide on all their various sufferings and misfortunes; while they perseveringly declared, they only wanted to be avenged of those who had actually done them wrong; and I was asked, if similarly circumstanced, would I not take revenge for such injuries as theirs? All this I endeavoured to answer, and strove to appease the wrath of the popular frenzy, by alleging that the laws of God were indefeasible, and that they dictated that good should be returned for evil. This had some little effect for the instant; but it was, indeed, but momentary. I, however, continued still unwearied in my exertions, particularly endeavouring to preserve my dear and beloved friend, Mr. Turner, whose death, and that of a Mr. Gainsfort, the populace declared indispensable to their satisfaction, as they had led out the army against them on Whit Sunday, and had burnt their houses. Although I knew that my friend had burned a house (of which he most sincerely and heartily repented), yet I appealed to the multitude, if any one could prove the fact alleged against him, and no one appearing to come forward for that purpose, I seized on the glimpse of hope I now entertained of his safety, thinking that his life might be preserved by demanding a trial, on which, if no proof of criminality could be adduced, it was natural to conclude that his safety must be certain. I then made the experiment; but was answered by this universal cry—"What trial did we or our friends and relations obtain when some were hanged or shot, and others whipped or otherwise tortured; our houses and properties burnt and destroyed, and ourselves hunted like mad dogs?" But I rejoined with some effect—"Do you mean to compare yourselves to the perpetrators of such deeds, or would you disgrace your conduct by such barbarous acts?"

This appeal to their principles produced the consequence, providentially, as I fondly hoped, of their consenting to a trial, but on the express condition that I should retire, and be present on no account. At this critical moment I perceived a person near me whom I had induced to return from the Three Rocks, and who, true to his promise of every assistance in his power, after a variety of difficulty had got close by me, together with some others of the like benevolent dispositions, to whom I stooped down from on horseback to listen to the arguments they humanely suggested; and I must declare that I derived great courage from their presence and advice to persist in my entreaties, in the course of which I find, on cool reflection, that I underwent great danger, of which I was by no means so sensible at the time, until afterwards informed by many, who were kind enough to hold me in regard, while they prevented different persons from shooting me. I entreated the particular person before mentioned to procure men whose humanity could not be doubted to try the prisoners; and when he should have succeeded, to give me notice, as I would endeavour in the meantime to delay the people, who were insisting that I should retire, "as," they declared, "I would go to the devil to save Turner." I did promise to retire as soon as I could have proper persons appointed to sit in trial over the prisoners, when my humane friend beckoned to me, signifying that he was ready. I then went into the committee house, where, although Captain Dixon and Morgan Byrne, whose sanguinary disposition I was well aware of, insisted that they should be on the trial, I could not oppose their appointment; but, however, four out of seven, which was the number chosen, humanely offered themselves, having previously promised me that they would not consent to put any one to death.

I made use of another stratagem by proposing an oath—that in their proceedings they would not be guided by public prejudice, but by justice and the evidence before them. This was with a view, if possible, to secure the assistance and co-operation even of the most sanguinary, and the seven were accordingly sworn to that effect. By this contrivance, and the solemn assurance of the four persons that they would not consent to the condemnation of any one, I fondly hoped that I had secured the life of my friend from danger; and being fully confident of the success of my plan, I left its subsequent management to a person on whose sincerity I could rely, and to whose worth I am sorry at not having the liberty to do justice by naming him; and having made sure of such a friend to humanity, I thought it most prudent to retire, in order to please the people, the inclinations of many of whom I had now thwarted for hours; and I had good reason to suppose they would then be more inclined to listen to a new man.

The seven persons appointed to sit on the trial proceeded from the committee house to the gaol, where they went into a small bed-chamber, inside the gaoler's kitchen, in which Captain Dixon had left five prisoners whom he had doomed as the first victims for condemnation; but he here met with an opposition of which he was not until that moment at all aware. The members of this kind of popular tribunal divided; three were for death; but the other four, true to their promise, and unwarped in their humane inclinations, firmly declared that they considered themselves merely

appointed to prevent massacre and to save the lives of
the prisoners, and would not attend or listen to any
representation from Dixon or his fellows. This produced a very violent altercation, and great danger was
to be apprehended by the friends of humanity, as Peter
Byrne actually rushed into the room, and threatened
them with instant destruction if they did not agree to
the death of the prisoners.

Some others of Dixon's bloodthirsty associates had
got into the gaol, and were selecting such of the
prisoners as they pleased to doom fit objects of destruction; but although Dixon's own designs cannot be
doubted of ravening for blood, and that he was willing
and eager to attempt anything to gain his object, yet,
as the four men resolutely persevered in refusing to
agree to the death of any man at such a crazy and
frenzied moment, he was going to retire from a place
where his sanguinary views and cruel sentiments were
opposed and overruled, and it is more than probable
that the sanguinary, retarded for hours in the onset,
would have cooled in their fury, and have recovered
sentiments of humanity sufficient to prevent them from
putting anyone to death, were it not for two informers,
Charles Jackson, a carver and gilder,* and ——
O'Connor, an organist, both of whom had not long
resided in Wexford, and who were cast off from the
society of the other prisoners then in the gaol. These,
as ill fate would have it, threw themselves on their
knees to Captain Dixon, acknowledged that they were
Orangemen, and ready to give every information, provided their lives might be spared. Dixon, before in
despair at finding his sanguinary hopes baffled and
blasted, readily agreed to their proposal, as it afforded
a new prospect of perpetrating his infernal designs.

* Author of Wexford Cruelties.

He instantly addressed the people assembled before the gaol, stating that two Orangemen had become informers, and that proceeding to trial was therefore unnecessary, as the evidence of these men must be conclusive. It may easily be conceived that on this communication, horribly vociferated by Dixon, and re-echoed by his wife, the populace became ungovernable! The people instantly approved of his plan, and demanded that all Orangemen should be sent out to them; but his first care was to turn the men who opposed his bloody schemes out of the gaol, of which he and his savage associates took complete possession.

Kenneth Mathewson, as one of the persons denounced by the informers, was then turned out, and immediately shot at the gaol door. John Atkins, a painter and glazier, was another against whom they gave information; and he being one of those whom Dixon had originally brought down for trial, as destined victims for immolation, he was still in the gaoler's kitchen, when, hearing himself called for by name, he ran into the inner room and hid under the bed, where he lay concealed until all danger was over.

While these unforeseen but melancholy events were passing, I had retired in full assurance that the people would be appeased; and, notwithstanding that they had peremptorily forbidden my being present at any trial, yet I was in hopes, as appearing no longer on horseback, that I might get into the gaol unobserved, and endeavour to assist those who had undertaken the humane and philanthropic task of protection. But great was my amazement, indeed, at finding the most violent threats uttered against me as I approached the multitude. I, therefore, thought it most prudent to suffer myself to be led by two young women, who hurried me into a house, the door of which happened to be open; and while they were explaining to me the cause of this sudden and unexpected tumult, a shot was fired, and it was instantly rumoured through the crowd that Colonel Le-Hunte was killed; upon which I could not help exclaiming that they had put an innocent man to death! I then declared my determination to go out and endeavour to stop such a scene of butchery. On this a man who knew me seized upon me, and positively insisted I should not leave the house, as, just before I had come up, he had heard the people vow vengeance against me in so vehement a manner that he was certain I must inevitably perish should I attempt to interfere. On finding that it was not possible for me to do any good, the share of courage I had hitherto felt quite forsook me at this juncture. I burst into tears, and sunk into a state of insensibility. When the mob had in some degree dispersed, I was supported homewards by this good-natured man, but was obliged from faintness to stop twice on the way before I reached my lodgings.

It is confidently asked by many why the clergy and principal inhabitants did not interfere to prevent massacre. There were but few of the inhabitants at all in the town, and I saw most part of the few that had remained in Wexford on that day, together with some clergymen, do all in their power to restrain the fury of the people, and prevent the spilling of blood; but I do believe that, under existing circumstances, it was impossible to control the multitude, inflamed as they were by the representations of Dixon and his associates; and in such imminently critical cases, it is not every one that has nerves strong enough to encounter the impending danger. For my own part, although I was courageous enough in the beginning of the day, yet I found myself afterwards in such a state as to be incapable of any exertion. I therefore doubt much whether any person asking such questions would have fortitude or charity enough to step forward on such an occasion and attempt to save any one's life, so much as by declaring a truth favourable to his preservation—a conduct that ought to flow even from spontaneous generosity or gratitude for material obligation; but such slight interference as this was extracted by no motive from humanity, but in some instances refused or perverted by the like hypocritical and mock philanthropists, with those who put these presumptuous interrogatories. But to judge fairly of the conduct of another, it is necessary to be placed in a similar situation.

After the death of Mathewson, Captain Dixon and his wife proposed that those who were to be put to death should be brought down to the bridge, whither the mob retired. Eighteen intended for execution were first conducted from the gaol, under a strong guard, headed by Dixon, flanked by the two *Orange* informers, whom he wished to exhibit as the grand support of his conduct. These informers were brought into a public billiard-room on the Custom-house Quay (and not at all to the bridge, to which it is adjacent), where they underwent an examination, at which Dixon presided. It is probable that these informers did not give information against every one that was put to death on this occasion. But it is a certain truth, and an evident fact, that the information of these men was esteemed of such consequence, even by such a sanguinary tribunal, that their services saved their lives. The fate of the prisoners was quickly decided, on their being conducted to the bridge, as the proceedings concerning them were summary indeed. It was asked, did any one know any good action of the intended victim, sufficient to save his life; and if no answer was made, the assertion of an individual of some deed against the people, was conclusive evidence of guilt, and immediately death was the consequence, on his primary denunciation by

Captain Dixon. Some, however, escaped with their lives, on the interference of some person stepping forward in their favour. A few were shot, but the greater number suffered by being piked, and some of those with aggravated circumstances of barbarity. All the bodies were thrown over the bridge, but neither stripped nor their pockets rifled, which I should scarcely have believed, but that I have been positively assured that watches and money were found upon them when afterward discovered.

Captain Dixon sent from time to time for different persons to the several places of confinement, and at intervals came out to announce further discoveries from the informers. This admirably suited his hellish purpose of putting all the prisoners to death; which he might unfortunately have effected, but that Providence was at length pleased to interpose, while the minds of the populace seemed wrought up to the most desperate pitch of cruelty! The Rev. Mr. Corrin, who had been absent from the town the whole of the day on parochial duty, had but just returned, when he was sent for by Mr. Kellett, then on his defence at the bridge. Thither the reverend gentleman instantly repaired, and having thrown himself on his knees, entreated they might join him in prayer; when he supplicated the Almighty to show the same mercy to the people as they would show to their prisoners; and with that he addressed them in such feeling, pathetic and moving language, that he thereby saved the lives of several who had been just ordered to the bridge from the market-house by Dixon. While the Rev. Mr. Corrin was on the fatal spot, Mr. Esmonde Kyan, who had been wounded in the shoulder at the battle of Arklow, lay in the most excruciating torture in a house at Ferrybank, on the country-side of the wooden-bridge; but on hearing what was going forward, he instantly got out of bed, ran to the fatal spot, and by his animated conduct and address rescued Mr. Newton King and Captain Milward of the Wexford militia, with some others, from the fury of the populace. General Edward Roche, also by his humane interference, snatched Mr. James Goodall and others from the jaws of death; while different other persons of inferior note, and some even of the lower class, interposed so as to save one or other of their neighbours; and at length it pleased God that this horrid butchery ceased!

The Catholic clergymen and all the principal inhabitants who remained in the town that day, exhausted every means in their power in endeavours to appease the rage of the populace, of whom it is necessary to observe, they could have little or no personal knowledge, as the outrageous multitude had collected from the northern parts of the county, and not at all composed of Wexford men, over whom they might be supposed to have some local influence. But such as have not been eye-witnesses, and who have not, even in that case, been sometimes among and conversant with the people, can have but a very inadequate idea of the danger of interference against the uncontrollable fury of a rabble exasperated to the highest pitch by the incidents I have endeavoured to describe. Dreadful and shocking events are most subject to misrepresentations, as individuals will imagine excesses according to their several feelings, and although it is confidently asserted, that ninety-seven were put to death on the bridge, I have good reason to believe that thirty-five was the number that suffered.

Among the various occupations assumed by different persons in the course of this melancholy catastrophe, one man, in a most audible voice, counted the victims one by one, as they were put to death; and I have further reason to believe, that thirty-five was the exact number of sufferers on the bridge, and one at the gaol door, amounting in all that day in Wexford to thirty-six, as on most particular inquiry, even with the help of the lists published, as well as from personal knowledge, I am enabled to know, that several who are stated to have been sacrificed on the bridge that day, suffered not then, nor there, nor at all in Wexford, so that I hope humanity will induce a future retractation of the lists alluded to, not only as the assertors have been evidently imposed upon, but as also their publication must help to keep up those animosities which they profess they do not wish to encourage. But if writers will persist in publishing those lists, why not, for the sake of general and true information, publish the number of the killed and wounded, by whatever means, on both sides, since it must stamp the character of a partisan to detail but one side of the question ?

On that ever-to-be-lamented day there are many who ran great risk of personal safety in becoming advocates for the unfortunate. I wish I could learn of as many who exhibited equal proof of sincerity in favour of the hapless and ill-fated people! Were this the case, I verily believe I should not have to relate the dreadful desolation in the county of Wexford. In critical times, such as those, certainly different circumstances will excite different sensations; but with respect to the business before us, the saying of a most liberal Protestant gentleman must be regarded as possessing peculiar force in repressing misrepresentation. He says, "I have heard of hundreds of Catholics in the county of Wexford who have, at the risk of their lives, saved Protestants; but I have not heard of a single Protestant who encountered any danger to save the life of a Catholic."

The black flag that appeared in Wexford on this day is, among other things, talked of with various chimerical conjectures, and its notoriety as denouncing massacre has been confidently recorded, notwithstanding that it is an absolute fact, that this identical black flag was, throughout the whole Insurrection, borne by a particular corps, and the carrying of banners of that colour was by no means a singular circumstance during that period, as flags of that and every other hue, except orange, were waved by the insurgents, and from their different dyes, ingenious conjectures, however groundless, for the maintenance of prejudice, may be made as to the several dispositions of the bodies who moved under them, as little founded in fact or intention, as was the original intention of the black ensign in question.

Although General Edward Roche had the nominal command of the great body of men that came into Wexford on this day, yet his authority appears to have been very limited, when he was not able to lead them to the intended destination; but it became still less on his arrival in that town, where Dixon, who was his brother-in-law, had gained such an ascendency, although possessed of not even any nominal command; being but a general blusterer, affecting great consequence, galloping from camp to camp, and seeking every opportunity of doing mischief, generally while the battles were going on, and at one of which he never appeared but in the background. His denomination of Captain was owing to his being master of a sloop which traded to and from Wexford. This man's conduct was in complete contradiction to the sentiments of Roche, who was, on his subsequent surrender in December, 1799, tried by a court-martial in Wexford, on a charge of "aiding and abetting the murders on the bridge, on the 20th of June, 1798." But his humane exertions appeared so meritorious before that tribunal, that he was acquitted of this charge, which could not possibly be, as he possessed command, had it not been perfectly proved that such command was merely nominal, as his orders and endeavours were counteracted by persons having no command whatever, but what arose from inflammatory addresses to the populace, urging them to take exemplary vengeance of their enemies, in which they were unfortunately but too successful.

In the first house I had been obliged to stop at on the way to my lodgings, I met a gentleman to whom I was endeavouring to give some account of what had occurred, while Dixon was passing by, with the two *Orange* informers, one on each side of him. The gentleman ran out and began to plead for mercy, expressing at the same time a hope that Dixon would come into the house and consult with me, before he would put his designs into execution. But on this Dixon exclaimed, "Is it to consult Mr. Hay, who has already deserved death for the part he has taken in stopping us so long from taking revenge of our enemies ? Here are two *Orangemen*, who have become informers, and there are the men I am going to have put to death (pointing to the prisoners that were following him under a strong military guard), and when I have done with these, I shall then treat Mr. Hay in the same manner." When Dixon had passed on, the gentleman returned and offered to conduct me home, but I was again obliged to stop on the way in a house where the wives and daughters of some officers, affrighted by the general alarm, ran to me in tears, while all I could do was to join in their lamentations. I certainly should not have had sufficient power to walk any farther, had I not taken a glass of wine they kindly offered me. However, I at length arrived at the house where I had been since the Insurrection, and there remained in a state of stupid insensibility, until I was roused by several ladies, who pressed me to come to dinner, which was unusually late that day; and although I was able to carve for the ladies, I could not taste a morsel myself.

Shortly after, a messenger came for me from Lord Kingsborough and his officers, requesting my immediate attendance. I instantly complied, although I had little hopes of being able to afford them any relief, yet I would not refuse to try my best endeavours. On getting into the street, I met a crowd of people proceeding to a particular house, with intention, as I soon discovered, of bringing out Mr. Joseph Gray, Lieutenant of the Wexford cavalry, who had transported his servant. I had the presence of mind to say that Mr. Gray was out fighting for them, and that they seemed to me not to be able to distinguish their friends from their enemies; which fortunately prevented them from proceeding any farther; for I knew he was in the house, and had too much reason to fear, that upon their forcing into it, his death and many more must have been the inevitable consequence. This device proving successful, gave me more courage to go on to Lord Kingsborough's lodgings, where I was refused admittance. However, I spoke to him and his officers, as they appeared at the windows, and declared that as long as I was alive myself, they might depend upon every exertion of mine in their behalf.

Shortly after I fortunately met General Edward Roche, whose humane exertions to prevent them were as conspicuous as his lamentations were sincere for the dreadful scenes then exhibiting. I conjured him to hasten down to the bridge, and there to represent the urgent necessity of the people's attendance at Vinegar Hill, suggesting that he could, with more propriety than any other, interpose his authority with a prospect of success, as he was himself called on to attend by all the chiefs in the camp; and as an express was sent from Vinegar Hill to Wexford demanding reinforcements, and expressing surprise that Edward Roche had not come, with the force of his neighbourhood, which he had been sent home to collect and bring along with him. These considerations inspired the General with new vigour to endeavour to lead these men out of the town, which he at length effected, and the people marched off under his command out of Wexford.

When the town was thus cleared of its dreadful visitors, about eight o'clock in the evening I obtained admission to Lord Kingsborough and his officers. We jointly took a retrospective view of the horribly distracted state of the country, as well as of its impending danger; and, after a variety of consultation between us, it was agreed that the only mode of preserving Wexford and all its inhabitants from destruction was, that early on the next morning I should accompany Lord Kingsborough to the army, and by an explanation of existing circumstances it was hoped that the town might be spared from the dreadful fate which seemed to await it every instant.

Wexford was, indeed, at this period in a most perilous situation. Intelligence had arrived there of the approach of three different armies—one of which was advanced as far as Oulart, another had arrived at Enniscorthy, and the progressive march of the third was conspicuous the evening before from the Three Rocks, by the insurgents stationed there, who on the morning of this day proceeded to meet it. The gunboats on the coast also made a formidable appearance, as announced by the men who had been stationed at the fort of Roslare, but who now abandoned that post and fled into Wexford, bringing the alarming news that several ships of war and other armed vessels were approaching the harbour.

By the time we had settled all matters relative to our departure on this expedition next morning, it was advanced in the night, and the Wexford men were flocking home from the battle of Fooks's-mill. I had then proposed to go and consult the principal inhabitants, whose co-operation and assistance were so necessary in such an undertaking, but which I made not the least doubt of obtaining, and took my leave of his Lordship and the other officers, promising to return to them early on the next morning. It was a considerable time before I could collect a sufficient number of the principal inhabitants to communicate my intentions to them; and even when it was at length effected, their confusion was such that it was agreed to postpone their business until early in the following morning, then to meet at Captain Keugh's house, where the subject would be taken into consideration by a general assembly, which could not be so well formed at that time of the night.

About three o'clock in the afternoon of the 20th, the army, under the command of General Moore, began to march from its encampment at Long-graigue, the seat of the Rev. Mr. Sutton, towards Taghmon, and had proceeded but half-a-mile when the insurgent force from the Three Rocks, led on by their General, the Rev. Philip Roche, appeared in view at a place called Fooks's-mill. Each party immediately commenced the attack, which lasted with various success and great obstinacy on both sides for four hours, when the insurgents, having expended the whole of their ammunition at the very moment that it is said the troops were on the point of giving way, thought proper to retire, and made a good retreat to their original station on the Three Rocks. In this engagement, from the nature of the ground, the great body of the pike-men could not be brought into action, so that there were not more of the insurgents engaged than about an equal number with that of the army against them, whose loss, too, is said to be considerably greater than theirs; but although General Moore's despatches concerning the engagement have been published, yet the list of the killed and wounded mentioned to have been sent with the General's letter has been suppressed, so that I have not been able to obtain the official account of this particular.

The insurgents, as usual, did not attempt to retreat until they had fired their last shot, when two regiments under Lord Dalhousie were perceived coming up to reinforce General Moore. The insurgents in the retreat brought away with them five out of the six small cannon which they brought out with them; all of which had been fastened on common cars with ropes, and the remaining one they lost, because the car upon which it was mounted, having been broken by falling into a ditch, it was left there. The Wexford men who were in this engagement attended their companions to the Three Rocks, and then proceeded to the town, where they arrived late at night.

General Johnston had smart skirmishing with the outposts of the insurgents from Enniscorthy on the 20th, on his arrival at Bloomfield, within a mile of Enniscorthy. Early on the morning of the 21st, a general assault was made on the insurgent force encamped on Vinegar Hill by General Lake, while the town of Enniscorthy was attacked by General Johnston, which he carried after an obstinate resistance for two hours, with great slaughter of the insurgents, whose defence of the place was most wonderful, considering that they had but a few pounds of powder to distribute to their whole force on the preceding evening; so that it is astonishing how they could venture with such a scanty provision of ammunition to give any opposition to an army of great force, perfectly equipped and appointed, and abundantly provided with every necessary. Even on Vinegar Hill there were but two charges for cannon ; one of which was fired against the army approaching from Solsborough, and the other dismounted cannon posted at the Duffrey-gate at Enniscorthy; and, although a great number of cannon and bombs were fired from the royal artillery towards Vinegar Hill, only one man was wounded and none killed by the shot from the ordnance.

The insurgents, notwithstanding their defenceless situation, displayed vast courage and intrepidity before they abandoned the hill, which they were at length obliged to do, and great numbers of them fell on this occasion. All suspected persons were put to death in Enniscorthy, and several houses were set on fire; among the rest that which had been used by the insurgents as an hospital, which, together with all the wounded men in it, were totally consumed. A free passage was left for the insurgents to retreat to Wexford, as the division of the army under General Needham, from some unaccountable reason, had not come up in time to join the battle; and, from the route this division took, it is surprising that it did not fall in with the insurgent force under General Edward Roche, who was also too late for the engagement, as he only arrived just at the commencement of the retreat of the insurgents, which, however, he recovered with his men from Darby-gap, and restrained the career of the cavalry that were in full pursuit of the insurgents dislodged from Vinegar Hill.

Lord Kingsborough was so anxious to carry the plan we had agreed on for the salvation of the town into execution, that he sent for me before three o'clock in the morning on the 21st, when I had scarcely time to have taken any rest. I instantly got up and went to him, when I found him arrayed in full uniform and completely equipped to set out at that moment, which he wanted me to do also; but I represented to him the danger of going through the country in such apparel as he then was, and that, at all events, our safety could not be secured without the concurrence of the people with our plan, which, however, I thought, would be easily obtained, as I related to him the conversation I held with the principal inhabitants on the night preceding; and that I expected to meet them again on the subject at an early hour that morning. He and his officers then entreated me to hasten the meeting, and to have the drum beat to arms for the people to assemble, that their consent might be obtained, as there was no time to be lost in carrying into effect the only means of saving the town from total destruction; for we distinctly heard the report of the cannon from Enniscorthy, where the battle had just then commenced. I immediately went and rapped up the principal inhabitants nearest to me, whom I commissioned to call up their neighbours; and thus in a short time was the whole town roused from slumber.

A meeting consequently took place at the house of Captain Keugh, where it was thought advisable that Doctor Jacob should accompany Lord Kingsborough and me. But on further contemplation, instead of one, it was judged necessary to send out three deputations from the town to the three different armies approaching, lest one might not be able to effect its purpose; and it was also thought most prudent, that Lord Kingsborough should not leave the town, but that it should be instantly surrendered to him as military commander; and Doctor Jacob, who was present, offered to reassume the office of Mayor; so that this was putting all kinds of civil and military authority into the same hands in which they were before the Insurrection. And thus did the inhabitants of Wexford do everything consistent with duty by taking the earliest opportunity of returning to their allegiance which, by the fundamental principles of the Constitution, could never be arraigned, as they were not only abandoned, but even surrendered to the insurgents by those who were bound, by every tie of duty and interest, to protect them, but who, instead of acting as they ought, sent a deputation of surrender, and shamefully fled, leaving even their own wives and families, together with the other inhabitants, under the uncontrollable sway of the conquerors, whom they thus constituted regular enemies.

Captain M'Manus, of the Antrim militia, and myself were appointed to proceed to the army at Oulart, with the proposal of the inhabitants of Wexford and Lord Kingsborough's dispatches. Captain O'Hea, of the North Cork militia, and Mr. Thomas Cloney, were deputed on the like mission to Enniscorthy; and Captain Bourke, of the North Cork militia, and Mr. Robert Carty were sent to the army of Taghmon. The meeting was then adjourned to the Custom-house Quay to propose these arrangements to the people, assembled there on parade for the purpose. They approved of every step that had been taken with three cheers; and the business was concluded by a most feeling address from Doctor Jacob, in tears, to the people, whose good opinion on all occasions he was so happy as to possess, by being very attentive in his duty as physician and surgeon to the wounded. A deputation then went to Lord Kingsborough's lodgings to inform him of the determination of the people; and his lordship, upon accepting of the military command of the town, applied to Captain Keugh for his sword. But he, taking a wrong impression of the solemnity of the previous proceedings, and imagining himself entitled to march out at the head of the people to meet the army approaching the town, proposed surrendering it and the sword together to the officer principal in command of the army approaching the town. But not finding one supporter of this proposed scheme, he reluctantly surrendered to Lord Kingsborough his sword and other arms, but with the greatest formality.

Lord Kingsborough, thus invested with the military authority in Wexford, set about writing dispatches to the several officers commanding the different armies approaching the town, informing them, "That the town of Wexford had surrendered to him, and in consequence of the behaviour of those in the town during the rebellion, they should all be protected in person and property, murderers excepted, and those who had instigated others to commit murder, hoping these terms might be ratified, as he had pledged his honour in the most solemn manner to have these terms fulfilled on the town being surrendered to him, the Wexford men not being concerned in the massacre which was perpetrated by country people in their absence."*

With these dispatches were enclosed, as a further document, the following proposals from the people of Wexford: "That Captain M'Manus shall proceed from Wexford towards Oulart, accompanied by Mr. Edward Hay, appointed by the inhabitants of all religious persuasions to inform the officer commanding the king's troops, that they are ready to deliver up the town of Wexford without opposition, to lay down their arms and return to their allegiance, provided that their persons and properties are guaranteed by the commanding officer; and that they will use every influence in their power to induce the people of the country at large to return to their allegiance; and these terms it is hoped Captain M'Manus will be able to procure.

"Signed by order of the inhabitants of Wexford,

"MATTHEW KEUGH.

"Wexford, June 21, 1798."

* See Appendix, Captain Bourke and Lord Kingston's Letters.

All matters being thus arranged, I went down to the gaol for Captain M'Manus, as well as to announce the news to all the prisoners. As I had on a former occasion consulted them on the letter written in their name and behalf, and as they were universally pleased with my sentiments, they all crowded about me, many of them even in their shirts, and when I communicated to them the purport of the mission of Captain M'Manus and myself, the joy they manifested can only be conceived by such as have been in a similar situation. They expressed sentiments of the utmost kindness to me in particular and hearty success to our undertaking. Captain M'Manus then accompanied me to Lord Kingsborough, who waited his arrival to consult with him and the principal inhabitants together; and when all things were adjusted between them, and that his lordship had written his dispatches, enclosing the proposal of the townsmen, the Captain and I set out, bearing these credentials, and proceeded as far as Castle-bridge, where, finding that the troops which had been stationed at Oulart had moved toward Enniscorthy, we thought it best to direct our course thither.

As yet we had met with none but women and children, who were bewailing their wretched condition in the most piteous strains. Shortly afterwards, however, we met Captain Dixon, who had been present at the approval of our deputation by the people of Wexford in the morning; but the plan not corresponding with his sentiments, he had set out with intention to gain over a party in the country to waylay and put us to death. But as all the men had gone to camp, he could not find accomplices to assist him in this undertaking. Soon after we met Morgan Byrne, a man of the same stamp, who was Dixon's associate the day before, and whose cowardice and cruelty were equally

conspicuous,* he accosted us in the most abrupt and
savage manner, vowing death and destruction against
numbers, amongst whom he was pleased to include
myself and my companion, whom he called a spy.
Upon my declaring that I was going to take observation of the position of the army, he insisted upon
accompanying us; and as he had a musket and bayonet,
two cases of pistols—one in holsters and the other
flung on his belts—while we had no arms whatever, I
thought it most prudent to humour him; which I did
for two miles that he rode with us, when we had the
good fortune to shake him off; and I then informed
Captain M'Manus of the danger we had escaped by
getting off such a ruffian. We then came to a resolution to be the first to address every one we met, to
show our confidence, and by this precaution we passed
unmolested by great numbers who were flying from
Vinegar Hill, and the more dangerous, as they were
stragglers from the main body of the insurgents that
had taken another road; and using many expedients
to elude all inquiry on our business, but particularly calling out to the fugitives to collect at the
Three Rocks (the place appointed for the insurgents
to wait until the conclusion of the negotiation then on
foot), we at last arrived in sight of the army at Darby-
gap, where Captain M'Manus threw off a great-coat
which I had the precaution to make him wear over his

* The conduct of this man exemplifies the usual infamy attendant
on *informers;* as immediately previous to the Insurrection he had
waited on Captain (now Major) Kavanagh, with a plentiful offer of
information from his father and himself, when the sudden Insurrection prevented its accomplishment. *He* and some of his *relatives*
were distinguished by their barbarous dispositions, as true co-
operators of Captain Dixon, whose conduct is a manifest proof how
unlike you sometimes find even *brothers*, as they were distinguished
by their tenderness and humanity, whereas he was a sanguinary
monster.

regimentals. We then hoisted a white handkerchief as our flag; and could descry the country all along between that and Enniscorthy in a most dreadful situation; houses on fire, dead men and women strewed along the road and in the fields; while the soldiers were hunting for such as might be concealed in the ditches, and bringing down every person they met. In fine, it was altogether a dreadful picture, exhibiting all the horrors of war!

A small party of the Antrim militia happened to be among the first of the soldiery that we met, and these hailed their officer with the most heartfelt demonstrations of joy, and conducted us safely to Drumgold, where we met Major-General Sir James Duff, who led us into Enniscorthy to General Lake, the Commander-in-chief, to whom we delivered our dispatches. The remains of the town exhibited a dreadful aspect, as the greater part of the houses, which had escaped until the arrival of the army, were still on fire; and the house which had been used as an hospital by the insurgents, and which was set on fire with all the patients in it, continued burning until next morning, when I saw a part of a corpse still hissing in the embers.

The news of our arrival having quickly spread through the town, numbers of officers, yeomen, and gentlemen of my acquaintance crowded around me; some anxious to hear of their friends, while others expressed how disappointed they would be if hindered to demolish Wexford with all the concomitant horrors and atrocities usual on such dreadful and shocking occasions! Some had the savage indecency even to mention some young ladies by name, who, they intended, should experience the effects of their brutal passions before they would put them to death; but these intentions they feared would be frustrated-by the account I gave them of the proposal and dispatches. Others wished the extermination of all Catholics! some inquired for their friends and relations, and amidst these horrors were not destitute of humanity. While I was thus conversing with many of various descriptions, Major-General Sir James Duff kindly came to me and entreated that I would go into the house where the Commander-in-chief was, and by no means to remain in the streets; for that if I did, he entertained great apprehensions I might fall a sacrifice to the furious disposition of many persons in military array; offering at the same time to bring me any gentleman I wanted, as he should be sorry I should endanger my person, of which I ought then to be particularly careful, as, if I were to meet with any accident, it might put a stop to any farther negotiation on so desirable an object as I was endeavouring to obtain. I then went into the house, where I continued the whole of that day and remained the whole night also, as upon soliciting an answer to the dispatches, the Commander-in-chief signified that we should not get it until the next morning. Some of my friends have since informed me, that they prevented several persons who were on the point of shooting me from putting their murderous intentions in effect, into the streets of Enniscorthy.

Captain O'Hea, of the North Cork militia, and Mr. Cloney arrived about two hours after Captain M'Manus and myself in Enniscorthy. They, having taken the road direct from Wexford, met the main body of the insurgents on their retreat; and the several chiefs, having first read the dispatches and proposal, permitted them to be forwarded without further interruption. They were not sealed, to obviate the danger such a step might occasion.

Captain Bourke, of the North Cork militia, and

Mr. Robert Carty proceeded to Taghmon, and delivered their proposal and dispatches to General Moore, who had already begun his march, which he pursued for a mile beyond Taghmon, when he halted on perceiving a great concourse of people on the mountain of Forth. He then sent back Mr. Carty to Lord Kingsborough, with directions to return to him with further accounts of the state of the country, and new dispatches. The insurgents, on their defeat at Enniscorthy and Vinegar Hill, retreated along the eastern bank of the Slaney, over Carrig-bridge, and so on to the Three Rocks, on the mountain of Forth, where they were now observed by General Moore, and so occasioned Mr. Carty's return to Wexford for further information.

On the arrival of the insurgents at the station of the Three Rocks, several discussions took place relative to the proposals for the surrender of the town of Wexford, into which they could not finally be restrained from coming. Among those who thus hastily rushed into the town, there were some turbulent spirits, a circumstance unavoidable on such occasions, and in such an assemblage. These, apprehensive of their situations, exerted every means in their power to prevent an accommodation, although earnestly wished for by all the chiefs as well as by the great body of the people.

Lord Kingsborough, after he had assumed the military command of the town, went to the house of Mr. Meyler, where he was when this concourse of people arrived, and they insisted that his lordship and the other officers should come out to their camp, in order, as they said, to procure the like terms for themselves as for the inhabitants of Wexford. His lordship and the officers should certainly have gone out to the camp on this occasion, but for the interference of Mr. Fitzgerald, who dissuaded them from consenting

P

to a measure that would endanger the lives of the prisoners should they leave the town. The principal inhabitants had before determined to march out with them, in order to protect them from any violence that might be attempted against them ; and their united efforts, assisted by the timely interposition of the Right Rev. Dr. Caulfield, the Roman Catholic Bishop of Ferns, prevented any further urgency. The people were addressed from the windows of the house, in which an assembly took place for the purpose of devising the best means of preventing mischief and irregularity. The people were entreated and supplicated to desist from their intentions, as Lord Kingsborough had given the most solemn assurances that they should have as good terms as he had promised the inhabitants of Wexford ; and he, moreover, advised them to go to their camp, and not to lay down their arms until these terms would be perfectly secured.

It was Lord Kingsborough's own proposal, that the insurgents should remain encamped at Three Rocks until they would secure the same terms with the inhabitants of Wexford, which it was naturally supposed would be ratified ; and it is much to be lamented that they did not return thither, as from the commanding situation of the Three Rocks it would be very difficult to dislodge them ; besides, by securing the pass at Carrig-bridge, the Slaney would have formed a very strong barrier against the approach of the forces coming from Enniscorthy ; and the insurgents would by these means have appeared so formidable as to induce the granting of the terms demanded, and which good policy so strongly dictated. This would have put an end to any further disturbance, and peace would have been immediately restored. Nor would the desolation which afterwards disfigured the country at all have taken place ; and the lives of many sacrificed to the fury of the times would have been secured; while it would have ensured the certain punishment of all murderers and assassins, many of whom, by the conduct that was pursued, escaped the end so justly due to their enormous crimes. The Amnesty Bill afterwards secured the greatest part of the benefits claimed by the proposals, with the exception of officers, who, if they had not relied on the granting of these terms, would not have remained in Wexford, but would have proceeded with the insurgents, and so have saved their lives and properties as well as others who fought their way, and at length obtained favourable terms: so that all the evil consequences that ensued are attributable to the impolicy of refusing the proposed terms, which, it is to be presumed, had there been a possibility of obtaining Lord Cornwallis's sentiments, would have been readily complied with. But unfortunately for the county of Wexford, he had landed in Ireland but the day before, and his system could not be sent forward to counteract that which existed before his arrival.

Captain John Murphy, whose humanity had been so conspicuous with his gunsmen on Vinegar Hill, was now posted on the gaol for the protection of the prisoners from the infernal fury of Captain Dixon, who wished to renew the diabolical cruelties he had been unfortunately able to put in execution the day before, in the absence of the inhabitants of Wexford, who were now returned, and determined to protect the remaining prisoners at the risk of their own lives. This they were happily able to effect, as the murderers were too cowardly to attempt anything that portended danger to themselves. No one was, therefore, put to death on this day, but Ensign Harman, of the North Cork militia, who was going out with Mr. Carty to General Moore, to whom they were now proceeding on a second mission with fresh dispatches from Lord Kingsborough. They had but just got outside the town, when unfortunately they were met by a furious maniac, named Timothy Whelan, who instantly shot Ensign Harman, and snapped a pistol at Mr. Carty, who then thought it prudent to return, thus narrowly escaping with his life. This ruffian afterward had the audacity to attempt the life of Lord Kingsborough, in order to put an end at once to all accommodation, not meeting with his approbation. He would have been ordered for instant execution by the chiefs but for fear of irritating the great body of the populace, too ready, on such occasions and in such turbid times, to mistake desperation for heroism, and to attempt the most violent deeds themselves if thwarted in their inclinations, or by meddling with their favourites.

The insurgents were at length prevailed on by the incessant entreaties and exertions of their chiefs, to quit the town of Wexford. They now divided themselves into two bodies; the one under the command of the Rev. Philip Roche marched into the barony of Forth, and encamped that night at Sledagh; the other under the conduct of Messrs. Fitzgerald, Perry, and Edward Roche, proceeded over the bridge to Peppard's Castle, where they took their station for that night.

General Moore, although he had orders not to proceed farther than Taghmon on that day, that he might co-operate on the 21st, in the general attack on Wexford; yet from the present complexion of affairs, advanced toward that town, having perceived the departure of the people from the Three Rocks; and having been also informed, by Captain Bourke, of the peaceable disposition of the Wexford people. Concerning the latter circumstance, Captain Boyd (now returning home in General Moore's train) very prudently made many cautious and strict inquiries, requiring several assurances of the fact, from Captain Bourke, who had been sent out in that direction from Wexford; in addition to which he could himself, from the commanding elevation of the road he took, observe the retreat of the insurgents over the bridge before he ventured into the town, which, after the most minute circumspection, he at length entered, attended by some yeomen, almost with as much precipitancy as he had formerly abandoned it.

Some straggling wretches of country people were put to death on this triumphant occasion. All the green ornaments that had been so conspicuously exhibited hitherto were now torn down, and some persons, who but the moment before appeared anxious to demonstrate their friendship for the people, changed sides as quick as lightning, and endeavoured to exhibit every symptom of loyalty. General Moore, on consultation with Lord Kingsborough, thought it most advisable not to let his troops into the town, which it had been determined to annihilate previous to the negotiation, and in consequence of this circumstance, of which the army was perfectly aware, it required the utmost precaution to prevent its being plundered, sacked, and destroyed, with the attendant atrocities. The townspeople now felt the utmost anxiety at not receiving any answer either to their own proposal or Lord Kingsborough's dispatches, and as even those which had been forwarded to General Moore himself, he had sent off requesting further orders from General Lake. General Moore now took his station on the Windmill Hills, taking every precaution, and having the advantage of a large park of artillery, while the situation itself completely commanded the town of Wexford. The Chapman sloop of war, commanded by Captain Keen, took her station outside the harbour, too shallow for her to enter, and three gunboats were sent to attack the fort of Roslare, which was previously abandoned, and, therefore, they thence proceeded opposite the town, completely commanding the wooden bridge and adjacent strand; so that Wexford was now thoroughly invested both by land and water. On the approach of the army, too, all the wounded men in the hospital were put to the sword, and some of the straggling inhabitants lost their lives, notwithstanding the express orders of General Moore, that no kind of excess should be committed.

At three o'clock A.M. of the 22nd the trumpet sounded for the army to march from Enniscorthy, and every one was on foot as soon as possible. Shortly after, Captain M'Manus and myself, as well as Captain O'Hea and Mr. Cloney, were required to wait on General Lake, who delivered me his answer to the proposal of the inhabitants of the town of Wexford, and desired me to read it. It was as follows:—

"Lieutenant-General Lake cannot attend to any terms by rebels in arms against their sovereign; while they continue so he must use the force entrusted to him with the utmost energy for their destruction. To the deluded multitude he promises pardon on their delivering into his hands their leaders, surrendering their arms, and returning with sincerity to their allegiance.

"Signed,   G. LAKE.

"Enniscorthy, June 22nd, 1798."

On reading this I expressed my fears that such an answer would not be pleasing to the people of Wexford, as it did not ratify the terms solemnly promised by Lord Kingsborough; but General Lake would not allow further explanation on the subject, as he declared he would not confirm any promise made by Lord Kingsborough, to whose dispatches he would not even return any answer. He then ordered that I should be conducted by an officer, whom he named, to the head of the army, whence I was to proceed to Wexford, and thence to return to him, with all convenient speed, with the determination of the inhabitants, as he mentioned he would not discontinue the march of the troops; and that if any fatality should happen Lord Kingsborough, or any of the prisoners, nothing should dissuade him from his original intention of annihilating the town. I was also warned by him, on pain of death, to return to him with a positive answer, and to bring Lord Kingsborough along with me; and if on my approach to Wexford, I should not think it safe for the officer accompanying me to go into the town, I should return with that information immediately; and that if anything should happen to the officer or to me, in consequence of having brought the dispatches and proposal, the town of Wexford was not to be spared. I was then questioned about the state of the country, the bridges, roads, and the like; and General Lake finding upon inquiry what road I was to take, that I should not want an escort until I would reach General Needham's division, encamped at Ballenkeele, he sent orders to him by me to furnish me with any escort I might require, to conduct me safe to Wexford. Captain O'Hea and I were then led to the head of the army by a general officer, and we set off with all expedition to avoid as much as possible the horrid spectacle of the dead bodies of men and women strewed along the roads and over the adjacent fields; some bearing marks of the most savage and indecent cruelty; some with their bowels ripped open, and others with their brains dashed out—situations which they did not at all exhibit the day before, when I saw them lying dead on my way to Enniscorthy!

On delivering my orders to General Needham, while the escort was getting ready, I was surrounded by several officers and yeomen who expressed like savage sentiments with those I heard the day before at Enniscorthy; and I was truly astonished to hear men of such rank and education as they were making use of such language. Some, however, expressed anxiety tempered with humanity. The escort being got ready, consisting of a troop of the Ancient Britons, and a trumpeter, commanded by Captain Wynne, we set off and could learn nothing along the road but the mournful lamentations of women, the country having been abandoned by the men.

When we arrived near Castle-bridge I proceeded for some distance by myself to reconnoitre, and, perceiving no interruption, I called on the escort to come on; and when we came in sight of Wexford, the trumpet was sounded, and I hoisted a white handkerchief to announce our arrival; but we did not learn that the town had surrendered to General Moore until we arrived at Ferry-bank adjoining the wooden bridge. As this was not as yet passable for horses, as the loose planks that had been laid on where the flooring was burned were thrown off on the retreat of the insurgents, Captain Wynne and I proceeded on foot as far as the portcullis, which had been hoisted since the preceding evening. We were, therefore, detained for half an hour, till orders were given to let it down. During the time that we were thus detained, I saw the prison-ship and several other vessels set on fire. Many more were afterwards burned; and all the ships in the harbour that were not consumed were so far considered as prizes taken from the insurgents, that the owners were obliged to pay salvage.

When the drawbridge was let down, we waited on Lord Kingsborough, to whom I made known the orders I had to bring him out to General Lake; but he declared he could not possibly comply, as he had been appointed by General Moore to command in the town. He, however, wrote a letter, excusing his attendance; and, on receipt of this, I set off with Captain Wynne and his troop of horse, which had by this time crossed the bridge, in order to return to General Lake; and we met him a little outside the town, as, on hearing what had happened, he moved forward with all expedition; and, on delivering him Lord Kingsborough's letter, we formed part of his suite on his entrance into Wexford. The preservation of this town may, indeed, be recorded as a wonderful event, as its destruction seemed as determined as that of Nineveh; and yet its state, then and now, bearing so few marks of depredation or direption of any kind, is a circumstance that has surprised all who have visited it since, and who observed the desolation that prevailed in all other directions where disturbances had existed.

Relying on the faith of Lord Kingsborough's promises of complete protection of persons and properties, several remained in the town of Wexford, unconscious of any reason to apprehend danger; but they were soon taken up and committed to gaol. The Rev. Philip Roche had such confidence in these assurances, and was so certain of obtaining similar terms for those under his command, that he left his force at Sledagh, in full hopes of being permitted to return in peace to their homes, and was on his way to Wexford unarmed, coming, as he thought, to receive a confirmation of the conditions, and so little apprehensive of danger, that he advanced within the lines before he was recognised, when all possibility of escape was at an end. He was instantly dragged from his horse, and in the most ignominious manner taken up to the camp on the

Windmill Hills, pulled by the hair, kicked, buffeted, and at length hauled down to the gaol in such a condition as scarcely to be known. The people whom he had left in expectation of being permitted to return quietly home waited his arrival. But at last, being informed of his fate, they abandoned all idea of peace, and set off under the command of the Rev. John Murphy to Fooks's-mill, and so on, through Scollagh-gap, into the county of Carlow.

From the encampment at Ballenkeele, commanded by General Needham, detachments were sent out to scour the country. They burned the Catholic chapel of Ballemurrin, situate on the demesne of Ballenkeele, on which they were encamped, besides several houses in the neighbourhood. The principal of these was that of Newpark, the seat of Mr. Fitzgerald, which, along with all the out-offices, haggard of corn, by far the largest in the county of Wexford, a malt-house containing fifteen hundred barrels of malt, and a thousand barrels of barley, were entirely consumed; as were also the house, offices, and malt-house, containing a thousand barrels of malt, at Ballimore, belonging to Mr. Edmund Stafford, mistaken, as I have been informed, for the dwelling and property of General Edward Roche, besides a great number of houses of inferior note. In short, death and desolation were spread throughout the country, which was searched and hunted, so that scarcely a man escaped; and the old, who were feeble and decrepid with age, and who could not, therefore, easily move out of the way, as well as the idiots or fools, were the victims on this occasion; as almost all such as had the use of their limbs and intellects had previously made off with the main body of the people. The dead bodies were to be seen scattered about, with their throats cut across and mangled in the most shocking manner.

It is scarcely possible to describe all the horrors and devastations that took place, as all the atrocities of war were most wofully exhibited. The fair sex became the prey of the lustful soldiery; and female beauty, which at all other times may be considered a blessing, now became a curse, as women paid dearly for their personal charms, which failed not to augment the general brutality of these odious and detestable deeds! What must be the pangs of a mother on seeing her beloved favourite child dragged from her by the ruffian hands of an unfeeling monster, glorying in his barbarity, and considering his crime meritorious in proportion to its enormity; spreading death and disease to the utmost extent of his depraved capacity! The Hompesch dragoons are held in peculiar remembrance on this occasion. Indeed, the ferocity of the soldiery in general was such at this period, that the women and children through the country even now are worked up to the highest pitch of horror at the sight of a military man, as bringing to their recollection all the barbarous scenes of which they had been formerly witnesses!

Notwithstanding the abominations of the vilest of pike-men, it is a well-established fact that during the period of their uncontrollable sway, no female, not even one of the wives or daughters of those whom they considered their greatest enemies, ever suffered any kind of violation from them; and their general respect for the sex is as true as it is wonderful; and their forbearance in this particular is as remarkably civilized as the conduct of the troops was savage, sparing neither friend nor foe in their indiscriminate and licentious brutality.

The northern part of the county of Wexford had been almost totally deserted by all the male inhabitants on the 19th, at the approach of the army under General Needham. Some of the yeomanry who formerly deserted it returned to Gorey on the 21st, and on finding no officer of the army, as was expected, to command there, they, with many others who returned along with them, scoured the country round, and killed great numbers in their houses, besides all the stragglers they met, most of whom were making the best of their way home unarmed from the insurgents, who were then believed to be totally discomfited.

These transactions being made known to the great body of the insurgents encamped at Peppard's Castle on the 22nd, they resolved to retaliate, and directly marched for Gorey, whither they had otherwise no intention of proceeding. The yeomen and their associates, whose conduct had been so conspicuous on the day before, made some show of resistance, having proceeded some little distance outside the town, as it were, boldly to meet the force coming against them. But, upon the near approach of the insurgents, they fled back with the utmost precipitation; and thence, accompanied by a great many others, hastened towards Arklow; but were pursued as far as Coolgreney, with the loss of forty-seven men. The insurgents had been exasperated to this vengeance by discovering through the country, as they came along, several dead men with their skulls split asunder, their bowels ripped open, and their throats cut across, besides some dead women and children. They even met the dead bodies of two women, about which the surviving children were creeping, and bewailing them—poor innocents!—with piteous cries! These sights hastened the insurgent force to Gorey, where their exasperation was considerably augmented by discovering the bodies of nine men, who had been hanged the day before, devouring by pigs in the streets, others recently shot, and some still expiring.

After the return of the insurgents from the pursuit, several persons were found lurking in the town and brought before Mr. Fitzgerald, particularly Mr. Pippard, sovereign of Gorey; but, from this gentleman's age and respectability, he was considered incapable of being accessory to the perpetration of the horrid cruelty which provoked and prompted this sudden revenge, and he and others were saved, protected, and set at liberty.

At this critical time the news of the burning of Mr. Fitzgerald's house, haggard, and malt-houses, by which he lost several thousand pounds, arrived; and, had the smallest seed of rancour or cruelty existed in the mind of such a sufferer, he might have so far felt it on this occasion as not to restrain the insurgents from exterminating Gorey, which they were loudly proclaiming as a just retaliation for the devastation committed on so great a favourite of the people. The magnanimity and forbearance of Mr. Fitzgerald at so trying a crisis are truly remarkable, as, forgetful of such great personal injury, he exerted his utmost endeavours to restrain the insurgents, vociferating vengeance for his wrongs, and succeeded in leading them off from Gorey; when, after a slight repast, they resumed their intended route, rested that night at the White-heaps on Croghan mountain, and on the 23rd set off for the mountains of Wicklow.

General Lake, with some other general officers, remained for some time in Wexford. The gaol of this town was now immensely crowded, as almost every one of the principal inhabitants were taken up and arraigned for treason. Many of them, however, were acquitted upon trial, which was by court-martial, and the greater number received protections, according to Lord Cornwallis's proclamation. Captain Keugh had remained at Lord Kingsborough's lodgings, and after the surrender of the town, two sentinels were placed on him there for two days, when he was removed to the gaol. Mr. Cornelius Grogan was taken at his seat in Johnstown, where he had remained, unconscious of any danger until conducted to prison. Mr. Bagnal Harvey had gone to his residence at Bargy Castle, having no conception that the terms agreed upon with Lord Kingsborough would not be ratified. Indeed, so confident was he of the contrary, that he sent some fat cattle into Wexford for the use of the army; but learning from the messenger who drove them thither, that no conditions whatever would be obtained, he hastened with the fatal news to Mr. Colclough. This gentleman had previously taken his wife and child to one of the Saltee Islands, where he thought to have weathered out the storm of the angry time in a cave, into which he had gone for concealment. Thither Mr. Harvey now also resorted; but they were all soon discovered, and the news of their being taken arrived in Wexford while they were being conveyed round to the harbour in a boat. This attracted a great number of people to the quay, curious to see them brought in, and amidst this concourse Mr. Harvey and Mr. Colclough and his lady were landed. The gentlemen were then led through the gazing multitude to the gaol, where they were confined in the condemned cells.

A court-martial was instituted for the trial of prisoners on charges of treason. The Rev. Philip Roche was the first tried and condemned by this tribunal. Captain Keugh was the next put on his trial, at which he made a very able defence; but was also condemned. The entrance of the wooden bridge was the scene fixed on for the place of execution. The sufferers were hauled up with pulleys, made fast with ropes to an ornamental iron arch, intended for lamps, and springing from the two wooden piers of the gate next the town. The large stature of the Rev. Philip Roche caused the first rope he was hauled up with to break; but another was soon procured, and his life was ended with double torture. The head of Captain Keugh, who suffered along with him, was separated from his body, and conspicuously placed on a pike over the front of the court-house. Their bodies, together with those of others executed at the same time, were stripped, and treated with the utmost brutality and indecency, previous to their being thrown over the bridge.

Mr. Grogan was brought to trial on the 26th, but the evidence which he hoped to obtain of his innocence did not attend, on account of the general apprehension that prevailed. His trial was therefore postponed, and he was remanded to gaol. Mr. Harvey was then put on his trial, which lasted for the best part of the day, and ended in his condemnation. Mr. Grogan's trial was then resumed; but this he did not expect until the next day, and consequently he had not been able to procure all the necessary evidence. It was indeed proved that he was forced to join the insurgents, but this did not prevent a sentence of his conviction. Such was the idea entertained at the time of the necessity of public example! The condemnation of these gentlemen was afterwards confirmed by the Irish Parliament, which passed an Act of Attainder against them, and a confiscation of their properties; notwithstanding that, on Parliamentary inquiry into the merits of the proceedings, it was clearly proved, that the court-martial had not been even sworn: so that although their condemnation and the confiscation of their properties be sanctioned by law, yet the justice of the process is very questionable, and the investigaton of it will employ the pens of future historians, particularly in the case of Mr. Grogan, who was undoubtedly sacrificed to the temper of the times.

On the 27th, Messrs. Harvey, Grogan, and Patrick

Prendergast, a rich maltster in Wexford, were ordered out to execution. When Mr. Harvey was brought out of his cell he met Mr. Grogan in the gaol-yard, and accosted him in a feeling, affectionate manner. While shaking hands with him he said, in the presence of an officer and some of the guards, and in the hearing of several prisoners who had crowded to the windows, "Ah! poor Grogan, you die an innocent man at all events!" They were then conducted to the bridge, where they were hanged, when the heads of Messrs. Grogan and Harvey were cut off and placed upon pikes on each side of that of Captain Keugh; while their bodies and that of Mr. Prendergast were stript and treated with the utmost brutal indecencies, before being cast over the bridge! Mr. Colclough was brought out to trial on the same day, and condemned. On the next day he was executed; but his body, at the intercession of his lady, was given up to her to be interred. Mr. John Kelly, of Killan, whose courage and intrepidity had been so conspicuous at the battle of Ross, now lay ill in Wexford, of a wound which he had received in that engagement. He was taken prisoner from his bed, tried and condemned to die, and brought on a car to the place of execution. His head was cut off, and his body, after the accustomed indignities, was thrown over the bridge. The head, however, was reserved for other exhibition. It was first kicked about on the Custom-house Quay, and then brought up into the town, thrown up and treated in the same manner opposite the house in which his sister lodged, in order that she might view this new and savage game of football, of which when the players were tired, the head was placed in the exalted situation to which it had been condemned—above that of Captain Keugh, over the door of the Court-house.

On the 28th, General Lake quitted Wexford, leaving

the command there to General Hunter, whose conduct must ever be remembered with gratitude by the people, as, on several occasions, he checked the persecuting spirit of the gentry and yeomanry; and this contributed much more than severity, or any other mode could possibly do, to induce the people to surrender their arms, take out protections, and return to their homes in peace. This desirable object would not have been so happily accomplished had he not interposed his authority so far, as to threaten some gentlemen with punishment, whose habitual zeal and mode of keeping the country quiet, he totally disapproved of, as he did not wish to see the people again roused by the continuance of their exertions. Brigadier-General Grose was stationed, under the command of General Hunter, at Enniscorthy, where he was distinguished for his pacific conduct. The First and Coldstream regiments of Guards were providentially placed in Ross, under the command of General Gascoigne, and their conduct there must be ever recorded to their immortal honour, as exhibiting true principles of justice and philanthropy —stepping in between the people and their oppressors, who were not only restrained in their career of persecution, but even shamed into compliance with the system of pacification. Many were released from prison after the severest treatment; and on inquiry into their cases, nothing could be alleged against them. They were consequently discharged; it being evident that their confinement had been most unwarrantable, and to be accounted for only as a part of the dreadful system of tyranny and oppression which preceded and produced so many evil consequences.

This is strongly exemplified in the case of Doctor Healy. This gentleman was a native of Ross, and had practised as a physician for some years in Wexford, whence he was on his way, on Whitsunday, to his native town, and stopping at Healthfield, the seat of Mr. John Grogan, he found that the latter wanted horses for some of his corps of yeomen, to conduct Sergeant Stanley to Waterford. The doctor then dismounted his servant, and gave the horse he rode to Mr. Grogan for the purpose required, and pursued his journey to Ross, where all his relations resided. Some of those who abandoned Wexford on the 28th of May, coming afterwards to Ross, had the inhumanity to get Doctor Healy confined, and the prevailing torture of whipping inflicted on him. His life was consequently endangered, and he continued to experience the most brutal treatment, and was in constant terror of being put to death, until relieved, along with many others, all of whom appeared perfectly innocent upon inquiry into their situation; and it is natural to suppose that their enemies would have come forward to accuse them, if they had any charge to make, were it only to give some colour of justice to their conduct, which appeared eminently tyrannical to the officers of the guards, who had no idea that such transactions could have taken place in any country.

I am induced to insert the following circumstance from Mr. Alexander's Account, as he was not liable to be imposed on, in this instance, by any misrepresentation:—" Corporal Morgan, of the First regiment of Guards, observing a country-protected rebel, whose house was burned for his crime, drop down at the word of command upon his knees to the gentleman who had burned his house, ran hastily to the fellow and lifted him off his knees, exclaiming, 'Get up, you mean-spirited boor, and do not prostrate yourself to any being but your God; surely you do not mistake *this* man for *that* Being?' 'Sir,' replied the gentleman, 'he shall go on his knees to me as he ought.' 'No, sir,' returned the corporal, 'he shall not; at least in my presence, and while I have the honour of being in the king's guards. We give the king but one knee, and that the *left*; reserving the right knee, as well as the honour of both for God; and I tell you to your fiery phiz (whether you believe me or not), that you are neither a god nor a king, nor shall you receive the honour of either.' This was a young man of good education, and in the same Latin class with me, at the late Rev. Mr. Wesley's academy at Kingswood, near Bristol. He was the son of an eminent Methodist preacher."*

The conduct of those commanders last mentioned was such as to induce the people to flock in with the greatest confidence to procure protections; and the country under their benign influence soon assumed quite another appearance. Had the county of Wexford enjoyed the blessing of being ruled by such men previous to the Insurrection, I am fully persuaded that no disturbance would have taken place there; and it is to be regretted that they did not continue longer in command than they did, as on their departure, former influence so far prevailed as to exhibit a tendency to persecution, by resuming, as much as possible, their former conduct, which dare not be attempted when properly checked and under due restraint. General Needham commanded in Gorey, and other officers were stationed at Taghmon and Ferns to grant protections.

Although I meant to confine myself in this narrative to what happened in the county of Wexford, yet it might be considered defective did I not relate what afterwards took place until the warfare of the Wexford men was closed by surrender in the county of Kildare, under Messrs. Fitzgerald and Aylmer.

The insurgents who passed west of the Slaney, under the conduct of the Rev. John Murphy, directed their

---

* See Alexander's Account, pp. 106, 107.

march to get into the county of Carlow through Scollagh-gap. Here they met with some opposition from a small body of troops placed there to oppose the passage. These, however, they soon overpowered, and burning the village of Killedmond on the Carlow side of the pass, they continued their march to Newbridge, where they arrived on the morning of the 23rd, and quickly defeating a party of horse and foot stationed on the bridge to prevent their passing it, they took twenty-eight of the Wexford militia, part of the force there stationed, but the cavalry hastily retreated to Kilkenny. From this town Sir Charles Asgill immediately set out to meet the insurgents at Newbridge, but was too late, as they had moved off towards Castlecomer, in expectation of being joined by the colliers, from whom they expected considerable assistance.

On the 24th the insurgents proceeded from the Ridge of Leinster, on which they rested the night before, to attack Castlecomer. Near this town they met a party of about two hundred and fifty men, whom they obliged to retreat precipitately before them into the body of the place. A thick fog, however, prevented them from observing the great inferiority of their opponents, and this, added to the town being on fire (of which each party accuses the other), also prevented their observing the approach of Sir Charles Asgill (who had moved after them with a large military force) until they began to be raked with grape shot from his artillery. This surprise forced the insurgents, with great loss, to quit their enterprise, the Wexford militia prisoners being retaken from them. But still Sir C. Asgill thought it prudent to retreat that evening back to Kilkenny, accompanied by a vast number of the inhabitants of Castlecomer, which, by-the-by, was instantly after taken possession of again and plundered by the insurgents.

After this they pushed on to the Queen's County, where they remained that night, and finding themselves greatly disappointed in not being joined by the inhabitants, and their own body being considerably weakened by desertion, they resolved to return home to the County of Wexford. They accordingly directed their course to Newbridge, and encamped that night on Killcomney Hill, where they were surrounded during the night of the 25th by a large military force, consisting of about five hundred of the Downshire militia, commanded by Major Matthews, who pursued them from Castlecomer, having first notified his intention to Sir Charles Asgill at Kilkenny, who accordingly set out from that place at the head of twelve hundred men, and arrived time enough to co-operate in the attack. A very thick fog prevented the insurgents from being sensible of their situation on the morning of the 26th, until they experienced a severe discharge of cannon on one side, which made them shift their ground a little; but on receiving a second salute of the same kind from another quarter, the rout became general; and they fled with great precipitancy; indeed, they must have been entirely cut off had not the horsemen that were among them rallied, and prevented the cavalry from pursuit; in which dangerous service they displayed great courage and intrepidity. The slaughter, however, proved very great; but it is lamentable that the greater part of the slain on this occasion were the people of the adjacent country, who had not at all joined the insurgents, nor left their houses; and great depredations in the way of plunder were also committed on all who happened to be placed near the scene of action. This body of Wexford insurgents, after again forcing their passage back through Scollagh-gap, against some troops who endeavoured to oppose them, never made its appearance again, as the people dispersed and retired to their several homes, except a very few who joined their associates in the county of Wicklow.

The other body of Wexford insurgents, which had proceeded, as before observed, after the attack upon Gorey, as far as the White-heaps, in the county of Wicklow, set off on the morning of the 23rd toward the lead mines. While resting in a posture of defence on an eminence near this place, they perceived a body of troops in the hollow beneath, and these fired some bomb shells at them from the opposite side of a river. The insurgents, having no cannon, retreated toward Monaseed, where they halted part of that night, and arrived on the morning of the 24th at Donard, which they found deserted. Here they waited for some time for refreshment, and then moved toward Glanmullen, where they met a small party of cavalry, who fled at their approach. They found the village of Aughrim laid waste, and many dead bodies bearing marks of cruelty.

From this place they proceeded to Blessington, and although their manner mostly was to rest as much as possible by day, and march during the night, to avoid the pursuit of a body of a cavalry that was observed to follow them, and which generally appeared in view, they, however, encamped this night at Ballymanus, where, uniting their forces with those of Mr. Garret Byrne, the whole moved on the morning of the 25th toward Hacketstown, before which they appeared about seven o'clock in the morning.

The military were drawn up in a small field outside the town, ready to receive them; but they were forced to give way, after the loss of Captain Hardy and four privates of the Hacketstown yeomen infantry, while the pikemen of the insurgents were wading across the river to attack the place on all sides. The cavalry retreated and kept aloof during the remainder of the action; but the infantry, consisting of about one hundred and seventy men, retired into the barrack, and a malt-house adjoining it, from which their fire did great execution, as did that from the house of the Rev. Mr. M'Ghee, who defended it with uncommon bravery, his force consisting of nine men only; but whose galling fire had the greater effect as it commanded the main street, and also that part of the barrack which was thought most vulnerable. This the insurgents endeavoured several times to set fire to, as they had before to the rest of the town; but all in vain. At length they made a desperate effort to accomplish their purpose. A few men proceeded up to the building, under the cover of feather beds and matted straw, fastened on cars; but they were only successful in obliging the military to abandon the malt-house, and could not by any means get possession of the barrack or of Mr. M'Ghee's house, both so situated as to support each other.

The insurgents, at last deeming it impracticable to effect their design without cannon, of which they had not a single piece, retreated from the place, after an action of nine hours, in which they had lost great numbers. Carrying off their wounded, and driving before them all the cattle from about the town, they encamped that night at Blessington. The loss of the garrison was but ten killed and twenty wounded; however, they thought it most prudent to abandon the place, which they did, and retreated that evening to Tullow, in the county of Carlow. During the engagement, it is said that a considerable force of cavalry and infantry stood on a hill at a small distance, in view of the scene of action, but did not venture to join in the battle.

Disappointed by the repulse at Hacketstown, the remaining Wexford insurgents, in conjunction with their Wicklow associates, directed their march towards

Carnew, which they were resolved if possible to carry; but General Needham, being informed of their approach, detached a strong body of infantry, and about two hundred cavalry from his camp at Gorey, to intercept them. The cavalry alone, however, as the infantry were recalled, came up with the insurgents on the road to Carnew. These, feigning a retreat, having timely notice of their approach, suffered the cavalry to pass until they brought them into an ambuscade, where their gunsmen were placed on both sides of the way, behind the ditches, to receive them. At the first discharge they were utterly confounded, and being unable to give their opponents any annoyance, they attempted to retreat in great haste towards Carnew. But here they had to encounter another part of the plan of ambush; for the insurgents, rightly conjecturing that when foiled they would attempt getting off in that direction, had blocked up the road with cars and other incumbrances. They were for some time exposed to the fire of the insurgents, and lost about eighty of their number, among whom were two officers, Captain Giffard, of the Ancient Britons, and Mr. Parsons, adjutant of the Ballaghkeen cavalry: the rest effected their retreat to Arklow. The detachment was commanded by Lieutenant-Colonel Pulestone, of the Ancient Britons, of whom twenty were among the slain. The animosity of the people against this regiment, which they charge with being guilty of great excesses, may be instanced in the case of a black trumpeter belonging to it who fell into their hands alive on this occasion. When seized upon, this man loudly declared, that he was a Roman Catholic, and besought them to spare him for the sake of his religion. But his deeds with which he was upbraided were too recent and too notorious, and he obtained no quarter.

The insurgents lost not a single man in this action; but they were foiled in their design upon Carnew, the garrison of which, being alarmed by the retreating cavalry, had just time to secure themselves, in a malt-house, before the approach of the insurgents, who, after an ineffectual attack, marched off to Killcavan Hill.

On the 2nd of July, as the insurgents began to move towards Shillelagh, they were pursued by a body of yeomen, cavalry and infantry, before whom they retired to an eminence called Ballyrabeen Hill. Here they took post, but as the yeomen moved up the hill, the insurgents poured upon them with such impetuosity and vehemence, that they were in an instant utterly discomfited, with the loss of seventy privates and two officers, all infantry, for none of the cavalry fell. The officers were Captain Chamney of the Coolattin, and Captain Nixon of the Coolkenna corps; besides numbers were wounded. Sixty privates, under Captain Moreton of the Tinahely, and Lieutenant Chamney of the Coolattin yeomen, retreated into Captain Chamney's house at the foot of the hill, whither they were pursued by the insurgents, who continued to attack them all night; but they were resisted with the utmost bravery and coolness, and at length repulsed with considerable loss, to which it is probable the light afforded by a house adjoining, that of Mr. Henry Moreton (which had been set on fire by the insurgents in their frenzy), contributed not a little, as it enabled those within to aim with precision at the assailants. It was several times attempted to fire the house, by approaching the door under the cover of feather-beds, which proved unsuccessful.

The Wexford insurgents next fixed their station near the White-heaps, at the foot of Croghan Mountain; from whence they moved during the night of the 4th, toward Wicklow-gap, but were met on the morning of the 5th by the army under Sir James Duff from Carnew; and after some salutes from the artillery, they were obliged to take another direction, and turned toward Gorey. But the fact is, that they were surrounded by four powerful detachments, before they could perceive the approach of any, in consequence of a fog so dense that it was impossible to distinguish objects at the distance of twenty yards; and finding themselves unable to withstand a battle, they broke through the pursuing cavalry of Sir James Duff's army, of whom they slew about eighty; and moved with great celerity in the direction of Carnew. But upon their arrival at a place called Craneford, by others Ballygullen, they resolved to make resistance and await the approach of the troops however numerous, although their own force was by this time considerably diminished. They, however, maintained the contest for an hour and a half, displaying the greatest valour, and most intrepid resolution; having repulsed the cavalry, and driven the artillery men three times from their cannon, all performed by the gunsmen; for the pikemen, as on former occasions, never came into action. But fresh reinforcements of the army, pouring in on all sides, they were obliged to give way, quitting the field of battle with little loss to themselves, and notwithstanding all their fatigue, retreating, with their usual agility and swiftness, in different directions; but agreed among themselves to assemble again at Carrigrew. A party of these refugees were met by the Rev. Peter Browne, Dean of Ferns, who was suffered to pass, and he instantly posted to Ferns, to inform the King's County militia, quartered there, of the route of the flying insurgents. The military accordingly set out, with all speed, on the pursuit, and killed such of the straggling peasantry as they met or came up to without mercy. The insurgents thus harassed and hunted, thought it advisable, upon meeting at Carrigrew, to disperse, and this put an end to the warfare in the county of Wexford.

A party of insurgents in the county of Kildare, under the command of Mr. William Aylmer, still held out in arms, and thither the remaining body of the Wexford men, commanded by Mr. Fitzgerald, accompanied by Mr. Garret Byrne, and some Wicklow men, directed their course to form a junction, which they accordingly effected. This associated force moved from Prosperous to Clonard, where they met a most determined and successful resistance from Lieutenant Tyrrel, a yeoman officer, who, with his corps, had occupied a fortified house in the town. These delayed the assailants until reinforcements arrived from Kinnegad and Mullingar, when they were forced to give up the enterprise.

After this repulse the few remaining Wexford men separated from their Wicklow associates, whom they deemed less warlike than themselves, and made different incursions into the counties of Kildare, Meath, Louth, and Dublin, eluding, as well as they could, the pursuit of the army, with different parties of which they had frequent skirmishes. The night of the repulse at Donard they committed some depredations in the village of Carbery, in the county of Kildare. On the next day, pursued by different parties of military, they marched into the county of Meath, where they were overtaken and put to flight by Colonel Gough, commanding a detachment of the county of Limerick militia from Edenderry. After this two of their leaders, Mr. Perry and the Rev. Mr. Kearns, endeavouring to make their escape by themselves, were taken, tried, and condemned by court-martial, and executed at Edenderry. Unable to effect anything in the county of Meath, the Wexford men crossed the Boyne, near Duleek, into the county of Louth, where, being pursued from place to place, they made a most gallant resistance to the cavalry of Major-General Wemys and Brigadier-General Meyrick, who overtook them between the town of Ardee and the Boyne; but the infantry and artillery coming up, they were defeated with some loss, and fled into an adjoining bog, where they were secure from pursuit. In the night a small party set off toward Ardee, and dispersed, each as he best could, making way by devious and circuitous routes homeward. The remaining body repassed the Boyne, and, with their usual celerity, were on the direct road toward Dublin, when intercepted by Captain Gordon, of the Dumfries light dragoons, at the head of a strong party of horse and foot, at Ballyboghill, near Swords, where they were finally put to the rout, and were never more collected.

Some Wexford insurgents, however, remained with Mr. Fitzgerald, along with Mr. Aylmer, who, as outstanding chiefs, negotiated with General Dundas, to whom they surrendered on the 12th of July, on condition that all the other leaders who had adventured with them should be at liberty to retire whither they pleased out of the British dominions. The same terms were afterwards secured by General Moore to Mr. Garret Byrne, who was sent into confinement in the castle of Dublin, together with Messrs. Fitzgerald and Aylmer. Here they continued until the beginning of 1799, when Lord Cornwallis permitted them to retire to England, where they remained until the 25th of March following, when Messrs. Fitzgerald and Byrne were arrested at Bristol (where they were for the recovery of their health), at the instance of persons connected with a strong Irish party for the Union, whom it was thought at that time advisable to indulge. These gentlemen afterwards retired to Hamburgh.

Messrs. Aylmer, Fitzgerald, and other outstanding chiefs surrendered, conditioning for themselves and others, by which they fared much better than those who laid down their arms in Wexford, depending on the faithful fulfilment of the terms entered into with Lord Kingsborough.

General Lake, previous to his departure from Wexford, appointed a committee to superintend prosecutions, and to grant passes to leave the country, consisting of the principal gentlemen then resident there. The appropriate duty of this body was to inquire specially into the cases of such prisoners as they should hand over to be tried by court-martial, to procure the evidence for prosecution, and to commit different persons to gaol. It was not, however, deemed necessary to send a committal to the gaoler, as the word of any of them was considered sufficient for the detention of any of those given in custody; and they were also to act as a kind of council to General Hunter, whose benevolent disposition they thwarted on several occasions; and this was so well known that many upon being put into confinement were induced by their apprehensions to petition for transportation rather than abide a trial under their direction. The tyrannical, unjust, and inhuman disposition of this body is strongly exemplified in their unwarrantable treatment of many besides myself, which I have endeavoured to detail in my preliminary discourse.

Different court-martials were instituted in Ross, Enniscorthy, Gorey, and Newtownbarry, and several persons were condemned and executed, and others were sentenced to transportation. Among those who were condemned to be executed I cannot avoid noticing the case of the Rev. John Redmond, a Catholic priest, who it seems during the Insurrection had done all in his power to save the house of Lord Mountnorris from being plundered, which he in some degree effected, but not at all to the extent of his wishes. Lord Mountnorris, however, to prevent the possibility of his being supposed by any one in future a friend to Catholics, sent for Mr. Redmond, upon finding that he was present at the plundering of his house, desiring that he would come to him directly. The reverend gentleman, conscious of his own integrity, and apprehensive of no danger, as involved in no guilt, obeyed the summons without hesitation. But his instantaneous, hasty trial, condemnation, and execution were the reward of his humane and generous exertions. His body, after death, underwent the most indecent mutilations. But to put this innocent man's conduct in its proper point of view, I do not think I can do better than the Rev. Mr. Gordon, a Protestant clergyman, has done in his History of the Irish Rebellion :—

"Of the rebellious conduct of Redmond, coadjutor to Father Francis Kavanagh, in the parish of Clough, of which I was twenty-three years curate, I can find no other proof than the sentence of the court-martial which consigned him to death. He was accused by the Earl of Mountnorris of having appeared as chief among a party of rebels who committed some depredations at his Lordship's house; while he alleged that his object in appearing on the occasion was to endeavour to prevent the plundering of the house, in which he had partly succeeded. Coming into Gorey on a message from the Earl, seemingly unapprehensive of danger and unconscious of guilt, he was treated as if manifestly guilty before trial—knocked down in the street, and rudely dragged by some yeomen. I mean not to arraign the justice of the noble Lord, his prosecutor, nor the members of the court-martial. The former, who had rendered himself in no small degree responsible for the loyalty of the Wexfordian Romanists, had doubtless good reasons for his conduct; and the latter could have no personal animosity against the accused, nor other unfavourable bias than what naturally arose from the turbid state of affairs, when accusation against a Romish priest was considered as a strong presumption of guilt. But his Protestant neighbours, who had not been able to escape from the rebels, assured me that while the latter were in possession of the country, he was constantly hiding in Protestant houses from the rebels, and that many Romanists expressed great resentment against him as a traitor to their cause. That he expected not the rebellion to be successful, appears from this, that when the wife of Nathaniel Stedman (one of my Protestant parishioners) applied to him to baptize her child,* he told her that he acceded to her request, merely lest the child should die unbaptized, in the necessary absence of her minister, on condition that she should promise to make the proper apology for him to me, on my return to the parish."

It is a melancholy reflection to think how many innocent persons were condemned. I have heard of numbers, of whose innocence the smallest doubt cannot be entertained, whose conduct merited reward instead of punishment; yet they fell victims to the purest sentiments of philanthropy, which dictated their interference: these have been perverted by their enemies, who are also those of the human race, into crimes utterly unpardonable. Is this any thing less than arraigning benevolence and humanity, the most amiable qualities of the soul of man, as criminal and atrocious? But every man's breast, whatever be his principles, will

* See Gordon's History of the Irish Rebellion, pp. 185, 186.

tell him with irresistible force, that crime and atrocity lie at the other side. From personal knowledge of the circumstances, I knew five or six who were innocent of the charges and of the deeds sworn against them, and who still were condemned and executed. In these turbid and distracted times I have seen persons sunk so much below the level of human nature, that I do believe they were not capable of judgment or recollection; which accounts to me in some degree for the various assertions, even testimonies on trials and affidavits made by different persons, who might as well relate their dreams for facts.

The dreadful prejudice, hateful as uncharitable, entertained against Catholics, has also occasioned the death of many; and the general excuse and impunity of Protestants, who joined in the Insurrection, has induced many to avail themselves of this favourable circumstance to change with the times; and to testify their loyalty, they accuse the very persons they themselves seduced to join the Association of United Irishmen, and thus cut off all the existing proof of their own delinquency by a consummation of villainy. The *loyalising* spirit, if I may be allowed the expression, has done a vast deal of mischief; for those in the predicament last mentioned are unprincipled *turn-coats* in religion, who scruple not to throw out every calumnious aspersion upon that which they have not only forsaken, but abandoned, in order, if possible, to impress an idea of the sincerity of their conversion in embracing the other. Vain effort—it only exposes the hypocritical apostasy in either case to the dignified contempt of every intelligent and principled man. I know two Protestant gentlemen, who if they had been Catholics, would not have escaped at this critical time. They also attribute the saving of their lives to gambling, of the good effects of which I never before heard an instance. However, certain it is that these gentlemen had lost some money at play, previous to the Insurrection, which luckily for them had not been paid at that period; and the gallant heroes who were the honourable creditors on the occasion, and who were eminently active in suppressing the rebellion, *humanely* considered that none of the debt could be recovered if the two gentlemen were hanged, and, therefore, they suffered their interest to work upon their mercy, which operated to the procurement of pardon and release for the gentlemen in question, as well as the consequent payment of these debts of honour. I know the two gentlemen well, and have often heard them relate this adventure, which is deemed to have preserved two fine fellows.

Mr. E. Kyan, whose courage and humanity deserved a better fate, was taken near Wexford, on his return home in the night, tried, condemned, and executed the next day; for although manifest proofs appeared of his humanity and interference, so conspicuously effectual on the bridge of Wexford, on the 20th of June, yet this was insufficient to save him, as he had arms about him when apprehended. His fate is the more lamentable, as Mr. Fitzgerald, on surrendering to General Dundas, had secured the same terms for Mr. Kyan as for himself; so that had any circumstance interfered to delay his execution for some time, the life of a brave man would have been saved.

General Hunter was indefatigable in his exertions to appease the minds of the people, and to restore confidence and tranquillity to this distracted country. In this he was very materially assisted by the address and exertions of Captain Fitzgerald, who, by the special appointment of the British Government, was attached as a proper person to attend the General as Brigade-Major on the service in Ireland; and to this station, besides his acknowledged military talents, a recent display of courage, independent of his knowledge of the country, certainly recommended him. He was even invested with the extraordinary privilege of recommending such as he thought deserving of the protection and mercy of Government.

Some principal gentlemen of the county, and others besides, attempted to interpose their authority to supersede the tenor of the general pardon held out by proclamation, pursuing the same line of arbitrary conduct which they practised previous to the Insurrection. They even proceeded to such a length as presuming to tear some of the protections which the country people had obtained; but this coming to the General's knowledge, he soon quieted them by threatening to have them tied to a cart's tail and whipped. Others had been rash enough to levy arbitrary contributions for the losses they had sustained during the Insurrection; but were glad, upon discovery, and refunding what they had received, to escape punishment, which favour was generally obtained through the intercession of Major Fitzgerald. Even a beneficed clergyman of the Established Church partook of the General's indulgence. Another who was but a curate was induced to wait on the General with an account of the *intended* massacre of the Protestants, which he detailed with appearance of the utmost alarm, and was patiently heard out, with the greatest complacency by the General, who, when the curate had ended, addressed him with this marked appellation and strong language:—" *Mr. Massacre*, if you do not prove to me the circumstances you have related, I shall get you punished in the most exemplary manner for raising false alarms, which have already proved so destructive to this unfortunate country." The curate's alarm now from general became personal, and on allowing that his fears had been excited by vague report to make this representation, his piteous supplication, and apparently hearty contrition, procured him forgiveness. Many and various were the representations of a similar tendency, made to General Hunter, which other commanders were led to believe, but which his superior discrimination deemed false and groundless, and were discovered so to be in several instances, by the activity and acumen of his Brigade-Major.

Annesley Brownrigg, Esq., a magistrate of the county of Wexford, received nine-and-thirty charges of pillage and slaughter against Mr. Hunter Gowan; and on the informations being submitted to General Hunter, he sent out a party of the Mid-Lothian cavalry to conduct him prisoner to Wexford, whither he was brought accordingly, and there it was determined to bring him to trial. Mr. Brownrigg returned home in the meantime to collect the evidence, but it was previously settled that he should have sufficient notice; but on the day appointed for the trial, no prosecutor attending, Mr. Gowan of course was discharged. An official letter had been dispatched in due time, yet he did not receive it until it was a day too late. Whether the miscarriage of the letter was by accident or design continues yet a secret.

The various outrages that were committed in the country prevented vast numbers from coming into the quarters of the several commanding officers to obtain protections, as many of the yeomen and their supplementaries continued the system of deflagration and shooting such of the peasantry as they met; and this necessarily deterred many from exposing themselves to their view, and prevented of course the humane and benevolent intentions of General Hunter from having due weight or extensive effect. The melancholy consequences of such a system of terror, persecution, and alarm were very near being wofully experienced in a shocking instance of dreadful severity—the extermination of all the inhabitants of a large tract of the county of Wexford. This was actually determined on, and the execution of it already planned and concerted, when its horrid perpetration was providentially prevented by the timely and happy intervention of Brigade-Major Fitzgerald, under the direction and orders of General Hunter. Incessant applications and remonstrances were made by different magistrates in Gorey and its vicinity to the Government, complaining that an entire quarter of the county of Wexford, extending from Courtown to Blackwater, which range of country is denominated the Macomores, was infested with constant meetings of rebels; and no means were left untried to prevent travellers from proceeding to Wexford in that direction without escorts; and many persons whose habitations lay in the neighbourhood of this district left their homes deserted from a belief that another rising of the people was inevitable; and it was daily expected to take place; nay, the reports laid before Government were even confirmed by affidavits; and so generally was it believed that persons resident within two miles of the confines presumed not to inquire into the veracity of the reports, to which, however, they gave implicit credit; while at the same time they were accredited by Government, to whom they were handed in under the specious, imposing, and solemn appearance of facts by a magistracy that should be deliberate, grave and respectable; and the noble Viceroy, who then held the helm of the Government, was rendered justly indignant by these reiterated complaints of the abuse of his clemency, on the represented imminent danger of the country.

Orders were accordingly sent to the different Generals and other commanding officers in and contiguous to the devoted tract, to form a line along its extent on the western border, and at both ends north and south, on the land side, so as to leave no resource to the

wretched inhabitants throughout its whole range, but
to be slaughtered by the soldiery, or to be driven into
the sea, as it is bounded by the channel on the east-
ward. Even women and children were to be included
in this horrid plan of terrific example. The chief
command in execution of this measure, the time for its
commencement, and the final determination of its
necessity, were intrusted to the discretion of General
Hunter; nor was the confidence, indeed, misplaced.
He was himself, with the Second or Queen's and the
Twenty-ninth regiments of infantry, together with the
Mid-Lothian fencible cavalry, stationed in Wexford;
Brigadier-General Grose was with the South Cork
militia at Enniscorthy; Lord Blaney commanded the
camp at Ferns, composed of the light brigades;
Brigadier-General Skerrett with his regiment of foot
in Gorey; and General Eustace with his brigade at
Arklow. These, together with the general assistance of
all the yeomanry corps throughout the country, were
to form the cordon round the country of the Macomores, and the troops were to move at once to the
dreadful expedition. So terrifying were the reports at
this crisis, that even some liberal but timid and
credulous minds approved of these melancholy means
of sacrificing thousands (that tract being very populous), as the only effectual resource for restoring tranquillity!

General Hunter, through the honest exertions and
bold scrutiny of Major Fitzgerald, fortunately discovered
in time the inhuman tendency of the misrepresentation that had dictated and determined this shocking
enterprise. The devoted victims found access to the
General, and he cheerfully acceded to their entreaties
to send an officer to inquire into their complaints,
imploring protection from the incursions of the black
mob (they thus denominated the supplementaries to

the different corps of yeomanry), who wreaked their vengeance even upon those who had received protections from General Needham at Gorey; as different parties of the soldiery and yeomanry waited their return in ambush, and slaughtered every one they could overtake! This naturally prevented great numbers from coming in for protections. Afterwards these *sanguinary banditti* made incursions into the country, fired into the houses of the peasantry, and so killed and wounded many. Several houses after being plundered were burned, and the booty was brought into Gorey. By the frequency of these horrible excesses and depredations, such houses as remained unburned were of course crowded with several families; and this multiplied the number of victims at each succeeding incursion.

At last most of the inhabitants of necessity took refuge on the hills, and armed themselves with every offensive weapon they could procure. The elevation of their retreats necessarily made their assemblages conspicuous, and this afforded some colour to the pretext for desolation, as it appeared a specious proof that a general rising was intended; and this was most strenuously urged by those who seemed bent on the extermination of the unfortunate inhabitants of the Macomores' territory, so as to work upon the minds of some well disposed but timid persons an approval of the dreadful expedient. General Hunter, however, having, along with his general orders, a discretionary power to act as circumstances might require, sent Major Fitzgerald to inspect the different military corps that were to be in readiness for the enterprise, in case his mission, for the purpose of conciliation, proved unsuccessful; he being vested with full powers to undertake that task of benevolence and mercy. Major Fitzgerald accordingly inspected the troops at Enniscorthy and

Camolin, and from the latter place dispatched Surgeon White of the Camolin cavalry (son of Mr. Henry White of Donoughmore, a gentleman much respected in the country of the Macomores,) to announce his intended visit to the inhabitants. The Major then proceeded on his inspection to Gorey, and here had great difficulty to procure an escort to accompany him, as the strongest fears were expressed for his safety should he enter into such a desperate quarter as it was represented; their dreadful accounts of its state being an echo of the representations that had been made to Government, and transmitted to General Hunter, who felt good reason to doubt their authority. However, the Major was not to be baffled, imposed upon, or disobeyed, and he perceived evident features of great disappointment exhibited by those who would fain dissuade him from his purpose, as they were conscious that the object of his mission was not according to their wishes, nay, that it must terminate directly contrary to them. The escort very reluctantly obeyed their orders, and on being dismissed galloped full speed back to Gorey, while the Major arrived in perfect safety at Donoughmore, in the Macomores, where he slept that night.

On the next morning, Mr. White and his son, who were beloved by the people, accompanied the Major to the place appointed for the meeting of the people; and soon after their arrival there, some yeomen, arrayed in military attire, were observed at some distance by the crowd. This instantly excited alarm, and a rumour was circulated that their extermination was determined on, and that they were led to this spot to be surrounded and cut off while the Major was to amuse them with terms and harangue! It is providential that the consternation and dismay produced by this incident did not operate to the Major's destruction, as it would have afforded the abettors of extermination every argument to fortify their representations; and it is to be hoped that the appearance of this military body was not intended for this purpose, in revenge for his unequivocally declared opinion of the misconduct of some of the yeomanry. The Major's death on this occasion would have put an end to all accommodation; and, from the very violent expressions used by the people, on thinking themselves betrayed, nothing but his coolness and presence of mind could have preserved him in so critical a juncture. He calmly waited for silence, and then offered himself as victim, should a military force of any consequence be seen to approach them, as his inspection the day before was to prevent all accidents of that nature; and stated that he could by no means account for that which occurred, but from the misconduct of some of the yeomanry.

This address instantly produced a thorough conviction of his indubitable sincerity and benevolent intentions, and the people unanimously surrendered to him, and continued to flock into Wexford for several days after, to give up their arms and receive protections. Major Fitzgerald considered it necessary to guard the roads with patrols of cavalry, to prevent the people from being insulted or interrupted in their return to their avowed allegiance; and General Hunter, being convinced of the expediency of protecting the harassed peasantry from the violence and machinations of party, ordered Captain Cornock, who was selected as an experienced officer, to protect the inhabitants of Macomores from the armed men closely adjoining their neighbourhood; and his corps was accordingly marched from Enniscorthy by Major Fitzgerald, together with a party of the Enniscorthy cavalry, under Lieutenant Sparrow, although there were five corps of yeomanry stationed in and near Gorey. Of these, that which attracted the greatest notice was under the command of Mr. Hunter Gowan, which it was found impossible to restrain from pillage and slaughter. It was after the rebellion was suppressed that this body received appointments as a cavalry corps, and as several of them were not owners of a horse, they took a speedy mode of mounting themselves without any expense. They scoured the country, as they termed it, and brought in without any ceremony the horses of the wretched cottagers. On a day of inspection by Major Fitzgerald, however, the poor claimants recovered their horses, and the *motley banditti*, as the Major termed them, were thus transformed into dismounted cavalry.

The false alarmists were not at all depressed or intimidated at these discomfitures; for although General Hunter reported the country as in a perfect state of tranquillity, they again returned to the charge and renewed their misrepresentations. Mr. Hawtrey White, captain of the Ballaghkeen cavalry, and a justice of the peace for the county, sent several informations to Government of the alarming state of the country; and the commanding officer at Gorey was so far persuaded of the intention of a general rising, that he quitted the town and encamped on the hill above it. These representations made under the semblance of loyalty, and by a person bearing the appearance and authority of a gentleman, had not, however, the wished-for weight with the Government. General Hunter was ordered to inquire into the information of Mr. Hawtrey White, and Major Fitzgerald was again sent out, and the result of his discriminating inquiry was, that the information was unfounded. Upon this the General ordered Mr. Hawtrey White to be brought to Wexford, and he was accordingly conducted thither with the greatest tenderness and humanity by Major Fitzgerald. He was then put under arrest at his lodgings, although it was first intended to have sent him to gaol.

Mr. White still persisted in maintaining that there was an encampment of the rebels (though not so numerous as he had previously represented it to be), on a rock of great extent in the sea, two miles from the land, whither the rebels retired in the daytime, after parading through the country at night; and he expressed a wish to be sent with a party by land, to intercept them in their progress to the shore. General Hunter, however, did not agree entirely to this proposal, as he was apprehensive that the people of the country might be alarmed at the appearance of Mr. White conducting a military force; and that they would be induced to fly at his approach, which might give some countenance to the information. But although he considered the island to be but imaginary, yet in order that truth should prevail over falsehood, he ordered a gunboat to convey Mr. White to the island he described, and that a party of military should be sent by land to cut off the rebels, when he should drive them from their sea-girt station.

In the meantime the captain of the gun-boat had orders to bring back Mr. White, to receive thanks for his extraordinary information, should it prove true, and to concert further measures for defence; but if found otherwise, to be dealt with accordingly. The sea and land expedition failed, in consequence of the described rock being found covered by the sea at the time, and, of course, if any rebels had been there, they must have been all drowned, when this new DELOS immerged into the deep! Mr. Hawtrey White was conducted back to Wexford, and General Hunter determined to bring him to a court-martial. Many gentlemen and ladies, however, interfered in the most earnest manner to prevent this investigation,

representing that Mr. White's great age might have
subjected him to the imposition of fabricated information; and the firmness of the General relaxed at the
instance of so many respectable persons. It is much
to be regretted that this inquiry did not take place,
as this and many other uncommon occurrences are
variously reported and believed, in different shapes
and forms, according to the bias or inclination, the
prejudice or the disposition of the narrators. The
General afterward regretted his clemency, as he was
not sensible at this period of the machinations
practised, and of the extent of party-prejudice, the
evil effects of which every day's experience convinced
him too fatally existed in the county of Wexford.
False alarms are always productive of the greatest
mischief, and are deemed in all countries offences of
the most dangerous tendency. Ireland has suffered
much by the tales of adventurers in these infernal
practices; but I am glad to perceive a growing
disposition to discountenance these pests of society,
who must, if continued to be encouraged, keep all
well-disposed persons in a constant state of alarm,
and screen the malignant intentions of their original
projectors from the infamy they so well deserve.

A court-martial, of which Lord Ancram was president, was instituted at Wexford for the trial of persons
accused of treason; and contrary to the expectation
and wishes of the committee for procuring evidence,
many were acquitted. Lord Ancram, however, soon
left the town, and his departure was much regretted
by the people; but his Lieutenant-Colonel, Sir James
Fowlis, of the Mid-Lothian cavalry, succeeded him as
president of the court-martial. To say merely that
he acquitted himself with honour and integrity, would
not be doing adequate justice to his merits. I believe
no judge ever sat on a bench that displayed more

judgment, discrimination, and mercy, in selecting the innocent and misled, from the criminal and the guilty; and his conduct inspired so much confidence throughout the country, as to induce such as were conscious of integrity to submit to trial, which they would not otherwise dare to do, from a well-founded opinion of the rancour of their accusers, who attempted at first to warp, and afterwards to counteract his upright intentions, which those who experienced them can alone appreciate. Was the character of Irishmen such, as too many have been led, from misrepresentation, to believe, would such a dignified character choose Ireland as his place of residence? Does it not rather appear that the result of numerous trials not only convinced him for the instant, but even left a lasting impression on his mind, that the people of Ireland were goaded into rebellion, notwithstanding the unnatural calumnies of those whose prejudice and bigotry urge them to revile their country!

General Hunter's object of conciliation was so evident, that many insurgent leaders were induced to surrender themselves to him, on obtaining protections. General Edward Roche surrendered on condition of transportation; and Major Fitzgerald accordingly brought him into Wexford, where he was lodged in the gaol. On the morning of the very day on which he submitted, a rumour had prevailed of the landing of the French in the west of Ireland, and although Mr. Roche accredited this rumour, it did not prevent him from surrendering. The landing of the French force, under Humbert, was officially transmitted to General Hunter, and he was ordered off with the Queen's and Twenty-ninth regiments of infantry. This sudden and unexpected news created great alarm, and many ladies and gentlemen were anxiously desirous to quit the country, as they had been at the commencement of the Insurrection, and were actually making preparations to that effect. The county of Wexford assuredly felt an impression of the general temper of Ireland at this critical period. The inhabitants of the territory of the Macomores, however (though led to believe on the first intelligence that their former enemies would resume their plan of desolation), were impressed with the fullest conviction, that they were rescued from extermination by the interference of Brigade-Major Fitzgerald, and the humane exertion of General Hunter's authority. Under this patronage and protection, therefore, they wished to remain (not knowing that the General had been ordered off). The spontaneous effect of their feelings on the occasion was manifested in an offer of their services to march against the French. The style and expression of their memorials to Major Fitzgerald and General Hunter, I will not attempt to describe in any language but their own: they are therefore inserted in the Appendix; and although altered, perhaps, and corrupted in style and orthography, as they have come to me, yet their force and sincerity are manifest.*

On the departure of General Hunter, the inhabitants of this county, as they received no answer to their memorials, were so alarmed, that they sent repeated remonstrances to Brigade-Major Fitzgerald, requesting his interference for protection. The Major, therefore, now thought it necessary to consult Sir James Fowlis, on the expediency of going into the Macomores, and Sir James esteemed it of such material consequence, that the proposal met his most hearty approbation. The Major, however was detained by his official situation for some days in Wexford; and during this time he received repeated messages, informing him that

* See Appendix, No. X.

Holt and Hackett had come from the county of Wicklow, and were tampering with the people, and using every means in their power to induce them to proceed with them to attack Dublin, which they represented at the time as destitute of regular troops, as Lord Cornwallis had led them all off to meet the French. From the general uncertainty of the public mind at this momentous period, with respect to the actual strength of the invasion; and from the subsequent accounts of the success of the French on the first onset, it may be very well supposed that the minds of a people so lately rescued from concerted extermination must be strongly affected, and ready to be influenced by the solicitations and remonstrances of the adventurers who came among them. It therefore required the utmost address and energy to fix their wavering opinions, and Brigade-Major Fitzgerald accordingly set out from Wexford for this purpose, and on the way he met different groups assembled in anxious uncertainty what to determine. These, however, on being assured by the Major that neither he nor Sir James Fowlis were to quit Wexford, under whom the people were sure of protection, all their fears and apprehensions were calmed. The Major represented that if they left the country, their wives and families who so lately escaped extermination, would be left destitute and defenceless at the mercy of their enemies, who would not fail to take advantage of their absence as a pretext for their destruction; and this argument prevailed.

Though many and various were the opinions Major Fitzgerald had to encounter, yet he pursued his intended course, and arrived that night at Donoughmore, and here he was further convinced of the representation of the people. He heard the signals of movement made by Holt and Hackett; but the people remained quietly at home, and suffered these adventurers to depart, accompanied only by those whom they originally brought along with them; and the intended attack upon Dublin was given up in consequence of the Wexford men not joining, for much reliance was placed on their exertions from the courage and intrepidity which they displayed in the course of the Insurrection.*

These incontrovertible facts give the lie so palpably to the calumniators of Ireland, that I cannot help adducing the testimony of an English lawyer of eminence nearly two centuries ago, but very applicable to our own time, of the character which the Irish have ever maintained. In 1620, Sir John Davies, then Attorney-General in Ireland, published a work on "The State of Ireland," in which he strongly asserts as follows:—"They will gladly continue in the condition of subjects without defection or adhering to any other lord or king as long as they may be protected

---

"Dublin, December 14, 1802.

* SIR,—I return, with my thanks for your polite attention, your manuscripts you were so kind as to leave for my perusal. Am exceedingly glad to find through the whole of your compilation so strict an observance of facts, which chiefly come under my cognisance as Brigade-Major. It is with pleasure I observe also your adherence to truth and impartiality—free from the rancorous spirit of party fabrication, which is the true criterion that exalts the historian above the class of party scribblers, who dissipate as rapidly as unerring truth unveils itself, strongly exemplified in the past and present times. I give you much credit in not retorting as you might for your unmerited sufferings, by exposing the crimes of some respectable persons; for, indeed, if they are not very forgetful and very insensible, the compunctions of their consciences must be sufficiently tormenting. There is little doubt of your labours meeting their due reward from an unprejudiced public, which is the wish of

"Your obedient humble servant,

"B. E. FITZGERALD.

"To EDWARD HAY, Esq."

and justly governed, without oppression on the one side or impunity on the other; for there is no nation under the sun that doth love equal and indifferent justice better than the Irish, or will rest better satisfied with the execution thereof, although it be against themselves, so as they may have the benefit and protection of the law, when upon just cause they do desire it." And again he says what is very applicable to the unfortunate situation of the people, "The Irish were out of the protection of the law, so that any Englishman might oppress, murder, or spoil them with impunity."

I cannot omit here mentioning the case of Mr. Walter Devereux, who, having obtained protections from several general officers, had gone to Cork to embark for Portugal. He was there taken up, tried, condemned, and executed. Mr. Gibson, a yeoman, and wealthy Protestant shopkeeper, and Mr. William Kearney, an extensive brewer, were summoned and attended at his trial, and proved that he was in Wexford, and even in gaol, at the very time some soldiers of the Wexford militia were shot thirty miles from that town; and the principal charge against him was, that he gave orders and was present at their execution, which some men of that regiment were hardened enough to swear! I myself saw him in Wexford on the alleged day. He was also accused of aiding and abetting the abomination at Scullabogue; and this charge was similarly supported by the testimony of some soldiers' wives; and yet it is an undoubted fact that he was all that day engaged at the battle of Ross, where he displayed the most heroical bravery and courage—qualities inconsistent with the odious crime it was falsely sworn he had perpetrated. But what puts the falsehood of the facts alleged against him beyond all question is, that after his execution, another Mr. Devereux was taken up on the discriminating sagacity of the same witnesses who prosecuted the former to death; but who (now as they said) discovered the *right* Devereux. The trial of the latter has been published, and I would recommend its perusal to such as wish for further proof of the miserable and lamentable condition of those existing in the county of Wexford during the Insurrection.

The following case is also distinguished for its peculiar hardship:—After the Insurrection the Rev. James Dixon was anxious to spend some time with his step-brother, Mr. Denis Butler, a merchant in Bristol, where he might enjoy that peace and tranquillity which the distracted state of his native country wholly precluded. His intentions were well known to the late Colonel Le-Hunte, who lived in the vicinity of Castlebridge, where Mr. Dixon resided, and had, therefore, the best possible opportunity of being acquainted with his unimpeachable conduct and demeanour, invited him to accompany his lady and family to England, where, on his landing, he was recognised by some of the incensed Wexford refugees, who immediately denounced him as a *Catholic priest*. By this outcry (and the prejudice against his order) those on the beach were roused to inflict severe treatment on him. It is probable that these *active prejudices* might have proved fatal, had not the *providential interposition* of the Rev. Mr. Draffen, the Protestant clergyman of the parish where the Rev. Mr. Dixon officiated as a Catholic priest, interposed in his favour, protected and covered him from the full exercise of their rage. This philanthropic divine was as distinguished for his loyalty as his attachment to the constitution of his country, and for his exemplary piety and abhorrence of rebellion. This act of manliness and goodness on the part of the Rev. Mr. Draffen cannot be too much extolled, and whilst it manifests the purest sentiments of Christianity, it cannot fail to impress the strongest conviction of the Rev. Mr. Dixon's innocence, which, along with other representations of the principal gentlemen of the county, laid before the Lord Lieutenant, did not prevent his transportation to Botany Bay. This innocent clergyman was brought back from Milford a prisoner, and lodged in Waterford gaol, where he was tried and condemned on evidence that is in every degree questionable; and, notwithstanding the strongest proofs of his innocence, yet prejudice was too triumphant on this occasion in preventing a reversal of his sentence.

The County of Dublin militia, who had distinguished themselves so much at the battle of Ross, under the command of Major Vesey, whose gallantry on that day afterward procured him the command of the regiment, were sent to Wexford; but a wound which the Colonel received at the battle of Enniscorthy prevented his coming with them, and the command, as well as that of the town, necessarily devolved upon Lieutenant-Colonel Finlay. On the night of the 8th of September, 1798, the turnkey of the gaol went round along with the guard (composed of Ogle's Blues, formerly the Shilmalier infantry) with general notice to all the prisoners, that if any riot should happen that night in any part of the county of Wexford, *the prisoners were all to be shot!* When these orders were so officially notified to me, I desired the turnkey begone about his business, for that *no officer would give such orders;* nor could I be persuaded that the orders were given, until the sergeant of the guard offered to save me from the massacre, as he said he had heard of my good actions during the rebellion. I could not but express my gratitude for such an offer of essential service; but I naturally felt great anxiety at the gloomy prospect before me, of which no doubt could now be entertained. The gaoler, whose humanity had been so successful in saving Mr. Bagnal Harvey, as I have related on a former occasion, was then in Dublin, being summoned before Parliament to prove that fact. I was, therefore, necessitated to write to Brigade-Major Fitzgerald an account of the transaction, and he without loss of time waited on Sir James Fowlis, and both instantly came down to the gaol, where, upon inquiry, they found my representation to be too true; but they took measures to counteract the execution of this denunciation, should it be attempted. The commanding officer of the town was supposed at that time to be too fast asleep (occasioned by a too free indulgence of the bottle) to attend to any remonstrance on the occasion.

The departure of General Hunter from Wexford was an irreparable loss to the county; but his presence proved a great blessing in Kilkenny, where he displayed his usual discrimination, judgment, and humanity in developing and unravelling the proofs of the melancholy situation of the persecuted inhabitants, who were consequently impressed with that confidence with which his noble and manly conduct never failed to inspire the oppressed. Although his absence was severely felt in the county of Wexford, yet his representation of its state to the Government had such a salutary effect as to prevent alarm from assuming so serious or formidable an aspect as before. Petty depredators, however, still continued their usual practices, and this they were enabled to do with the greater impunity, as, under general orders and martial law, the inhabitants were liable to be shot, and their houses burned, if discovered out at night.

The regular military, with the yeomen and their supplementaries, were the only persons privileged to be out between sunset and sunrise; and as the latter description of persons now received military pay, they were rendered independent of industry and labour (which ever and anon depraves the minds of working people), and having the enforcement of the general orders entrusted to them, depredations and excesses were committed by persons unknown, until the frequency of robbery and murder urged the necessity of furnishing the country farmers, at the discretion of the commanding officers, with arms for the defence of their families and properties. Some yeomen and supplementaries were consequently shot in attempting houses, and this plainly discovered who were the marauders. Indeed, it must be observed, that some outstanding insurgents were sometime after taken into company by the primary robbers, and that the religious and political differences of both parties were united in the consideration of mutual assistance in robbery and rapine. This multiplied the evil tenfold; and motley gangs of this description infested several parts of the country the winter after the Insurrection. This evil was remedied in some degree by sending out parties of soldiers from the towns into different parts of the country, to be there stationed; and it was considered an indulgence by most of the people, that a soldier was permitted to quarter upon them, and his protection was purchased by every kind of care and sedulous attention. It merits singular observation, that men were called upon to deliver up the identical sum they had collected or received by the sale of substance at fair, market, or by private hand, on the day previous to the night of attack; and although numbers could give information against the perpetrators of these enormities, yet they preferred silence of their wrongs to the risk of being murdered or burned in their houses, which others had experienced, and with which all were threatened if they would dare to inform.

The Orange system now became very prevalent throughout the county of Wexford, and was strengthened by the accession of almost every Protestant in it. This general promotion was forwarded by a received prejudice, that no man could be *loyal*, who was not an *Orangeman*. Doctor Jacob, who was captain of a yeomanry corps in Wexford, however, did not deem it at first an essential of loyalty to become an *Orangeman;* but he was afterward induced to alter his opinion, by a resolution entered into by a majority of his corps, that they would resign if he would not join the association. Not willing, therefore, to possess the mere *empty* title of *captain*, he condescended to gratify their wishes.

It has not yet come to pass, that any political association has invariably adhered to the principles that dictated their original formation; as some individuals generally dictate to the body at large, and raise themselves to consequence by the support of their adherents, who cannot recede without deviating from an avowed principle of honour, which binds them together; and the society thus shoves its leaders into consequence, and these frequently, when they find another opportunity of benefiting themselves, secede and make way for new adventurers to succeed them, and the same routine takes place, so that the individuals of a political society are so far not their own masters, but are led on by party on various occasions, to give public sanction to what they inwardly disapprove. I, however, know valuable and estimable characters possessing the utmost integrity, members of political societies, and whose motives and conduct are unexceptionable; and although I approved of their principles and actions, yet I have ever and always avoided entering into any political society, from a consideration, that I might thereby be obliged to surrender my opinion contrary to my inclination, and would not, therefore, feel myself thoroughly independent.

From a review of the many and various political societies and parties in this unaccountable age, I have observed, that in the most perilous times well-disposed persons, unconnected with party, have escaped, where others, venturing into societies, have been cut off, for no other reason but their association has been inimical to some other that in the turn of affairs gained an ascendency. And thus has one political society risen on the destruction of another; while a true lover of his country, individually engaged in the pursuit of whatever is for its advantage, has outlived the storm. Most political societies avow their sentiments publicly, with a view of obtaining general approbation. My information does not, however, enable me to give a sketch of the two rival societies of *United Irishmen* and *Orangemen*, whose rivalry has indeed been productive of such serious consequences in Ireland. I must therefore refer my readers to the *memoire* and examination of Messrs. O'Connor, Emmet, and M'Nevin, published in London and Dublin, since the rebellion, as the most authentic account extant of the rise, progress, and ultimate views of the former society; but I must also observe, that the utmost extent of the information during the Insurrection in the county of Wexford was the oath of admission and secrecy: and with respect to the latter society, I can make no authentic reference whatever.

Orange associations became at length so general and indiscriminate, that their members could by no means be considered capable of constituting a select assemblage, as multitudes of them were of the lowest and most uninformed vulgar, and of course subject to the weakest passions, prejudices and frailties of human nature. Many of them certainly did no honour to the association. But it must be also said of United Irishmen, that individuals of them, contrary to the avowed principles of union and brotherhood, which they were sworn to preserve, disgraced themselves by acts quite opposite to the spirit of their institution. Freemasonry, though very generally embraced throughout Ireland, has yet escaped similar imputation, which I believe is owing to its being rather a social and moral than political fraternity.

I have conversed with many gentlemen who avowed themselves *Orangemen*, and whose conduct and principles I have every reason to suppose honourable; yet, I have heard them declare, that they would by no means graduate in the society, but remain in the state of simple *Orangemen*, not meaning in any degree to compare these honourable men to the *Orange informers* in Wexford, on the 20th of June, 1798, who said they had not taken the *purple* degree of the order. How the conduct of persons assuming the name of *Orangemen*, in the county of Wexford, may be viewed by the association at large, I know not; but truth imposes on me the task of relating the melancholy consequences of the conduct of some who avowed themselves *Orangemen*. After the Insurrection in the county of Wexford was suppressed, *Orangemen* wore ribands and medals without any disguise; and on the death of an *Orangeman*, the general decorations of black were laid aside, and orange substituted at their wakes and funerals. After the interment, houses have been burned, alleged to be in retaliation for the previous conduct of *Croppies*, whose houses were adjacent to the church-yard. Not unfrequently, on the night of a well-attended funeral, or after a rejoicing day, a Catholic chapel was consumed; and the frequency of these conflagrations manifests the most rancorous spirit of intolerance and inveterate party prejudice!

What makes these transactions more lamentable is, that not a single person has as yet been punished or even arrested for the perpetration of these crimes. Is it possible this could be the case but through the supineness of the magistracy? How could the repetition and impunity of such acts be otherwise accounted for, but from their not doing their duty? and does not such neglect necessarily imply connivance? From my knowledge of the country, I would venture to stake my existence, that I would discover the perpetrators, had I the assistance of an English or Scotch regiment to protect those who could give information from the merciless fury of these incendiaries; and it is much to the disgrace of the country that this is not accomplished. A reward of one hundred pounds was offered for the discovery of those that had burned Catholic chapels by the grand jury of the county of Wexford, at the Summer Assizes in 1799, published in some Dublin papers, which however produced no information.

Chapels burned in the County of Wexford and Diocese of Ferns, with the Dates of their respective Conflagration.

Boolevogue	. May 27, 1798	Ballegarret	. Jan. 15,	1799
Maglass	. May 30, 1798	Ballinamonabeg	. Jan. 18,	1799
Ramsgrange	. June 19, 1798	Askamore	. Feb. 24,	1799
Drumgold	. June 21, 1798	Murntown	. Apr. 24,	1799
Ballemurrin	. June 21, 1798	Monamoling	. May 3,	1799
Gorey	. Aug. 24, 1798	Kilrush	. May 15,	1799
Annacurragh	. Sept. 2, 1798	Marshalstown	. June 8 or 9	1799
Crane	. Sept. 17, 1798	Munfin	. June do.	1799
Rock	. Oct. 12, 1798	Crossabeg	. June 24,	1799
Balleduff	. Oct. 19, 1798	Killeneerin	. June 29,	1799
Riverchapel	. Oct. 19, 1798	Monageer	. July 1,	1799
Monaseed	. Oct. 25, 1798	Kiltayley	. Oct. 1,	1799
Clologue	. Oct. 26, 1798	Glanbryan	. Mar. 13,	1799
Killeveny	. Nov. 11, 1798	Kaim	. Sept. 3,	1800
Ferns	. Nov. 18, 1798	Ballimackesey	. Sept.	1800
Oulart	. Nov. 28, 1798	Courtenacuddy	. Aug. 13,	1801
Castletown	. Nov. 1798			

The Protestant church of Old Ross was burned on the 2nd of June, 1798.

These and many other shocking deeds could not have been constantly reiterated throughout the country, were the magistrates willing to do their duty; and it is astonishing that the country gentlemen could so far forget their own real interests, which are superseded by the narrow and prejudiced notions with which they are blindfolded. It will scarcely be believed that such neglect was possible; and the gentlemen themselves will lament it hereafter, when they come to their sober recollections, and feel the melancholy effects of religious prejudice, in the inevitable consequences of leaving such acts unpunished; which, although they did not actually commit themselves, yet they have encouraged them by their inactivity and negligence.

It is to be observed that the Insurrection was completely suppressed in the county of Wexford, in June, 1798, previous to, and during which period, five Catholic chapels appear to have been burnt, and the remaining conflagrations took place when the country was not disturbed by any other transactions but these enormities, perpetrated when the utmost tranquillity otherwise prevailed. Various depredations and excesses were also committed through the country. Murders were prevalent, houses were burnt, and notices were posted on the doors of many Catholics, desiring them to quit their habitations, of a similar tendency with those in the county of Armagh in the year 1795. The notices in the counties of Wexford and Wicklow, prevalent in 1798, 1799, and 1800, were conceived pretty nearly in the following terms:—"*A—— B—— we give you notice in six days to quit—or if you don't, by G—, we will visit your house with fire, and yourself with lead. We are the grinders—Moll Doyle's true grand-sons.*"

These and such like notices were posted on the

doors of Catholics in the night, and many quitted their houses and habitations in consequence of some of these threats being put into actual execution. I shall cite an example of these dreadful practices, exemplified in the case of Mr. Swiny, a Protestant gentleman, who resided for several years in Yorkshire, and had an estate called Court, between Oulart and Ballecanow, which was tenanted by many Catholics, whose leases expired in 1799; but who, by the prevailing system, were rendered incapable to retake their farms, as their houses were all burnt, and all the property they possessed destroyed. But what manifested this business quite systematic was, that notices were posted up afterwards through the country, purporting that *no Papist should presume to take the lands;* and that, *if even a son of Moll Doyle should offer more than half-a-guinea an acre* (worth fifty shillings), *he should forfeit all privileges of the fraternity, and undergo the same punishment for his transgression as if he was a Papist.* The lands of Court thus proscribed, remained waste for nearly two years! Is it not melancholy to reflect that this and many such manifest outrages, but more prevalent in the Macomores than any other part of the county, did not rouse the feelings of landlords, at a time that their own interests were so closely connected with the suppression of such deeds? And yet the tribe of middlemen seems to have so much influence, as to be able still to keep up the like occurrences, in the hope that they might benefit by the destruction or banishment of the great majority of the people. Miserable policy, that low minds alone, debased by prejudice, can harbour! These cannot be sensible that the population of a country constitutes its principal advantage, and is what enables them to raise themselves on a foundation of which they meditate the destruction, and thus endanger the superstructure which they wish to enjoy; not perceiving that it must totter, when so undermined, and involve themselves in the general ruin!

Courts-martial continued to sit in Wexford for nearly three years after the Insurrection, although the regular assizes and general gaol delivery were resumed in the spring of 1799. Prisoners confined in the gaol of Wexford were parcelled out into different lots, to be tried by the civil and military tribunals, according to the discrimination of the gentlemen of the county! Others have been arraigned at an assizes, and on showing legal cause had their trials put off to the next; when the judge has called for prisoners not produced, although returned on the Crown book, then it has been discovered that they had been handed over to a military tribunal, and according to their sentences had been transported or hanged. With the utmost respect and veneration, I look up to that great bulwark of the Constitution, TRIAL BY JURY; and shall always esteem juries less liable to bias than any other mode of trial. However, it so came to pass in the county of Wexford, from various occurrences that took place, that many prisoners preferred to be tried by a *military* rather than a *civil* tribunal, which the conduct of Sir James Fowlis contributed to inculcate. It would, however, be great injustice not to mention that the judges of the realm who presided in the criminal court in Wexford distinguished themselves by their benevolent humanity, and the most liberal construction of the Amnesty Bill; and whenever religious prejudice or party spirit broke out, they were not backward in expressing their dissatisfaction. They supported their just judgment with manly dignity, and by their recommendations rescued some from execution, on whom the laws of the land obliged them to pronounce sentence, and thus were actuated by the god-like virtues of justice and mercy. I most sincerely hope no other opportunity may ever occur of making any comparison between *courts-martial* and *trial by jury*. God grant that juries will ever hold in their minds the true spirit of impartiality, and then we shall ever consider them as the true basis of a free constitution.

Another kind of depredators made their appearance in the county of Wexford in the course of the winter of 1798 and 1799. They assembled in the wood of Kilaughrim, between Enniscorthy and Scollagh-gap, and were denominated among other appellations "*the babes of the wood.*" Independent of some outstanding insurgents, deserters from different regiments associated in this band, and they levied small contributions throughout the country. Those immediately in their vicinity were to supply their quota in provisions, while those at a distance were called upon for money, which was supplied in general without opposition, to avoid greater violation, as they, for the most part, behaved civilly if freely given, and did not at all pursue the merciless conduct of the depredators already noticed.

Different military detachments were sent out from Ross and Enniscorthy, and these endeavoured to surround the extensive woods of Kilaughrim, supposed to contain them, but their efforts proved fruitless, as they never could come up with the *babes in the wood*, who generally had a rendezvous in the night, and dispersed towards morning, into such a variety of lurking places that but few of them were apprehended, and though several plans for their annihilation were contrived, they all proved ineffectual. The activity of Brigade-Major Fitzgerald was again called forward, and he brought them to a consent of surrender; but, however, since the recall of General Hunter, who would have immediately put a final stop to their proceedings (his absence on this occasion was productive of serious evil), instead of the *babes of the wood* surrendering on condition of being suffered to enlist in the army, they continued their predatory system, during which they were occasionally visited by Holt and Hackett, and some of their associates, but most of them at last surrendered to Captain Robinson of the South Cork militia. Some of these were sent to Prussia, others enlisted into different regiments, and some were executed at Newtownbarry. A few who did not surrender, not thinking it prudent to continue in their old haunts, abandoned the county of Wexford, and joined the marauders in the county of Wicklow.

Estimates of the actual damages in consequence of the conflagration of the Catholic chapels were made out by order of the Government of Ireland, and the sums so awarded paid out of the Treasury for rebuilding them. Many persons who at stated times had received certain proportions of their losses during the rebellion have bitterly complained and expressed their apprehensions that the rebuilding of the Catholic chapels was to be defrayed out of the fund for the relief of the suffering loyalists. This scheme of supply must be considered very political, had it the effect of preventing the reiteration of these enormities, which many consider it had. Government has thus interposed in favour of *public Catholic property*. I therefore cannot conceive it is intended to exclude *Catholics individually;* yet it is almost exclusively the case in the county of Wexford, occasioned by the existing deep-rooted religious prejudice! Was the conduct of these *public accusers* to undergo the same scrutiny they have subjected others to, they would not appear in so favourable a light to the world as they wish to maintain. Poor claimants have been constrained to *prosecute* against their inclinations, to prove their *loyalty* sufficiently not to exclude them from payment! I, therefore, imagine that all

Catholics against whom there does not exist any charge but general prejudice ought not to be debarred of this privilege, as well as all those who on trial have been honourably acquitted, as many have withheld their just claims from the apprehension of the general prejudice entertained against Catholics. The case of Mr. Edmund Stafford is peculiarly apposite. This gentleman claimed as a suffering loyalist, and I am confident no person in the county was more deserving of that title; yet for daring to do so, he was accused and arraigned for murder on the discriminating sagacity of evidence that had been the cause of the execution of many, but whose villainy was not *publicly* known until the trial of Mr. Stafford could not be put off, and he was discharged without trial after a confinement of several months, *for presuming to enrol his name among the suffering loyalists.*

Although the conduct of the militia regiments, it might be naturally hoped, was such as to defy the possibility of any reflection on their behaviour, yet prejudice operated so strongly in some of them that the officers behaved in so partial a manner as to induce Catholics particularly to offer themselves as volunteers to serve in different regiments of the line. These afterward formed a considerable part of the army sent to Egypt. Many, who were doomed to transportation, were also sent on that expedition. Then it was considered a fortunate circumstance that these were sent out of Ireland, not from any idea, however, that they would have been the means of redounding to the fame of the British army, and immortalising their glory, by the courage and intrepidity they displayed, that must for ever silence their indiscriminate calumniators. I wish those who have been in the habit of dealing out illiberal opinions respecting Irish Catholics, may keep the conduct of these in recollection, as it may induce them to join in praise of men whom they ought to endeavour to imitate. They might thus too become sensible of the inestimable value to any country of such men, as with proper encouragement, they would be invincible, and so prove the most impenetrable bulwark and consequent support to the Constitution, far superior to anything which the system of coercion can possibly effect, and this irrefragable truth, I hope, may have its due weight.

At the Summer Assizes of Wexford, in 1801, James Redmond was tried and condemned for the murder of the Rev. Robert Burroughs, a Protestant clergyman, at Oulard, on Whitsunday, the 27th of May, 1798; and pursuant to his sentence, was executed on the 30th of July, and his body delivered to the surgeons, who after dissecting it permitted it to be taken away, and it was buried. The corpse was dug up out of its grave, and placed in the shed erected for the priest to officiate, on the site of the Catholic chapel of Monamoling, which had been burned. This exhibition was not discovered till the congregation had assembled to hear Mass on the Sunday following, the 3rd of August, 1801. Although this man was guilty of murder, yet there is something so vastly shocking in disturbing the dead in their graves, and repugnant to human nature, that the vilest of pikemen never were guilty of such a transaction in all their uncontrollable sway. Independent of the savage disposition of this occurrence, the disregard for religion is so manifest, that it is the more lamentable, as it keeps alive those prejudices which it is so much the interest of all parties to suppress.

The ratification of the Treaty of Peace with the French Republic has brought back many who were distinguished in fighting for their country in the navy and army; and these, upon their return home, found many of their relatives destroyed; and on being informed who the depredators were, they were induced to accost them at different fairs and *patrons* throughout the country, intimating that they had proved themselves loyal men by fighting the enemies of their country, and not by murdering their neighbours or friends, or burning their houses. These altercations constantly produced fights, and the result, though it has disturbed the public peace, yet it has corrected, in some degree, the overbearing contempt in which some high-spoken gentry held the generality of the people, whom they now condescend to respect through these their relatives; nay, they treat with more reserve some of the very insurgents who have returned from transportation, after having obliterated all stain of previous political delinquency by their subsequent exploits in the service of their country —and thus do the brave ever awe cowards into shame and submission! The rooted aversion, however, which has been by various means encouraged and inculcated against the great body of the people, has led many to adopt the most illiberal expressions; and I am sorry to learn that it is a prevalent notion to deplore the existence of the Amnesty Bill, as it precludes the accomplishment of the views of exterminating those who are protected by it from indiscriminating vengeance!

Those who make use of such language seem to have no notion of the crimes which call to heaven for vengeance! I would recommend to those who express such an illiberal and shocking sentiment to reflect seriously, whether they are not protected by the Indemnity Bills, as they might otherwise be exhibited on the gibbet. Let these unreflecting assertors of prejudice look to the fate of Governor Wall of Goree. The recurrence of their own deeds to their minds, by such a contemplation, may, perhaps, produce hearty contrition for their past misconduct, and may induce them to make what reparation remains in their power for the many injuries, in various shapes, which they have committed!

Though justice did not overtake the Governor of Goree for twenty years, yet then the recital of his horrid crime of ordering a soldier, whom he considered refractory, to be lashed, which produced death, roused the English nation, and exemplary punishment was the consequence! If this solitary case which regarded a distant colony, excited so much indignation in the breasts of Englishmen, can the same people overlook similar and greater deeds of atrocity committed a thousand times over against the Irish now incorporated with themselves? Can the feelings of any wise, just, and good man be withheld from most earnest endeavours to contribute all in his power to the coalescence and harmony of all parts, as well as of all ranks of the United Kingdom? and if that desirable object be attainable—and I do believe that by proper management it can be effected—who is the monster that will oppose its accomplishment? But it must not, it cannot be opposed. A merciful and benevolent sovereign, whose throne is now supported by consolidated dominion, and the united attachment of all his people, will not suffer so valuable a portion of them as the great majority of the Irish to be debased and degraded by thraldom the most intolerable, while they are deemed to man his fleets and armies in a proportion greater than the one-half, and display the most unrivalled bravery in his service, bearing terror and dismay to his enemies. He will certainly recommend them for relief from oppression to his Imperial Parliament, who will not forfeit the character of wisdom and justice, or the name of the most dignified legislature on earth, by being swayed by the tales of rancour, misrepresentation, and prejudice. They will redress, as truth and reason direct, a magnanimous and virtuous people, groaning under a partial tyranny, in the midst of an empire denominated free, to which they would be an incalculable accession of strength, if pro-

T

tected from oppression, persecution, torture, and the dread of threatened and meditated extermination—if secured *effectually* in their lives, liberties, and properties, without impeachment of their religion and principles; but should this be neglected and their grievances left a galling incumbrance upon them, in consequence of malevolent and fabricated calumnies, there will surely abide a rankling discontent, likely at all times to produce disturbance and distraction, which must necessarily weaken and paralyse the energies of the State, and, perhaps, eventually annihilate the connection between these countries. I would earnestly advise the most violent and unthinking supporters of division to consider their own real interests as connected and involved with the peace and happiness of the nation (which an impartial picture of the miseries experienced can best inculcate), as well as to dissipate the misconceptions of error, and to disprove the false representations which have been sent abroad, with zealous industry, to impose on and mislead public feeling.

My real object and earnest wishes are for conciliation; but if a doubt can possibly arise respecting my statements, I can only say that I could detail more numerous enormities than I have, and of which I entertain as little doubt as of those I have related. I have, therefore, confined myself to facts and circumstances vouched to me beyond the possibility of doubt, for which I can produce good authorities, and on this occasion limit my narrative to my native district, where my local and personal knowledge were least liable to deception or misinformation; and should the Members of both Houses of the Imperial Parliament deem it necessary, in their wisdom, to investigate the truth decisively, I will stake my existence that my relation shall be found, on an impartial scrutiny, extremely moderate.

APPENDIX.

No. I.

THE SPEECH OF EDWARD SWEETMAN,

CAPTAIN OF A LATE INDEPENDENT COMPANY,

At a Meeting of the Freeholders of the County of Wexford, convened by the Sheriff, on September 22, 1792, to take into consideration "Mr. Edward Byrne's letter, recommending a plan of Delegation to the Catholics of Ireland, in order to prepare an humble Petition to the Legislature."

MR. SHERIFF—I rise with a diffidence proceeding from the magnitude and awfulness of the subject, not from respect to the resolutions I have heard, which I deem exceptionable in every part; a circumstance which the silence of those who bring them forward would seem to acknowledge. I implore your attention whilst I deliver some thoughts, which are the fruit of my best researches, my honester feelings, and the unextinguishable love I bear this ill-fated country. I shall not consider the language or grammar of Mr. Byrne's letter—it is beneath the dignity of this meeting, and this great question, to descend to an altercation with inquisitors of words and dissectors of syllables: I shall enter into the subject at large, and speak to the scope and object of the letter, as it affects Ireland, and as it is the expression of Catholic hopes and desires. You will not expect brilliant remarks and exquisite deductions of reasoning from a man born a victim to the

Popery laws, and driven at an early period into foreign climes, for prohibited, imperfect education, and scanty bread. I shall speak like a soldier, with candour and with frankness, yet with respect and fear of offending, unmoved by slander, uninfluenced by any thing but truth. Truth is libel, faction, sedition, and treason in the eyes of those who live by its opposite, but it is the only criterion of honesty, the only basis of lasting settlement to your country, and every lover of it should utter it with courage, and hear it with patience. I belong to no party; I am an Irishman; I care as little for those who are in as for those who are out: I am the humble but the sincere and unbought advocate of a woe-worn people. I therefore conjure you to hear me, and forgive my inaccuracies and inexperience in speaking.

I know that honoured names, illustrious patriots, characters which Ireland must ever revere and love, men who led her to freedom and to fame—one of whom (Mr. Ogle) I behold in this assembly, with many mixed sensations—and who won the principle of prosperity from our common tyrants, a principle which remains a dead letter without the union of your people; I know, I say, that some of these differ in opinion with the persons whom I take to be the best and most enlightened friends of Ireland: I know this, and I lament it; and in it I lament the deplorable inconsistency of human nature, with the same poignancy that I lament the unaccountable but most certain fact, that the wise, the virtuous, the philosophic, the magnanimous Julian was a persecutor. In the face of those men whom I revere, as I hope I should in the face of death, I venture to stand forward the advocate of this woe-worn people, because I think it is for the honour of the Irish Crown, for the credit and consistency of Protestantism, for the prosperity and fame of your country, that British privileges should be restored to all who are the supporters of British and Irish freedom.

I wish for equal fate and equal freedom to every loyal subject in his Majesty's dominions. Upon no other terms do I wish Ireland connected with any country. Upon those conditions I wish it for ever confederated with England. Those objects cannot be attained till Catholics are emancipated, and Catholics cannot be emancipated till they obtain the elective franchise, and an equal participation of the benefits of trial by jury. Whilst their liberties, their properties, and their lives are at the mercy of those over whom they have no control, nor can acquire a control, it will not be contended the Catholics are free. Taxed without being represented, bound without their consent, and tried by their *superiors*, the Protestants, and not by their peers, their situation is the very definition of slavery, unmitigated, unqualified by any thing but a fleeting liberality, which may perish with the fashion of the hour.

I have said, it was for the honour of the Irish Crown that Catholics should be emancipated, because I conceive that honour to be deeply interested in, and inseparably interwoven with, the question. The honour of the Irish Crown has been perpetually violated by a perpetual breach of faith with the Irish, ever since our English ancestors first landed in this island. They were induced to come hither by a tyrant and a ravisher, and their political conduct and yours (for we have been all guilty alike) has never once belied the principles of their introducer. Henry the Second granted the Irish the common law of England, and they gratefully received and swore to the observance of it. They, in justice, became entitled to the benefit of that law. Instead of this, every means

which fraud could invent, avarice suggest, or violence
enforce, were employed to plunder and destroy the
brave and simple aborigines of the isle, whilst the duty
of their kings, whom they had sworn to obey, and
who from that instant were bound to protect them,
slumbered, or rather presided over these cruel outrages
upon human nature. Sir John Davies says, the old
Irish were out of the protection of the law, so that
any Englishman might oppress, spoil, or murder them
with impunity. Sir John was certainly possessed of a
better understanding, and had more honesty than most
Englishmen who have ever blessed us with their
presence in this island: yet he was an *Englishman,
that is, a foe to Irish freedom,* and wished to throw
the whole blame of these horrible and absurd oppressions, as Hume phrases them, upon the English settlers.
Those settlers were guilty of innumerable villainies to
the ancient Irish; yet they wished not that their
enmities should be immortal, like modern settlers, but
sought at last to bury all animosity in the mutual
peace and harmony of a final coalition and incorporation. What did the English-Irish king of the day?
Alarmed at this incipient incorporation and prospect
of happiness held out to the people, he dispatches his
grandson, Lionel, Duke of Clarence, to counteract it,
and to revive the dying embers of civil discord. This
prince passed the famous statutes of Kilkenny, so
much extolled by England, and the slaves of England,
that once more sowed the seeds of that everlasting
hostility which divided the sons of Ireland from each
other, and has subsisted in one horrid shape or other
to this very day. The English settlers, inflamed by
those diabolical laws, became the executioners of
English vengeance and hatred, and the base procurers
to English passions. The proscribed natives were
driven into rebellion, and then dispossessed of their

property, for the unavoidable effects of the crimes of their oppressors. You see I feel little propensity to canonize the vices and follies of my ancestors, like some noble lords,* who might justify the massacre of St. Bartholomew's day and the fires of Smithfield upon the same silly principle of mistaken pride. Near four hundred years passed away, during this dreadful scene of misery, rapine, and blood, in all which period, every virtue was invoked, whilst every crime was perpetrated. The sword of war was at length sheathed, and the sword of justice commenced the work of extermination. The English now availed themselves of every chicanery of law to oust the natives from their remaining lands. They did this without danger, for they did it with fraud, by the safe and bloodless methods of statutable plunder. In these iniquitous proceedings they were sanctioned by their king—the king of Ireland! This royal miscreant confiscated six entire counties without having found or looked for an evidence of guilt, whilst he boasted of his descent from the ancient inhabitants whom he spoiled. Subsequent kings have not been less faithless to Ireland. The insincerity and tyranny of the blessed martyr—the profligacy and ingratitude of Charles the Second—the holy impositions, the cowardice and bigotry of James, have been all equally fatal to, all equally levelled against Ireland. Your glorious deliverer's open and avowed suppression of our native and favourite manufacture will be no recommendation to any body who is a lover of Ireland. That he confirmed you in your estates is partly true ; but it is much more true, that you dearly bought that advantage by the sacrifice of the independence, trade, commerce, manufactures, prosperity, and name of your country. He drove a

* Lords Enniskillen and Aldborough.

Dutch bargain with you, and you bartered your freedom for a paltry consideration. You and the Catholics since have been set at variance, in order to govern you with a more easy iniquity, contrary to the duty and honour of your kings—the solemn faith of treaties has been violated by the house of Hanover, in the first of George the Second, by which the Catholics were deprived of the elective franchise, their inalienable right—the price of their blood—the honourable condition of their capitulation at Limerick. I therefore say, it is for the honour of the Irish Crown that King George the Third should repair the wrongs of his predecessors to a loyal and unfortunate race: for though he is not the original author of these wrongs, yet as the king never dies, he is in some degree chargeable with the wrongs continued under his government, and stands accountable in his reputation for the evil he is at no pains to prevent. The recommendation of this late act of justice from the throne, will become him full as well as the recommendation of charter schools. He should at last remember, that allegiance and protection are reciprocal. He should bear in mind, that he no longer deserves to be a king, who systematically ceases to be just to millions of his subjects.

The credit of Protestantism and its consistency is equally involved in this great question of Catholic Emancipation. The Protestants abandoned the Roman Catholic religion for one fundamental reason amongst others: because they pronounced its followers to be persecutors upon principle, and to want charity, that grand desideratum in Ireland, without which religion itself is rather a curse than a blessing. They should now abandon the Protestant religion for the same reason, if they are true to their original principles: for the Protestants of Ireland have been persecutors—unrelenting, inquisitorial persecutors, for upwards of two hundred years. But the spirit of neither religion is persecution—bad priests, bad ministers, bad Parliaments, and bad kings have perverted the principles of both, for the purpose of fixing a lawless yoke on the necks of their fellow-creatures. *Sanctis nominibus rapere imperium*, has been their maxim. Good Protestants and good Catholics have ever reprobated these sanctified iniquities. The worthy Cardinal Pole, in the reign of the sanguinary Queen Mary, though a Catholic upon principle, recommended toleration; Bishop Gardiner, though ready to conform to any religion for interest, taught that persecution was lawful. The history of the Jewish and the Christian religions incontrovertibly proves the truth of that axiom in the schools—that what is best, when corrupted, becomes worst. The purer the worship, the more abominable has been the persecution it gave rise to, and the more corrupt the morality practised in its name. The name of God has been the watchword for the abominations of man. The religion of the Jews was pure and sublime—their manners and disposition detestable: the religion of the ancient Egyptians was absurd and impious—their manners and government were the glory of humanity and model of nations. The same moral mischief I have described amongst the Jews must unquestionably be produced again, when more trust is reposed in faith than in charity; in profession than good works. The knave professes anything—the honest man practises without profession. A poet, who knew man and woman well, writes:—

> Whoever's faith is than his neighbour's more,
> If man, believe him rogue.

Your Popery laws engender and propagate this evil with a foul increase. They punish a belief in Catholics, which, being harmless, should be allowed without the infliction of disabilities; and they condemn principles which Catholics have abjured in words, and ever proved to be false charges by their actions. You give the reward of honesty, loyalty, and patriotism—I mean the right of citizenship—to oaths, to nugatory declarations and abjurations. For a bare recantation of the faith of his fathers, and hard anti-Christian swearing, puts your Catholic neighbour instantly upon a footing with yourself, whilst all the virtues which Christ or Socrates ever thought or practised, would leave him a slave without it. Do you not daily see the effect of these laws? Does it not require great fortitude in an honest man to become a convert, and expose himself to the obloquy and suspicion of both parties? Are not the generality of those who apostatize to your religion the basest of mankind? Do they not slanderously abuse, and rancorously persecute the wretches they have forsaken? And yet, those creatures are caressed and courted, whilst honest Catholics are despised and trampled on! Thus your laws become a premium to vice — a penalty on virtue. Judge, then, if the continuation of this vile system can do credit to the Protestant religion. No!—it takes from you at once all pretensions to Protestantism and Christianity.

It is equally fatal to the prosperity and fame of your country in every particular. It has been truly said, that oppression is a smothered warfare: it annihilates the peace and comfort of society. Can the Protestant esteem the Catholic he dooms to slavery? Can the Catholic love his oppressor? They are both hypocrites if they pretend to it. They must in the present state of things most inevitably hate and fear one another. It is the law of nature, which laughs to scorn the unnatural institutions of man, and what can you expect from such a situation? Does not the tranquillity of your country hang by a thread, and are you still determined to leave it in this feverish, tremulous existence? You have been bred in a contempt for Catholics—a contempt originally instilled by your oppressors, the English, and which they are by no means sparing of to yourselves. And indeed none of us have been totally wronged by our kind and affectionate sister: for we have not respected ourselves. America has respected herself, and therefore she is respected. She has performed a very arduous task —she has taught Englishmen manners. But the English have grossly deceived you in their description of your countrymen. They have refused them credit for every good quality, and fixed the stigma of every bad one upon them. They have denied them courage and understanding—that they persuade them and the world that they had neither sense to perceive, nor spirit to assert their rights. But I tell you again they have grossly deceived you.

There is not in Europe a nobler peasantry than the peasantry of Ireland, the great body of the people you have enslaved. The English began their system of calumny against the Irish, not before they began to despoil them. Had they reported them as an innocent people, they would have wanted a pretext for their undoing. You will find the proof of this in the Venerable Bede, who loads them with the highest praise, and the lying Giraldus Cambrensis, who covers them with foul reproach. Sir John Davis acknowledges this race of men to be endued with extraordinary abilities of mind and body ; and that there is no people under heaven who love equal and indifferent justice better than the Irish. The enlightened Doctors Young and Campbell do them the same justice. The immortal Swift, in a posthumous work which has lately appeared, declares that the common Irish who understand English, have a much better taste for reason and raillery than the English of the same description. Lord Chesterfield and Adam Smith call them the most able-bodied and handsome men in Europe. Camden testifies that they are incredibly active, ingenious, and warlike. British adjutants inform you that they are made soldiers sooner than any subjects in the three kingdoms; and America, Hindostan, and Europe bear witness to the ardour and firmness of their courage. See then the gallant race of men you have to govern, and reflect how you have governed them! You have endeavoured to unman them, and reduce them to the level of the beasts that perish. Bereft by law of almost every stimulus to industry — precluded from education, foreign and domestic—from conjugal connection with their favoured brethren—from every blessing, civil and political—it is a miracle that they have retained anything human but the shape. The prototype of your policy, Machiavel, in the eighth chapter of his *Prince*, lays it down as a maxim, that cruelty may be necessary in a recent settlement acquired by war and crimes, but if prolonged beyond that necessity, that it ultimately proves the ruin of its upholders. You have outstripped your model: take care how you verify his prophetic observation. When the city of Sparta was overthrown by an earthquake, the helots surveyed the visitation with rapture, and redoubled the horrors of the calamity. Your Protestant settlement is secure beyond the probability, nay, the possibility of dangers, if you do not continue the temptation, and the language of the Constitution might add the duty to uproot it, in the hearts of those whom you mean to destroy. You have nothing to fear from those miserable beings whose ancestors' estates the chance of war delivered into your hands one hundred and thirty-eight years since. Most of them have perished in exile and in want. Some of them are fighting the battles of foreign kings, being incapacitated even from DYING for their own. Their sad remains are the porters of your towns, the clowns of your country, and beggars of your streets. They do not look for power; they ask but leave to die. The Catholics have given you every security which the most solemn declarations can give: you have a much better security in their uniform demeanour, and still a better in their interest—that interest

> Which, like the sword of kings,
> Is the last reason of all things.

It is the interest of every honest and independent mind in Ireland that the smothered warfare of oppression should cease; that the feelings, the prejudices, the passions, the faculties of all should be collected into one common focus, to cheer, re-animate and illumine this aggrieved, palsied, and long-benighted country. Have you not had enough of vengeance and petty despicable monopoly, or are you still resolved to persist in it even at the expense of your own well-being and honour? Is not your country a prey to foreigners through the imbecility entailed upon it by emasculating four-fifths of your people? Were the provisoes, indulgences, and mortmains of Popery in any degree so pernicious as the ruin and ignominy of English influence? Impostors delude you, whilst they are practising ancient villainies under new names. Does not this influence yearly drain you of two-thirds of your whole revenue? Does it not send undeserving Viceroys to rule over you to the degradation of your own nobility, many of whom were known in Europe long before the great majority of the present English nobility had crawled from their original obscurity? Does it not quarter the worthless followers of those insignificant Viceroys—the buffoons, panders, and parasites of a corrupted court—the trash and refuse of another land, upon the most productive spots of your island? Does it not exalt the most unprincipled and shameless politicians to the very highest stations—and for what? for reviling your country and denying its independence!* Has it not made you a by-word amongst nations, and the very sound of your name a subject of laughter? Are not your mines unexplored, your fisheries neglected, your trade and commerce restricted, your manufactures unprotected, your lands unimproved, your country denuded of its wood and shorn of its beauty and means of naval strength, nay, your very character debased through this influence? Whence the want of employment in Ireland? whence the rack-rents of absentees? whence the squalid appearances and concomitants of poverty? Whence the wanderings of your people to every corner of the earth; the alarming emigrations of northern industry to America; of southern hardihood to England, France, and Spain—to the East and to the West? Whence, I say, does all this proceed, but from the wide-wasting, pestilential influence of England? Even now it is clandestinely aiming at the extinction of your Parliament and your lately-recovered name.

I myself heard the Marquis of Downshire express his ardent wish for a union in the House of Lords of England! Ireland appears loosened from its foundations by this influence, and floats at the breath of every bold and flagitious English undertaker who is

* If such a man as I have here portrayed had not carried the audacious impurities of the Senate to the judgment seat, but administered law in justice and in mercy, as became his great abilities, the circumstance should be a drawback on the detestation of his countrymen—it should take but little from the distrust of the character. *Nemo unquam imperium flagitio quæsitum bonis artibus exercuit.*

sent to defame and to devour it. She might most happily maintain more than double her population, were she not inhibited from availing herself of the bounties of heaven. But your Draconian laws against Popery, the loathsome but unacknowledged offspring of the influence I have been describing, have worn her natives down to a degree of wretchedness not to be equalled by that of slave or freeman in any quarter of the globe; they have given your country the melancholy pre-eminence amongst nations of being supreme in misery. But she has borne her adversities with fortitude. You may thank your stars that the suicide principle of those laws has not utterly eradicated the spirit of your people. If it had, you would have looked in vain for freedom. Had they stood aloof in the day of trial, or joined with your enemies —had they not listened to the dictates of their own virtues, but followed your example in wounding themselves through the heart of their country, you had still been in bondage. They disdained the inglorious example—they pledged their lives and their fortunes for your freedom, and YOU PLEDGE YOURS to hold them in chains!

They are a conquered people, you say. But when they resigned their power in 1691, after their glorious defence of Limerick, they stipulated for freedom with arms in their hands. What did you? When you got them in your power, you stripped them of their arms and robbed them of their freedom—YOU KEPT NO FAITH WITH CATHOLICS! They ask for restitution, therefore, and they would be unworthy of it if they did not. They ask for the liberty their ancestors planted and preserved in this island; for nine-tenths of them are descendants of those English who first won the country by fraud and by force from the ancient Irish. They and their forefathers are your

benefactors, and you are still bent upon remaining
their destroyers; for slavery is the destruction of the
people. Such being their conduct and yours, is it
decorous to talk of their ingratitude? Would it not
be more decorous to retrieve the honour you have lost
by your own? You say they want to intimidate you
into a compliance with their humble supplications.
The assertion is falsified by the fact. They presented
a petition to Parliament praying for a share of that
freedom they contribute to support. They did not
make the compliance of Parliament the condition of
their allegiance: they have evinced the contrary by
the unvaried tenor of their conduct; for though refused in no very flattering manner, amidst scoffs, and
scorn, and indignity, their enemies have not gained
their point: they have not driven them into violence:
they have remained unaltered in their loyalty, their
love of order, and obedience to the law. A brave
General in your House of Commons invites these
defenceless citizens to draw their swords, and make
their appeal to heaven. These oppressed men have no
swords, and if they had, they would only draw them
in defence of their king and country. They and their
fathers have so demeaned themselves in every vicissi-
tude of fortune. I wish this great officer may be as
well disposed. Shame on the man who can thus
mock at the unfortunate, and pour new misery into
the agonising bosom of a tortured generation!

That the Catholics are not prepared for freedom is
a proposition unfounded in reason and contradicted by
the experience of every age and the feelings of every
heart. Liberty, which is equal justice to all, is taught
by nature to all—the savage and the barbarian feel
its sacred impulses as completely as the philosopher.
The liberty of England originated in the woods of
Germany. We know that the Germans were not a

lettered race—they had no property but what was in common; yet these sturdy barbarians were at least as free and as zealous assertors of their independence as their descendants the English. Many of the mighty Barons who extorted Magna Charta from John were unable to read or write; yet the rude feelings of their untutored breasts fitted them admirably to wrest that palladium of happiness from a tyrant. I hope we shall hear no more of this insidious and hypocritical cant, invented by the designing to mislead the unwary. To be fit for freedom, it is sufficient to be born, and it affords an additional aptitude to be bred a Christian —for I hope it is unnecessary to inform you that the service of the Catholic God and yours is perfect freedom.

I should imagine the requisite knowledge for choosing a representative does not lie far beneath the surface. Surely a Catholic has as good an opportunity of learning the acts of wisdom, justice, humanity, and fortitude which distinguish a neighbouring gentleman, and recommend him to notice at an election, as a Protestant; or do the magic syllables of Protestantism bestow sense and sensibility, while the execrated name of Papist bereaves its unhappy owner of every organ of feeling and understanding? Away with such fooleries! Were their absurdity not lost in the immensity of their mischief, they would be as contemptible as the dreams of dotards. If your execrable laws had unfitted the Catholics for freedom, freedom only could re-create that moral and political fitness your laws had done away. Slavery is the worst of all possible schools to teach the principles of liberty: you would not manacle the limbs of the man you would enable to start in the race! Be not afraid of overpowering the tender optics of your brethren with the new light of liberty. The eagle eye of nature looks steadily at the sun of liberty in every stage and every condition of this many-coloured and wearied life.

It is also said that the Catholic Committee* is an unlawful meeting. Those who say so do not understand the law, or misinterpret it with an evil intent. No meeting is unlawful which is peaceably met for a lawful purpose—whether the mode of meeting be borrowed from Constantinople or Paris, whether from the empire of slavery or the seat of democracy. The Catholic Committee is not acknowledged by the law, *totidem verbis*, but everything is allowed by the law which is a quiet assertion of right, and hurts no man. Now, the object of this meeting is not, as has been foolishly or maliciously said, to consolidate the power of the Catholics, but to ascertain their utter impotence to protect themselves, to concentrate their miseries and their tears, to lay them at the foot of the throne, to supplicate Parliament to give freedom, consequence, and union to Ireland. They hope it is no offence to wish to add dignity, strength, and stability to their country, and they are sure petitioning is lawful. The Catholics labour under grievances, and there are two ways of removing them—the one is by war; the other by peace. They seek not relief through the calamities of war: they adore their country. They desire that peace may be the harbinger of their freedom. That peace can be preserved by no better means than by quietly assembling and humbly proposing their grievances to the consideration of the Legislature. The Legislature may refuse granting the prayer of their

---

* Posterity will honour the memories of those prudent and undaunted citizens of Dublin who, unshaken by the secession of their deceived fellow-sufferers, brought those very men back to their opinion by the irresistible force of truth, and cast the foundation of Catholic Emancipation amidst the intrigues, and lies, and calumnies, and menaces of their enemies. Their names will live when court prostitutes, and hirelings, and slaves will be forgotten.

petition, but they have no right to spurn the begging, prostrate, and obedient subject from their door. You are angry with these miserable people for stating their numbers at three millions. You are then angry that they were born. You are then angry that they tread the earth, breathe the air, or survey the heaven. By that heaven I conjure you to dismiss those deadly sentiments of shocking uncharitableness from your otherwise generous hearts, and dare to have the magnanimity to forgive those you have so deeply and so cruelly injured. Be united, be Irishmen, be free.

I hear a great deal of the favours already conferred upon Catholics, and that their emancipation should be gradual.—The Catholics are a grateful people, but the fashion of the day and your own exigencies gave them most of what they have got, and your liberality wears too much the appearance of selfishness to entitle you to much gratitude. Recollect that you only lately set your hand to a partial restoration of their rights, and that those acts of grace were accompanied with no small share of reluctance, no small portion of contempt. By giving the Catholics the power of purchasing land, you converted a flux, monied property, which might be employed against you, into an immovable pledge for their abiding by your fate, and binding their own chains the faster; and by withholding the elective franchise from them, you refuse them the shield by which they might protect their new acquisition. So that the privilege you rate so high makes them but the more dependent upon your good will and caprice. As to gradual emancipation, if you mean to treat your brethren as the English Parliament has the negroes, you should mark a period for their emancipation, as that Parliament has done for the more fortunate Africans. But you do not wish it; you are withholding their rights from your fellow-creatures, and indulging them now and then with a few fragments from your table, fondly hoping that an opportunity may arise to dash their hopes for ever, and plunge them back into that unfathomable abyss of misery from whence they have but just raised their heads. But the opportunity will not arise: the imperishable spirit of freedom has gone abroad and cheers the heart of the meanest peasant. He trusts in the justice and virtues of his king and the tardy humanity of his brethren. His king longs already to burst his chains; for he can do no wrong; and many of the fathers, restorers, and preservers of political Protestant freedom in the North are working seriously, honestly, nobly, and independently in their cause. Your really and truly glorious deliverer, Mr. Grattan, and many of the most exalted natures in Ireland, are at the same God-like work of redemption. The Catholics will deserve it—for I know them—and, of course, they will be free. They have nothing to dread; they walk in the fearlessness of virtue.

But what shall become of the Protestant ascendency? I revere the Protestant ascendency, if, like the prerogative of kings, it is limited by justice and the safety of the people. I cannot revere it if it is nothing but an uncontrollable sway. Such a sway I could never respect, though seated on the throne of Great Britain or the chair of St. Peter. If by Protestant ascendency you mean that the great power of the country should remain in the hands of the present possessors, more than three hundred years would not transfer the power (for property is the power) into the hands of Catholics, even if the whole Penal Code was swept away at this moment; and, I believe, it requires no inspiration to foretell that the folly and wickedness of religious animosity will have died with those who harbour it long, long before that period. But if you define the Protestant ascendency, a Protestant king, a Protestant peerage, a Protestant House of Commons, a Protestant constituency, and make no account of your Catholic brethren, but wish, with the representative of the whole Irish nation, as he was pleased to denominate himself,* that their liberties should be for ever extinguished; while you but half retain your own, I abhor the inhuman idea as I do the author of evil, and exactly upon the same principle, because it is the enemy of mankind.

I have now done; and I implore mercy for your brethren and justice for your country. If you refuse that mercy and withhold this justice, you should prepare for a union: things cannot remain in their present situation; you must either give freedom to the Catholic or abdicate it for yourself. Your ancient oppressors are on the watch to inflame your passions and re-insnare you into worse than your former bondage. A union would be advantageous to the Catholic. By it the Protestant would lose his all, if freedom be all to the noble-minded and the brave. The Catholic would not be raised to the Protestant, but the Protestant would be levelled down to the Catholic, and sunk into a slavish acquiescence in the will of a country accustomed to despise him. The Catholic would be more happy; for that liberty he is never doomed to taste would be removed far from his wounded ear, his aching sight. The Protestant would have no consolation for past glories and present shame. He would experience a servitude more grievous than death.

* The late Richard Sheridan, Esq., then M.P. for Charlemont.

ACCOUNT OF THE COUNTY MEETING AT WEXFORD.

Extracted from *The Wexford Herald* of Monday, Sept. 24, 1792.

Saturday being the day appointed by the High Sheriff to take into consideration a letter, purporting to have been written by order of the sub-committee of the Catholics of Ireland, and signed Edward Byrne, about one o'clock the Sheriff took the chair, and the letter having been read, the following resolutions were moved by the Hon. Francis Hely Hutchinson:—

1. Resolved—That it is the undoubted right of all his Majesty's subjects to petition every branch of the Legislature.—*Adopted.*

2. *Resolved—That it appears to this meeting that the object of the plan referred to by the letter which has been read this day from the chair is to collect the sense of all the Catholics of Ireland, in order that their wishes may be laid by the petition at the foot of the throne.*—Rejected.

3. *Resolved—That the said plan is agreeable to law, and that those who shall endeavour peaceably and quietly to carry it into execution will not, by so doing, commit any act, either illegal or unconstitutional.*—Rejected.

A debate for some hours having taken place upon the above resolutions, and the question having been put, the first was passed in the affirmative unanimously; and a division having taken place upon the two last, they were rejected by a majority of one hundred and ten to forty-five.

This division having taken place, Mr. Maxwell moved the following resolutions, all of which were carried in the affirmative:—

We, the freeholders of the County of Wexford, convened by the High Sheriff, at the requisition of the last Grand Jury, to take into consideration a paper, signed "Edward Byrne," purporting to come from a body of men, styling themselves "The Sub-Committee of the Catholics of Ireland," think it highly incumbent on us to express in the strongest terms our disapprobation of the contents of it.

Resolved—That we see, with much surprise, the many favours so liberally conferred, of late years, by the Legislature on the Roman Catholics of Ireland do not meet with the return of thanks and gratitude to which they were so justly entitled.

Resolved—That since the proceedings of Catholics are unwarrantable, and their demands unreasonable, it is time for the Protestants to make a stand, and to be firm in refusing to make further concessions.

Resolved—That we firmly rely on the wisdom of our most gracious Sovereign, that he will not give his sanction to any measure that may militate against the principles that placed his family on the throne, or tend to diminish the Protestant ascendency of this kingdom.

Mr. Maxwell moved an address to the representatives of the county, to entreat them to give their opposition to any Bill which might be introduced either now or any time hereafter, extending to Catholics the benefit of the elective franchise, or a participation of the trial by jury.

The address having been a long time debated, was at last withdrawn. Mr. Hutchinson then moved the thanks of the meeting to Matthew Derenzy, Esq., the High Sheriff, for his very correct and proper conduct in the chair, which motion was carried unanimously; and the question of adjournment having been put and carried, the meeting was dissolved at a very late hour of the night.

RESOLUTIONS OF THE CATHOLICS OF WEXFORD.

Extracted from *The Wexford Herald* of Thursday, the 27th of September, 1792.

We, the Roman Catholics of the town and vicinity of Wexford, ever anxious to cultivate the friendship of our Protestant brethren, and to unite with them in all the bands of social happiness, embrace this flattering opportunity of testifying our gratitude to the virtuous and independent *forty-five*, whose united efforts and interests supported our cause at the County Meeting, convened by the High Sheriff on Saturday last.

The malignant shafts of calumny, directed by the iron hand of arbitrary power, will never awe us into an acquiescence of *guilt*, which we most solemnly abjure. We are, have been, and ever shall be *grateful* and loyal. Were we possessed of more our noble friends should participate thereof, did their generous and disinterested patriotism permit the idea of a transitory reward; nay, we respect our enemies as members of the State, but hope they will not expect *gratitude* from us until they become our benefactors—that is, proselytes to the true political faith, on which depends the salvation of our country.

We hail our illustrious and glorious protectors, who, with irresistible energy, eloquence, and truth, pleaded the cause of injured innocence and degraded humanity, attempting to raise its head amidst its implacable oppression! We hail them as being invaluable co-operators with the saviours of our country; on whom alone, and on men of such minds, depends the perpetuity of the Constitution as established at the Revolution.

Signed by order,
JAMES E. DEVEREUX.

No. II.

REQUISITION OF THE MAGISTRATES OF THE COUNTY OF WEXFORD.

To the Gentlemen, Clergy, Freeholders, and other Inhabitants of the County of Wexford.

We, the undersigned magistrates of the county of Wexford, convinced that you have not a wish nearer your heart than to have an opportunity of expressing your loyalty and inviolable attachment to our king and excellent constitution (in the absence of the High Sheriff), request your attendance at the County Courthouse, on Friday, the 11th of January next, for that purpose. A measure we conceive at this time not only highly becoming, but also essentially necessary, thereby to contribute so far as in us lies to the restoration of public and private credit, which we have experienced to be materially injured by the seditious practices of a few designing and turbulent incendiaries.

Walter Hore,
Henry Hatton,
John Harvey,
Ebenezer Jacob,
James Boyd,
Robert Hawkshaw,
John Heatly,
Richard Newton King,
William Hore,
John Cox,
William Glascott,
Miller Clifford.

RESOLUTIONS OF THE COUNTY MEETING.

At a Meeting of the Freeholders and Inhabitants of the County of Wexford, convened by Requisition of the Magistrates thereof, and held at Wexford, on Friday, the 11th January, 1793.

WALTER HORE, Esq., in the Chair.

We, the freeholders and inhabitants of the county of Wexford, convened by the magistrates, think it right at this time unanimously to declare our attachment to the Constitution, consisting of King, Lords, and Commons; and have resolved—

That the principles of the British Constitution are founded in wisdom and justice, equally providing for the liberty and happiness of the people.

That an hereditary monarch, an assembly of the nobles, and a body of representatives derived from the people, by free and general election, are each of them integral, vital, and essential parts of our Constitution, insomuch that the decay or corruption of any of them will taint or destroy the whole system.

That the representative part of our Legislature is not derived from the people by that free and general election which the fundamental principles of our Constitution require, and the state and condition of this nation would warrant.

That the permanent peace and welfare of Ireland can only be established by a radical and effectual reform in the Commons House of Parliament, and that this object once obtained, the people ought to remain content and grateful.

That we will, by all constitutional and lawful means, promote a radical and effectual reform in the representation of the people in Parliament, including persons of all religious persuasions; and we rely on the wisdom of Parliament to grant such reform.

That we are happy thus publicly to declare that the people of this country are perfectly peaceable and quiet, and we know of no seditious practices therein, nor do we see the least shadow of, or tendency to, riot or tumult in this country; but lest any such should be entertained or intended by any factious persons, we do declare that we will resist all attempts to introduce any new form of government into this country, or in any manner to subvert, corrupt, or impair any of the three essential parts of our Constitution, consisting of King, Lords, and Commons.

Resolved—That copies of the above resolutions be forwarded by our chairman to the Right Hon. George Ogle and the Hon. John Loftus, representatives in Parliament for this county.

Resolved—That the above resolutions be inserted three times in the *Dublin Evening Post, Morning Post,* and *Wexford Herald.*

(Signed) WALTER HORE.

Walter Hore, Esq., having left the chair, and Cornelius Grogan, Esq., being called to it, the thanks of the meeting were unanimously voted to Walter Hore, Esq., chairman, for his impartial and upright conduct this day.

(Signed) CORNELIUS GROGAN.

No. III.

CERTIFICATE OF SOLOMON RICHARDS, ESQ.

At the request of Mr. Edward Hay, late of Ballenkeele, in the county of Wexford, I certify that I became acquainted with him in the year 1793, for which year I was high sheriff for said county, and at which time the country was much disturbed. I thought necessary to consult the gentlemen of the county, and called meetings for this purpose. Mr. Hay attended these meetings, and was, with other gentlemen, as active and zealous as possible in endeavouring to suppress the disturbances, and to restore peace to the country. From Mr. Hay's actions and expressions I had every reason to consider him a loyal man; I have often heard him declare that he did not, nor never would belong to any political society, and that he disapproved being of all such societies. I was appointed, in the year 1797, administrator during a suit respecting the Hay property. On the 1st of May, 1798, I attended at Ballenkeele as administrator, on which day Mr. Edward Hay, or Mr. Fitzgerald, as his trustee, gave me up possession of the house and demesne of Ballenkeele, and other lands, part of the disputed property; and delivered what furniture he had in the house to his brother, with whom I understand he had settled, and declared he would want immediate payment for this furniture, as he intended to go without delay to America, and settle there. Mr. Edward Hay was much dissatisfied with me about that time, but this did not prevent him from rendering me the most essential services in the rebellion. The rebels attacked the town of Enniscorthy in great force on the 28th of May, 1798, on which day, after a severe engagement, and the town being in flames, I retreated with my corps, and the rest of his Majesty's troops stationed there, to Wexford. On my arrival in that town I saw Mr. Edward Hay in the street, who seemed and expressed himself much distressed at what had happened at Enniscorthy and elsewhere. On the 29th of May I again saw Mr. Hay, when he was approved of as one of the securities for Mr. Edward Fitzgerald, who was then confined in Wexford gaol, but was liberated that day, on giving bail, and sent out to endeavour by his supposed influence with the rebels to disperse them. On the 30th of May, after the rebels had cut off a detachment of the Meath militia, near the Three Rocks, the troops which marched from Wexford to oppose the rebels at that place, retreated to the town; we found the greatest confusion prevailing there. After some time the town was evacuated, and finding it impossible for me, situated as I was, to retreat by land, I made an unsuccessful attempt to effect my escape by sea, but was taken and brought back to Wexford, where I was in the most perilous situation, not knowing the instant I should fall a victim to popular fury. I was taken to a house where a number of ladies and gentlemen were. A furious mob came to this house and called for me to be put to death. A particular friend of mine, who was then in the house, assured me lately, that Mr. Edward Hay went to the door, stood there, and declared they should kill him before they should hurt a hair of my head, and he succeeded in sending them away. It being generally understood that every person who had not taken the United Irishman's oath, or did not know their signs, would inevitably be put to death, I asked Mr. Edward Hay to swear me, which he assured me he could not do; and I have further reason to think he was not an United Irishman, as the week before the rebellion broke out, when I was, as a magistrate, giving certificates to the people on their taking the oaths of allegiance, surrendering their arms, and giving on their oaths such information as they could, respecting the intended rebellion, not one of them—*and I was very strict in my inquiries*—mentioned Mr. Edward Hay, though they gave me information against most of those who in a few days after, in this country, were leaders in the rebellion.

While a prisoner in Wexford, some people intimated a wish to take me home, and I thought I would be safer, if where I was well known, than at Wexford. Mr. Hay told me he would not let me go, as I would be certainly put to death, as the rebels acted with greater cruelty at Vinegar Hill, near which my house is situated. An order was sent by the rebels for twelve prisoners to be taken from Wexford to Vinegar Hill. Mr. Edward Hay told me of this order, and said he would endeavour to prevent these men being sent, as he feared they would be executed, and he succeeded for some time. The event proved he was right, as some of the same persons were afterward taken there and put to death. The house in which I was for about ten days was often searched for arms and *Orangemen*. Mr. Hay, when in the house, endeavoured to save me by attending the searchers, and conducting them to different parts of the house from where I was. When at last a party of those searchers found I was in this house, my destruction was considered inevitable had I remained there. I was conducted to the prison-ship as a place of safety, and I do believe, had it not been done I most probably would have lost my life. Considering the popularity of Mr. Hay, and he being a Catholic, I am surprised he was not obliged to take a command amongst the rebels, and I am confident he could have had an high one was he so inclined. I do not believe Mr. Edward Hay had any command in the rebel army, nor did I ever see him appear in arms of any kind ; and I consider it a fortunate circumstance for some of the Protestant loyalists that he was in Wexford during the rebellion, as I knew that he expressed his earnest desire, and I believe he exerted himself for the preservation of many of them. I think it but justice to give Mr. Hay this certificate, the substance of which I would have proved on his trial had I been called on, and to which I had been summoned.

SOLOMON RICHARDS,
Captain Enniscorthy Cavalry, and Magistrate
of the County of Wexford.

Solsborough, August 30, 1799.

CERTIFICATE OF MARTHA RICHARDS.

I hereby certify, that on the 20th of June, 1798, while the massacres were perpetrating on the bridge of Wexford, Mr. Edward Hay came into the room where I was with other ladies. He was in tears and seemed much distressed at the cruelties that were going forward. I earnestly entreated him to use his influence to save the prisoners' lives. He replied it was in vain for him to try, as he had no influence with the people. I also know that he prevented twelve prisoners from being sent to Vinegar Hill, on a belief that they would be massacred there, and I do believe that he had no command in the rebel army.

Given under my hand this 30th of August, 1799.

MARTHA RICHARDS.

AFFIDAVIT OF MR. TAYLOR, AN ENGLISHMAN.

County of Wexford, } Mr. Thomas Taylor, of the town of
to wit. } Wexford, merchant, who was a prisoner in the gaol of Wexford during the rebellion, freely and voluntarily maketh oath on the Holy Evangelists, and saith he has known the prisoners to express the comfort and consolation they experienced from Mr. Edward Hay's deportment and manner towards them, and had always heard them express their joy on Mr. Hay visiting the gaol. Deponent being an Englishman, and not long in Ireland, had no kind of acquaintance with Mr. Hay, but always approached him when he saw him conversing with his fellow-prisoners, and experienced the consolation of his conversation, although not addressed to him, but considered Mr. Hay the greatest friend of the loyalists, as the purport of his

visits to the gaol evidently was, to give general comfort
to all he saw in distress, as he communicated his sentiments openly and candidly to them, and undeceived
the prisoners with respect to many false reports that
were circulated. Deponent has heard Mr. Hay express
his horror and detestation of the barbarous proceedings of the rebels; and that he would lose his life or
put a stop to the cruelties that were committing on
Vinegar Hill had he been there. Deponent remembers
to have heard of an order for several prisoners to be
sent to Enniscorthy, which order might have been complied with had not Mr. Hay gained intelligence that
they were to be put to death; and at the earnest
request of the prisoners from the neighbourhood of
Enniscorthy, Mr. Hay declared he would make such
representations to the principal inhabitants of Wexford
as to have them detained in gaol as their only place of
safety, on which occasion he has heard the prisoners
express their utmost gratitude to Mr. Hay, whom they
consulted on all occasions of distress, and from whom
they received every possible comfort. Various reports
were propagated which tended to rouse and irritate the
passions of the people to revenge—that the army had
committed the greatest excesses, which alarmed the
prisoners very much, who consulted Mr. Hay about a
proposal they had drawn up to be forwarded to Government, intimating their great danger, and hoping that
the prisoners taken by the army might meet with the
like good treatment that they did, otherwise reprisals
might be made, and their destruction inevitable. Mr.
Hay undertook the task of endeavouring to forward
this proposal with the greatest alacrity, and conducted
Captain M'Manus to consult with Lord Kingsborough,
who accordingly wrote a letter in the name of all the
prisoners, among whom were many officers and principal gentlemen of the county, which proposal was

dispatched by an officer to be forwarded to the next commanding officer of his Majesty's forces, but who would not be allowed to proceed farther than the rebel camp at Enniscorthy, and was obliged to return to Wexford, at which disappointment we considered our situation more critical than ever, and experienced in a greater degree the consoling visits of Mr. Hay, who truly sympathised in our feelings, and felt this disappointment as much as any of us. Deponent never saw Mr. Hay appear with arms, or with any kind of green ornament, then usually worn by all descriptions of persons; and from what he has seen and every information he could learn, believes that during the rebellion Mr. Hay was solely actuated by principles of philanthropy, in any interference of his during that period.

Sworn before me this 28th day of August, 1799.

EBEN. JACOB.

THOMAS TAYLOR.

No. IV.

EXTRACT FROM THE DEBATES OF THE HOUSE OF LORDS,
10th of July, 1793,
On the Convention Bill, as it appeared in the public papers.

Lord Farnham declared "That he had received letters from the county of Wexford, perfectly agreeing with what had been mentioned by the noble lord on the woolsack. In that county the people had held meetings at night, and from parish to parish had sworn the inhabitants not to pay rents, tithes, or taxes, expressing their disappointment that they had not received ten pounds each man annually for the emancipation, but a lease for which they were obliged to pay." He approved of the Bill.

x

No. V.

RESOLUTIONS OF THE CATHOLICS IN WEXFORD.

At a Meeting of the Catholics of the Town and Neighbourhood of Wexford, on Tuesday, the 30th of July, 1793, James Edward Devereux, Esq., in the chair.

We, the Roman Catholics of the town and neighbourhood of Wexford, having acquiesced in the resolution and recommendation of our late general Committee, notwithstanding the many degrading and injurious distinctions still existing against us, to act no more as a body, but as IRISHMEN, united by one will and interest, find ourselves most reluctantly compelled by different attacks, immediately pointed at our honour, to defend ourselves as a distinct people; our loyalty has been traduced, our views misrepresented, and our conduct defamed; we conceive that sinking under such infamous and audacious slander would be the ruin of our country, and bereave us of the affections of our king and our fellow-subjects, for we have learnt from the history of all nations, but particularly from our own, that unrefuted calumnies lead from the extinction of the honest fame of a nation, to the final extinction of her liberties.

Resolved therefore—That it is a base and scandalous falsehood that the Catholics of Ireland ever entertained the thought or harboured the project, either in private or public, of severing the sister countries from each other, or of renouncing their loyalty and gratitude towards a sovereign, to whom, of all who ever sat upon the throne, they are the most indebted.

Resolved—That the Catholics of Ireland never sought any other boon but that of equal law and equal liberty, such as Englishmen possess, and such as is equally the right of Irishmen, and that they are satisfied for ever to abide by one common fate with Englishmen, so that they may for ever enjoy the common blessings of the Constitution, as established in King, Lords, and Commons, under a separate Legislature and a common King.

Resolved—That the general Committee of the Catholics never exercised the right of taxation in any one instance, nor in any other right but in absolute subordination to the laws of their country; nor can we understand how these proceedings and pursuits can be accounted criminal, unless it is proved that the British Constitution—the sole object of those pursuits—is a code of iniquity and vice, which ought to be rejected with detestation, and not contended for at the hazard of every thing dear to man.

Resolved—That we are unalterably attached to the peace, happiness, union, and liberty of Ireland, and, therefore, from our hearts abhor and reprobate any disturbances which may endanger the possession of those invaluable objects, and that we recommend most seriously and earnestly to our Catholic brethren to join and co-operate in every loyal and constitutional measure to suppress them, be their authors whom they may.

Resolved—That we highly approve of the conduct of our late Committee, who have proved us not unworthy of freedom, by evincing our loyalty to our King, our gratitude to the Legislature and our friends, and our unceasing desire to fulfil his Majesty's gracious wish to unite all classes and descriptions of the people in support of our most excellent Constitution.

Resolved—That the silly assertion which has been publicly made—that the Catholics of the county of Wexford were induced to join the Committee by the promise of ten pounds a year, freehold, to the lower classes—is equally devoid of probability and truth, and deserves nothing but our contempt.

Resolved—That these resolutions be published, and that our chairman do transmit a copy to each of the gentlemen who were delegated to the late general Committee.

No. VI.

REQUISITION TO THE HIGH SHERIFF.

To GEORGE GILES, Esq., High Sheriff of the County of Wexford.

We, the undersigned freeholders of the County of Wexford, request you will convene a meeting of your bailiwick on as early a day as possible, to prepare an address, &c., &c., to the Lord Lieutenant, on his Excellency's apprehended departure from this kingdom.

Cornelius Grogan
Isaac Cornock
Arthur Meadows
John Grogan
Matthew Keugh
William Hatton
Anthony Lee
John Colclough
Thomas Richards
William Talbot
Edward Sutton
Patrick Keating
Richard Waddy, M.D.
John Meyler
Loftus Hatton
Harvey Hay
Matthew Talbot
Solomon Richards
John Richards
Edward Hay
Bartholomew Sparrow
Joshua Pounden
Clement Wolseley
James Drury
Robt. Shap. Carew
Matthew Derenzy
Joshua Nunn
Goddard Richards
John Pounden
William Wheeler
John Wheeler Pounden
Stephen Lett
Joseph Stringer
William Barker
John Stringer
Anthony Rudd
Michael Masterson
William Barrett
Loftus Richards
Thomas Esmonde
John Johnston
William Fitzhenry
Robert Meyler
Frederick Flood
Thomas Grogan Knox
Joshua Nunn
John Harvey
William Kellett
Armstrong Browne
James Furlong
Charles Vero
Dudley Colclough
William Harvey
B. B. Harvey

The foregoing requisition to the High Sheriff, as well as the following to the Magistrates, are copied from the public papers, from some unaccountable accident without dates, as the original has been lost or mislaid. The author is particularly cautious not to introduce a particle that is not clearly substantiated; however, it is certain that many days intervened, which he hopes at a future period to be able to ascertain exactly.

REQUISITION TO THE MAGISTRATES.

To the Magistrates of the County of Wexford.

GENTLEMEN,—We, the undersigned freeholders of said county, being informed that the High Sheriff is not in his bailiwick, and deeming it highly necessary, at this awful and alarming crisis, that this respectable county should meet for the above purpose, request that you will please to convene the freeholders and inhabitants of said county as soon as possible.

Frederick Flood	Richard Waddy, M.D.
Joshua Nunn	Edward Hay
William Hatton	B. B. Harvey
Matthew Talbot	William Kellett
John Harvey	Armstrong Browne
Edward Sutton	John Colclough
Matthew Keugh	Thomas Richards
John Johnston	Loftus Richards
William Talbot	William Harvey
Loftus Hatton	

In compliance with the above requisition, we, the undernamed Magistrates of said County, request a meeting of the freeholders and inhabitants of the County, at the County Court-house, on Monday, the 23rd instant, at twelve o'clock.

Cornelius Crogan	Harvey Hay
Isaac Cornock	John Grogan
Thomas Grogan Knox	

Wexford, 17th March, 1795.

RESOLUTIONS AT THE COUNTY MEETING ON THE RECALL OF EARL FITZWILLIAM.

At a numerous Meeting of the Freeholders and Inhabitants of the County of Wexford, in the County Court-house, on the 23rd of March, 1795, Cornelius Grogan, Esq., in the chair, the following Resolutions passed unanimously :—

Resolved—That the resolutions of the freeholders and inhabitants of this county in favour of Catholic Emancipation and Reform, adopted by them at a county meeting held at Wexford on the 11th day of January, 1793, be now read.

Resolved—That we continue of the same opinion as declared by us at the above meeting.

Resolved—That Earl Fitzwilliam, by the wisdom of his measures, and by calling to his councils those men who have at all times promoted the union and supported the interests of the people, and proved themselves the true friends of their King, the Constitution, and their country, has deservedly obtained the confidence and merited the gratitude of Irishmen.

Resolved—That we have good reason to be convinced that the sudden recall of so PATRIOTIC a nobleman, at that moment when those friends of Ireland who had obtained his confidence were bringing forward measures that would have promoted the UNION of the *people*, and increased the strength of the Empire, could have no other source than in the malignant schemes and interference of a late Administration (supported by the influence of certain members of the British Cabinet), who knew that whilst his Lordship remained in the Government they could no longer pursue a detested system of measures—which seemed more calculated for the purposes of corruption, oppression, and persecution than the prosperity of the State.

Resolved—That strongly impressed by our past

experience of so dangerous an administration, it is not without reason we dread the return of the men who formed it into power, and the revival of a system which filled the minds of the people with terror and alarm, and had a fatal tendency to create disunion and disaffection, and we call upon every man who regards the safety of the empire to come forward and deprecate the return of that administration into power, and thereby rescue the nation from plunder, dissatisfaction, and disunion.

Resolved—That an humble petition to the king, expressive of our sentiments on this occasion, be forthwith drawn up and laid before us for our approbation, and that a committee be appointed to prepare the same—which being read—

Resolved—That we approve of said petition, and that Cornelius Grogan, Edward Hay, and B. B. Harvey, Esqrs., do present the same to his Majesty.

Resolved—That we should ill deserve the patriotic intentions of Earl Fitzwilliam to this country, if we did not declare our sense of them previous to his Lordship's departure from this kingdom.

Resolved therefore—That an address be prepared by the committee accordingly—which being read—

Resolved—That we approve of the said address, and that Sir Thomas Esmonde, Bt., Sir Frederick Flood, Bt., and William Harvey, Esq., convey said address to Earl Fitzwilliam.

Resolved—That we congratulate our countrymen of the Roman Catholic persuasion, on the liberal and honourable testimony which so many counties, cities, and towns have borne to the justice and policy of their claims.

Resolved—That the thanks of this meeting are justly due to Mr. Grattan, for his honest and patriotic attention, as well in as out of power, to those measures which on former occasions he had supported and brought forward, and also for his spirited and constitutional answer to the address of the Roman Catholics of Dublin.

Resolved—That we do publicly thank and entertain a due sense of the merits of those members of both Houses of Parliament, who have uniformly stood forward the advocates of those indispensably necessary measures for the preservation of our Constitution, the emancipation of our Catholic brethren, and a reform in the representation of the people in Parliament.

Resolved—That these our resolutions of thanks be communicated by our worthy chairman to his Grace the Duke of Leinster, and the Right Hon. Henry Grattan.

Resolved—That our peculiar thanks are due to the Magistrates who so properly and spiritedly complied with the requisition to convene this meeting in the absence of the High Sheriff, who was not in the county.

PETITION TO THE KING.

At a numerous Meeting of the Freeholders and Inhabitants of the County of Wexford, convened by public notice, held at the County Court-house on the 23rd of March, 1795, the following Petition to the King was unanimously adopted.

May it please your Majesty,—We, your Majesty's most dutiful and loyal subjects, the freeholders and inhabitants of the county of Wexford, convened by the Magistrates thereof in absence of the Sheriff, beg leave to approach your throne, and with permission of our most gracious sovereign to express our attachment to your Majesty's family and government, in full confidence that our benevolent sovereign will vouchsafe to hear his subjects in whose hearts he reigns, and whose

love for his sacred person will ever lead them to
support with their lives and their properties his throne
and his government.

With gratitude we received as a signal instance of
our august sovereign's beneficence to his Irish people,
the appointment of Earl Fitzwilliam to the government
of this kingdom—a nobleman whose wisdom and whose
virtues peculiarly qualified him to be the beloved
Viceroy who would administer to the inhabitants of
Ireland that happiness and union we know your
Majesty would wish to be the lot of all your people;
and we anticipated the happy consequence from Earl
Fitzwilliam's administration, when we had observed he
had called to his councils those men who were most
conspicuous in the nation for their abilities, and their
attachment to the interest of their king and the
constitution of their country; and whose measures
promised a just appropriation of the public revenues,
and additional strength to the empire. But particularly we contemplated with the most heartfelt joy, the
union of all your Majesty's subjects, by the removal of
those civil distinctions arising from difference in religious opinion—a measure of such invaluable wisdom,
as would for ever shield the throne of our revered
sovereign with the unconquerable phalanx of a loyal
and brave people. But these our most flattering
expectations being suspended by the removal of Earl
Fitzwilliam from the government of Ireland, we beg
leave to represent to our most gracious sovereign our
fears and apprehensions lest these men whose advice
had for several years past directed the administration
of affairs, should again be called into the confidence
and councils of government. We beg leave to represent that a contempt for your people, and a prodigality
and waste of the public revenues, distinguished their
administration; we therefore deprecate the return of

such men into power and confidence, as dangerous to your Majesty's interest and the welfare of your people; and at this awful and alarming crisis, most humbly throw ourselves for relief on the benevolence and affection of our most gracious sovereign in humble confidence that his Majesty will be pleased to restore to a grateful nation the prospect of those blessings which we so anxiously hoped for, and call again to your councils those men whose measures must ensure the prosperity and strength of the empire, and in whom your people place their hopes and their confidence.

Subscribed by twenty-two thousand two hundred and fifty-one signatures, presented to the king at St. James's, 22nd of April, 1795.

ADDRESS TO HIS EXCELLENCY EARL FITZWILLIAM.

To his Excellency, WILLIAM, EARL FITZWILLIAM, Lord Lieutenant, General, and General Governor of Ireland.

The Address of the Freeholders and Inhabitants of the County of Wexford, convened by public notice, at the Court-house at Wexford, 23rd March, 1795, Cornelius Grogan, Esq., in the chair:—

May it please your Excellency,—We, the freeholders and inhabitants of the county of Wexford, beg leave, in the present alarming state of affairs in this kingdom, to express to your Excellency the sentiments of regret which we feel at the information we have received of your Excellency's departure from this kingdom.

When we beheld your lordship commencing your government in this country by the proposition of measures the most just and the most politic, the removal of civil distinctions on account of differences in religious opinions, and the investigation of abuses which time and corruption had introduced into some departments of the State—when we beheld your lordship calling to your councils those men who were most conspicuous in the nation for their attachment to its interests and the true spirit of the Constitution—men in whose integrity the people placed their hopes and their confidence, we exulted in the glad proposal of union and harmony, and we anticipated with joy the approaching happiness of the people. The honest and virtuous were inspirited, the corrupt, the factious, and the rapacious oppressor alone felt disappointment and chagrin.

But should your Excellency withdraw from the government of Ireland, these our most anxious hopes must yield to apprehension and despondency: we dread lest a set of men, as odious as they are vindictive and tyrannical, should return into power, and revive a system of measures which disunited the people, and were dangerous to his Majesty's interests and the safety of his kingdom. The memory of the unhappy discontents and divisions, which were produced by the evil councils of such men, heightens our regret at the recall of a governor whose wise and conciliatory measures would have infallibly promoted the union of the people, the strength of the nation, and the stability of the Constitution.

Happy then in that reward which the good and virtuous alone can know—the consciousness of an upright mind—receive, from a grateful people, their thanks and their gratitude. And may our gracious sovereign, when he shall have dismissed from his councils those men who have, unfortunately for this country, too long beset his throne, finally bestow on your Lordship every royal favour to which your services and your virtues so justly entitle you.

Signed by order of the meeting,
CORNELIUS GROGAN, Chairman.
THOMAS RICHARDS, Secretary.

Among the many losses the author sustained during the distracted state of the county of Wexford, he has, on this occasion, particularly to lament the answer of Earl Fitzwilliam. Independent of its prophetic allusion, it also contained sentiments that would be highly gratifying to the friends of Ireland. This, and many other unavoidable wants in this work, it is to be hoped may be given to the public in a future publication.

No. VII.
LORD GOSFORD'S ADDRESS.

At a numerous Meeting of the Magistrates of the County of Armagh, convened on the 28th of December, 1795, at the special instance of Lord Gosford, governor. His Lordship having taken the chair, opened the business of the meeting by the following address:—

GENTLEMEN,—Having requested your attendance here this day, it becomes my duty to state the grounds upon which I thought it advisable to propose this meeting, and at the same time to submit to your consideration a plan which occurs to me as most likely to check the enormities that have already brought disgrace upon this county, and may soon reduce it into deep distress.

It is no secret, that a persecution, accompanied with all the circumstances of ferocious cruelty which have in all ages distinguished that dreadful calamity, is now raging in this county. Neither age nor sex, nor even acknowledged innocence as to any guilt in the late disturbances, is sufficient to excite mercy, much less to afford protection.

The only crime which the wretched objects of this ruthless persecution are charged with, is a crime, indeed, of easy proof—it is simply a profession of the

Roman Caholic faith, or an intimate connexion with a person professing this faith. A lawless banditti have constituted themselves judges of this new species of delinquency, and the sentence they denounce is equally concise and terrible! It is nothing less than a confiscation of all property, and an immediate banishment.

It would be extremely painful, and surely unnecessary to detail the horrors that attend the execution of so rude and tremendous a proscription—a proscription that certainly exceeds, in the comparative number of those it consigns to ruin and misery, every example that ancient or modern history can supply: for where have we heard, or in what story of human cruelties have we read of more than half the inhabitants of a populous country deprived at one blow of the means as well as of the fruits of their industry, and driven, in the midst of an inclement season, to seek a shelter for themselves and their helpless families where chance may guide them.

This is no exaggerated picture of the horrid scenes now acting in this county; yet surely it is sufficient to awaken sentiments of indignation and compassion in the coldest bosoms. These horrors are now acting with impunity. The spirit of impartial justice (without which law is nothing better than an instrument of tyranny) has for a time disappeared in this county, and the supineness of the magistracy of Armagh is become a common topic of conversation in every quarter of the kingdom.

It is said in reply—the Catholics are dangerous; they may be so—they may be dangerous from their numbers, and still more dangerous from the unbounded views they have been encouraged to entertain; but I will venture to assert, without fear of contradiction, that these proceedings are not more contrary to humanity than they are to sound policy.

It is to be lamented, that no civil magistrate happened to be present with the military detachment on the night of the 21st instant; but I trust the suddenness of the occasion, the unexpected and instantaneous aggression on the part of the delinquents, will be universally admitted as a full vindication of the conduct of the officer and the party acting under his command.

Gentlemen, I have the honour to hold a situation in this country, which calls upon me to deliver my sentiments, and I do it without fear and without disguise.

I am as true a Protestant as any gentleman in this room. I inherit a property which my family derived under a Protestant title; and, with the blessing of God, I will maintain that title to the utmost of my power. I will never consent to make a sacrifice of Protestant ascendency to Catholic claims, with whatever menace they may be urged or however speciously or invidiously supported.

Conscious of my sincerity in this public declaration, which I do not make unadvisedly, but as the result of mature deliberation, I defy the paltry insinuations that malice or party spirit may suggest.

I know my own heart, and I should despise myself, if, under any intimidation, I could close my eyes against such scenes as present themselves on every side, or my ears against the complaints of a persecuted people.

I should be guilty of an unpardonable injustice to the feelings of gentlemen here present, were I to say more on this subject. I have now acquitted myself to my conscience and my country, and take the liberty of proposing the following resolutions:—

1. That it appears to this meeting, that the county of Armagh is at this moment in a state of uncommon disorder—that the Roman Catholic inhabitants are grievously oppressed by lawless persons unknown, who

attack and plunder their houses by night, and threaten them with instant destruction, unless they immediately abandon their lands and habitations.

2. That a committee of magistrates be appointed to sit on Tuesdays and Saturdays in the chapter-room in the town of Armagh, to receive informations against all persons of whatever description, who disturb the peace of this county.

3. That the instruction of the whole body of magistrates to their committee shall be, to use every legal means within their power to stop the progress of the persecution now carrying on by an ungovernable mob, against the Roman Catholic inhabitants of this county.

4. That said committee or any three of them be empowered to expend any sum or sums of money, for information or secret service out of the fund subscribed by the gentlemen of this county.

5. That a meeting of the whole body of the magistracy be held every second Monday at the house of Mr. Charles Reynolds, in the town of Armagh, to hear the reports of the committee, and to give such further instructions as the exigency of the case may require.

6. That offenders of ever description in the present disturbances shall be prosecuted out of the fund subscribed by the gentlemen of this county.

From " The Dublin Journal" of January the 5th, 1795, and copied in all the papers in Ireland.

No. VIII.

GENERAL ORDERS OF SIR RALPH ABERCROMBY.

Adjutant General's Office,
Dublin, 26th February, 1798.

The very disgraceful frequency of courts-martial, and the many complaints of irregularities in the conduct of the troops in this kingdom, having too unfortunately proved the army to be in a state of licentiousness, which must render it formidable to every one but the enemy,—The Commander-in-chief thinks it necessary to demand from all Generals commanding districts and brigades, as well as commanding officers of regiments, that they exert themselves, and compel from all officers under their command, the strictest and most unremitting attention to the discipline, good order, and conduct of their men, such as may restore the high and distinguished reputation the British troops have been accustomed to enjoy in every part of the world. It becomes necessary to recur, and most pointedly to attend to the standing orders of the kingdom, which, at the same time that they direct military assistance to be given at the requisition of the civil magistrate, positively forbid the troops to act (but in case of attack) without his presence and authority; and the most clear and precise orders are to be given to the officer commanding the party for this purpose. The utmost prudence and precaution are also to be used in granting parties to revenue officers, both with respect to the person requiring such assistance, and those employed on the duty; whenever a guard is mounted, patrols must be frequently sent out to take up every soldier who may be found out of his quarters after his hours.

A very culpable remissness having also appeared on the part of officers, respecting the necessary inspection of barracks, quarters, messes, &c., as well as attendance at roll calls, and other hours, commanding officers must enforce the attention of those under their command to those points and the general regulations, for all which the strictest responsibility will be expected for themselves.

It is of the utmost importance that the discipline of the dragoon regiments should be minutely attended to, for the facilitating of which the Commander-in-chief has dispensed with the attendance of orderly dragoons on himself, and desires that they may not be employed by any general or commanding officer, but on military and indispensable business.

Lieutenant-General CRAIG,
Eastern District.

Barracks, Dublin.

No. IX.

OATHS DURING THE INSURRECTION.

By Order of the Council for Directing the Affairs of the People of the County Wexford.

Oaths to be taken by all the United Army, in the most public and solemn manner.

TEST OATH.

In the awful presence of God, I, A. B., do voluntarily declare, that I will persevere in endeavouring to form a brotherhood of affection among *Irishmen* of *every* religious persuasion; and that I will also persevere in my endeavours to obtain an equal, full, and adequate representation of *all* the people of Ireland. I do further declare, that neither hopes, fears, rewards, nor punishments, not even death, shall ever induce me, directly or indirectly, to inform on or give any evidence against any member or members of this or similar societies, for any act or expression of theirs, done or made collectively or individually, in or out of this society, in pursuance of the spirit of this obligation. So help me God.

OATH OF A PRIVATE.

I, A. B., do solemnly and sincerely swear, and take God, and His only Son our Lord Jesus Christ, to witness that I will at all times be obedient to the commands of my officers; that I am ready to lay down my life for the good of my country; that I have an aversion to plunder, and to the spilling of innocent blood; that I will fight courageously in the field, and have mercy where it can be given; that I will avoid drunkenness as tending to disorder and ruin; that I will endeavour to make as many friends and as few enemies as possible; that above all, I detest a coward; and that I will look upon him as an enemy who will stand back in the time of battle. So help me God.

OATH OF AN OFFICER.

In the awful presence of God, who knows the hearts and thoughts of all men, and calling my country to witness, I, A. B., officer in, &c., do solemnly swear, that I do not consider my life my own when my country demands it—that I consider the present moment calls for a proof of the sincerity of that sentiment; and I am ready and desirous to stand the test; and do aver, that I am determined to die, or lead to victory; and that all my actions shall be directed to the prosperity of the common cause, uninfluenced by any inferior motive; and I further declare my utter aversion to all alarmists, union breakers, and cowards, and my respect and obedience to the commands of superior officers. So help me God.

By order of the Council,

B. B. HARVEY, President.
NICHOLAS GRAY, Secretary.

Done at the Council Chamber,
Wexford, June 14, 1798.

No. X.

THE ADDRESS OF THE INHABITANTS OF THE MACOMORES TO MAJOR FITZGERALD.

To Bregaddeer-Magar Figgerald, in Waxford.

Plaise your honour, as you war good enof get the general to give us pardon, and as you tould us, that if there was an occasion youd expect that weed fite for our king and cuntry, and as ever willin' to be up to our word, we send this paper about the bisness; and if your honour 'ill give us leave to fite, weel do everything your honour bids us, and we minded nothing else to-morrow but to fite for the king's officers against the French; and hopes your honour will excuse this haste, an we wished to lose no time, and excuse our not nowing how to write to such generals; but if your honour will get a memoral drawn rite, your honour may depend on us and put our names to it for us as in the inclosed.

O'BRIEN,
WALSH, and
SULLIVAN.

THE ADDRESS OF THE INHABITANTS OF THE MACOMORES TO GENERAL HUNTER.

To the General Hunter, or Governor of Waxford, belonging to King George the Third.

We, the Macomore boys, was in the turn out against the Orangemen, and to who your noble honour gave your most grasous pardon, for we never desarved any other if we war let alone, and being tould that the French was cumeing to take this cunttry from his Royal Highness the King, who we swore to fite for, and in regard to our oath and to your lordship's goodness in keeping the Orrangemen from killing us all, weel fite til we die if your honour will give us leave, and weel go in front of the battle, and we never ax to go in the back of the army your honour will send wid us, and if we don't bate them weel never ax a bit to eat, and as you gave us pardon and spoke to the king about us, as the bregaddeer-magar tould us and as we tould him weed never deceive your honour, tho' the black mob says weel turn out a bit again, but we'el shew them and the world if your honour will bid us, that weel fite and won't run away from the best of them, and if your honour will send down the magar that was wid us from your lordship afore, or the Honorable Magar Curry, or the Lord Sir James Fowler, general of the Middle-lothin sogers in Waxford, and let them lave word at Pepper's castle and weel march into Waxford, go where your honour bids us, do anything atal to fite for your honours, and weel expect to hear from your honour what weel do; or, if your honour will order a signal to be made with a red flag, weel draw up and march as good as any sogers, and, as far as one or two thoughsand good stout boys goes, weel fite for your honour to the last man, and weer sure all the barneys 'ill do the same if you will give them lave.

Signed by the desire of all the parishes in the Mack-omores.

O'Brien,
Walsh, and
Sullivan.

August 27th, 1798.

The Author applied to Major Fitzgerald for authentic copies of the addresses to him and General Hunter from the inhabitants of the Macomores, offering their services to march against the French, and received for answer, that he had no copies by him, although such addresses had been forwarded, but not exactly in the

APPENDIX. 341

form in which the foregoing are therefore unavoidably introduced, which it is hoped may be sufficient apology for the burlesqued manner they appear in, however intended to undo the innate spirit and intention of the originals.

Major Fitzgerald got several messages and notices from the Macomores, respecting the arrival of Holt and Hackett, but was induced to set out immediately on the receipt of a letter from a respectable gentleman, who does not wish to have his name appear in print, but is authenticated by a copy in the hand-writing of Major Fitzgerald, with his initials as follows:—

"DEAR SIR,—I am requested by the respectable farmers of this county to entreat you to come here without delay, as the people are much agitated. The industry and domestic happiness which you established among them seems suspended; and to-morrow appears to be an appointed day for general meeting. Your appearance would certainly quiet the distracted people, and I trust your humanity and ardent exertions will induce you to interfere. If you honour me with an answer, and that you promise the people the pleasure of a visit, the most respectable farmers are ready to attend your arrival, and accompany you through the Macomores. I remain in anxious expectation of seeing you, &c., &c., "G. S."

"C—h—e, September 2nd, 1798.
"To Brigade-Major FITZGERALD."

No. XI.
AFFIDAVIT OF MR. STEPHEN LETT, JUNIOR.

County Wexford, to wit. } Stephen Lett, jun., upholder and auctioneer, of Enniscorthy, in said county, came before me this day, and maketh oath on the holy Evangelists, that Captain Philip Hay called upon deponent to value the furniture at Ballenkeele, which he was to take from his brother, Edward Hay, and which he understood formed part of a settlement between them, previous to Mr. Edward Hay leaving Ballenkeele. Deponent accordingly attended at Ballenkeele about the middle of May last, and, on the valuation being made, Captain Philip Hay declared they were too dear, and would not take them. In consequence of which Whitsun-Monday was, as a holiday, considered the best day for a country auction, requiring at least two market days to post up printed advertisements, which was accordingly done. Deponent avers that Mr. Edward Hay was distressed at this delay, as it was quite contrary to his inclinations, as he declared his intentions of leaving the country as speedily as possible. Deponent had often heard Mr. Edward Hay declare in the most solemn manner that he would never become a member of any political society. Deponent retreated from Enniscorthy to Wexford along with the army, on the 28th of May, 1798, and the day after, Wexford was taken by the rebels, while deponent was in a boat along with Mr. O'Toole and family, with Mrs. Lyster, going to Edermine; verily believes that he would have been put to death, had not Mr. Edward Hay thrown himself between the mob and the boat, and with great difficulty kept them off with a stick until he shoved the boat from the quay.

Sworn before me this 15th of November, 1798.

ISAAC CORNOCK.

STEPHEN LETT, jun.,
Sergeant in the Enniscorthy Cavalry.

LETTER FROM LIEUTENANT MURPHY.

Wexford, 6th January, 1799.

DEAR SIR,—I received yours, and shall with pleasure say every thing in my power consistent with honour and justice touching your character, so far as I am capable of judging, during the rebellion. At that time I considered myself honoured by your acquaintance, and the frequent visits I paid you at Ballenkeele, and the intimacy that existed between us, leads me to believe I could form a just opinion of your principles in political matters, which we constantly talked over. I most solemnly declare I never heard you drop one sentence that was inimical to the Constitution or Government of our country, but the reverse—reprobating the conduct of such as were disturbing the peace of the country and condemning their proceedings; and I have heard you declare most solemnly that you never would belong to any political society whatever. Since my return to Wexford, after the country was recovered, I have not heard any man say you committed an act that would disgrace your name, which I verily believe, from what I experienced, and also was informed of your humane and tender actions to individuals of every description. I remain, with warmest wishes for your speedy liberation,

Dear Sir, yours most truly,

ARTHUR MURPHY,
Lieutenant Healthfield Cavalry.

To EDWARD HAY, Esq.,
Wexford Gaol.

AFFIDAVIT OF EDWARD ROCHE.

County Wexford, to wit. } Edward Roche, of Garrilough, who acted as a rebel chief in the late rebellion, voluntarily maketh oath, that the rebels vowed vengeance against Mr. Edward Hay, for aiding and assisting the late Edward Turner, Esq., who was a magistrate for said county, on the surrender of their arms and pikes at Newpark, on Saturday, the 26th of May, 1798, thereby supposing him their enemy. Deponent saith that the rebels constantly, during the rebellion, called for Mr. Edward Hay to go out to their camps and take the command; and if said Edward would not, he should be put to death by them. Deponent saith that, from the hate and violence of the rebels, and their threats against said Edward, his personal safety became uncertain and precarious; and the more so, as frequent representations were made to the rebels by certain persons that had influence among them, that said Edward was inimical to them. Deponent saith that said Edward never carried arms, attended the rebel camps, or did anything to conciliate the rebels. Deponent saith he was in Wexford on the 20th of June, 1798, being the day of the massacre on the bridge, where deponent saw Mr. Edward Hay exert himself with zeal and activity in preventing the wicked and blood-thirsty designs of the rebels; and saith that the said Edward, in so doing, exposed himself to almost inevitable destruction. Deponent saith that the rebels loudly declared Mr. Hay to be their enemy—that his whole designs were to protect their enemies, the *Orangemen*; and, if he was not one himself, he would not oppose them (the rebels) and exert himself for the protection of *Orangemen*.

Sworn before me this 18th day of April, 1799.

EBEN. JACOB.

EDWARD ROCHE.

APPENDIX. 345

LETTER FROM CAPTAIN BOURKE.

DEAR SIR,—In compliance with your request, and having received a summons to attend your trial, I shall relate the circumstances I recollect of your conduct during the rebellion, as you mention you want to have your instructions made out for your lawyers previous to the Assizes. I was taken prisoner along with Lord Kingsborough and Captain O'Hea, on the 2nd day of June, 1798. We were confined together in a house in Wexford, with a strong guard on us. From the great fury of the people against Lord Kingsborough, we expected every moment to be put to death. Mr. Edward Hay visited us frequently, and we clearly perceived his disposition to afford us every consolation in his power, as he took every opportunity he could of softening our captivity, and has frequently conducted my wife and family to see me at a time it was extremely dangerous to seem or appear friendly to us. Whenever we experienced any kind of distress, we always sent for Mr. Hay, who readily came to us, and never left us without our being convinced he would do his utmost to be of service to us. I have every reason to believe he saved our lives on several occasions, when the mob were for bringing us out and putting us to death. One day in particular I perfectly recollect his standing with his back to the door of the house in which we were confined, where he remained until the tumultuous crowd had dispersed who sought our instant destruction. I always heard Mr. Hay express his horror at any barbarous proceedings of the rebels, and his earnest wish that peace and good order might be restored. Various reports being circulated, that tended to rouse and irritate the passions of the people to revenge, that the army had committed the greatest excesses, which alarmed us and all the rest of the prisoners in Wexford for our situation, we, as usual, consulted Mr. Hay on this peculiar cause of distress, and found him particularly anxious to forward a treaty of negotiation of prisoners, proposed by Lord Kingsborough as the best mode of re-establishing peace and good order. During this dilemma letters had been forwarded through the rebel camps from Dublin to Lord Kingsborough, in answer to which was considered a favourable opportunity of forwarding this measure, which Mr. Hay readily undertook; and he accordingly conducted Captain M'Manus to consult with us, and in consequence a letter was written by Lord Kingsborough, in the name of all the prisoners, among whom were thirteen officers, a great number of yeomanry officers, and principal gentlemen of the county, intimating that they were well treated, and in every respect prisoners of war; hoping, therefore, that the prisoners taken by the army might meet with the like good treatment that they did, otherwise they feared reprisals might be made, and our destruction inevitable, which proposal was confided to my charge, and with which I was to proceed to the next commanding officer of the army, and to return with the answer with all convenient speed. I accordingly set out from Wexford on the 14th day of June, 1798, and proceeded as far as Enniscorthy, where I was stopped by the people, and not allowed to proceed any further, and obliged to return to Wexford the next day, at which disappointment we felt our situation more alarming than ever, and experienced in a greater degree the consoling visits of Mr. Hay, who was truly concerned at this disappointment. I never knew nor heard of Mr. Hay having any command among the rebels, nor did I ever see him appear in arms or wear any mark or distinction of uniform, which I had a daily opportunity of witnessing had it been so, as the house in which we were confined was situated in the bull-ring, and commanded a full view of the most frequented streets in Wexford, through which all the armed men in the town passed and repassed twice a day.

Among the many attentions paid us by Mr. Hay, he brought us letters that had been directed to us, and had fallen into the hands of the rebels, which if made public to them might have proved our instant destruction, for which piece of service Mr. Hay narrowly escaped with his life, as Captain Keugh, who then commanded in Wexford, expressed great anger on hearing it from Lord Kingsborough, who inadvertently mentioned Mr. Hay having done so, and Mr. Hay was afterwards constantly prevented from visiting us by order of Captain Keugh.

On the 20th day of June, 1798, the day of the massacre on the bridge of Wexford, considering our situation more critical than ever, we wished to see Mr. Hay; Lord Kingsborough sent for him, and he immediately attended, but was denied admittance to us, but he spoke to him out of the window, and he declared to us, that as long as he was alive himself, we might depend upon every exertion of his. We had at last the consolation of Mr. Hay being admitted up stairs to us at eight o'clock in the evening. We found him beyond expression affected at the cruelties that had been committed, which he had in vain done every thing in his power to prevent, and anxious to undertake any thing for the safety of the prisoners. After a variety of consultation, Lord Kingsborough and Mr. Hay agreed to go out to meet the army that was approaching Wexford, in order to save the town from destruction. The Wexford-men that had gone out of the town that day returned from the battle of Fooks's-mill, whilst Mr. Hay was still with us; he then proposed to go and consult the principal inhabitants

who he had not the smallest doubt would agree to
and facilitate the plan ; it being then late at night, he
promised to return early in the morning to set off along
with Lord Kingsborough, who was so anxious to carry
this project into execution, that he was dressed in full
regimentals, and completely ready to set out at three
o'clock in the morning of the 21st of June, 1798, at
which time he sent for Mr. Hay, who instantly came,
represented to Lord Kingsborough the danger of his
going out equipped as he was, for it would prove their
inevitable destruction, if they went without the consent
of the people. Lord Kingsborough then entreated
Mr. Hay to hasten a meeting of the principal inhabitants, and to have the drum beat to arms, and the
men would speedily repair to parade, where their
consent might be obtained, as the smallest delay would
prove the destruction of the town and all its inhabitants. Mr. Hay instantly complied, and returned with
an account of the Wexford-men having agreed to the
plan with the greatest alacrity, and it had been further
resolved on, that Lord Kingsborough should not leave
the town, which should be instantly surrendered to
him as military commander; and that Doctor Jacob
had re-assumed the office of Mayor, all of which was
immediately carried into effect with some opposition
on the part of Captain Keugh, who wanted to retain
the command, but was most spiritedly opposed by
Mr. Hay. Mr. Hay set off with Captain M'Manus, as
soon as Lord Kingsborough could write out the
necessary dispatches to the next commanding officer
of his Majesty's forces, announcing the town of
Wexford being surrendered to him; and that in
consequence of the behaviour of those in the town
during the rebellion, they should all be protected in
person and property, murderers excepted, *and those
who had instigated others to commit murder*, hoping

that these terms might be ratified, as he had pledged his honour in the most solemn manner to have these terms fulfilled on the town being surrendered to him, the Wexford-men not being concerned in the massacre which was perpetrated by country people in their absence. I saw Mr. Hay on his return from General Lake on the 22nd day of June, 1798, when Lord Kingsborough considered himself under so many obligations to him, which he acknowledged in the strongest terms, and insisted he should live in the house with him, where Mr. Hay remained with us until we left Wexford on the 29th of June, during which period I have repeatedly heard him express a desire to be brought to trial if any thing was alleged against him, as he would wish to have the benefit of our testimony before we went to Waterford. I consider myself bound on all occasions that may be afforded me, and I think it an indispensable duty, to do justice to the meritorious conduct of Mr. Hay during the rebellion in Wexford; and actuated by principles of honour and gratitude I think myself bound to prove and subscribe to.

MICHAEL BOURKE,
Paymaster North Cork Militia.

Sallins, June 3rd, 1799.
To EDWARD HAY, Esq.,
Wexford Gaol.

I believe the above account of Mr. Bourke, with the alteration I have made to be true.*

KINGSTON.

LETTER FROM LORD KINGSTON.

Colney, December 14th, 1799.

SIR,—From what I saw of your conduct whilst I was at Wexford a prisoner, I am convinced that you did all in your power to save the people whom the

* Alteration alluded to is in italic.

rebels wished to murder, and myself among that
number; and it was through you that the town of
Wexford was given up to me, which circumstance I
believe saved the lives of many; and by what I have
heard from you of your trial, do think you have been
very unjustly persecuted.

I am your most obedient humble servant,

KINGSTON.

To EDWARD HAY, Esq.

LETTER FROM MAJOR FITZGERALD.

Dublin, March 19, 1800.

SIR,—According to your request I have made a
proper retrospect on the circumstances you allude to in
your letter of the 17th, and recollect perfectly when a
memorial was presented to Major-General Hunter on
your part, from on board a prison-ship, denying that
you had ever petitioned for transportation, and to be
liberated under the general proclamation; that the
General had a very good disposition to liberate you,
and believe would have complied with your petition,
but on questioning the Committee, they still asserted
you had petitioned for transportation. General Hunter
declared if so, you should apply to his Excellency the
Lord Lieutenant, and if you wished it would forward
such memorial. When you were afterwards removed
from the prison-ship to the gaol on account of ill
health, through the interference of General Craddock,
a recommendation came by which I was sent to you to
inquire more particularly into your situation, when you
demonstrated the facts so clearly to me by documents,
etc. I had every reason to believe the General would
liberate you on discovering the iniquitous designs of
the Committee, as I conceived you had sufficient proofs
to show the falsity of their assertions; but unfortunately for you at that period, the landing of the French

in this kingdom obliged the General to depart hastily from Wexford, which left you and many more innocent persons the victims of a persecuting sanguinary party, which I call that vile body, commonly called the Committee!

However, I congratulate you on your happy escape from becoming the victim of suborned perjury, which to my knowledge was too commonly resorted to in that town, under the pretext of law.

I regret exceedingly General Hunter is not in the realm, as you would be certain to meet from him every honourable testimony of your situation, as he never countenanced party of any kind, and was always ready to relieve the oppressed. I shall be happy at any time to come forward to attest any thing that comes to my recollection, and should long since unveil the horrid atrocious practices of that town, if my public duties did not interfere. I wish you may succeed in getting redress; and have the honour to remain,

Sir, your obedient humble servant,

B. EDWARD FITZGERALD,
Major of Brigade.

To EDWARD HAY, Esq.

AFFIDAVIT OF MRS. BREEN.

County of Wexford, to wit. } Margaret Breen, the wife of Matthew Breen, of the town of Wexford, mariner, came before me this day, freely and voluntarily maketh oath on the holy Evangelists, and saith that she was on board the sloop Liberty in the harbour of Wexford, on the 29th day of May—the day before Wexford was surrendered to the rebels. Saith that on the same day deponent saw Mr. Edward Hay take shipping on board the vessel called the Adventure of Wexford, as deponent believes, to make his escape from the said town. Saith that on the 31st day of

May, 1798—being the day after the town was possessed by the rebels—a furious mob came calling loudly for Edward Turner, Esq., deceased, late magistrate for said county; declaring they would put him to death at the same moment, and were about to destroy the house wherein he the said Edward Turner was concealed. Saith that the said Mr. Hay being informed of the designs of the said mob, interfered for Mr. Turner's protection, and expostulated with them, saying that Mr. Turner was his most intimate friend, that he was a good charitable man, and a protector of the poor. Saith that the mob, on the warm solicitations of Mr. Hay, were induced to withhold their design of murdering Mr. Turner; but insisted on his being sent a prisoner to the gaol. Deponent saith that in some few days after the town was so possessed by the rebels, she saw a great multitude assemble in a clamorous and riotous manner near the house where Lord Kingsborough and two other officers of the North Cork regiment of militia were prisoners: saith the rebels seemed furiously determined to bring the said prisoners out and put them to death. Deponent saith she saw the said Edward Hay interpose for their preservation, and addressed the mob in terms strongly reprobating the idea of killing in cold blood, and that the vengeance of God would overtake all murderers. Deponent saith that she has frequently heard the rebels threaten the lives of Lord Kingsborough and his officers; and believes their safety and protection in a great measure attributable to the efforts of the said Edward Hay. Deponent was summoned on Mr. Hay's trial, and this affidavit is the substance of her testimony, had she been deemed necessary to be called on.

Sworn before me this 17th day of August, 1799.

EBEN. JACOB.

MARGARET BREEN.

LETTER FROM ARMSTRONG BROWNE, ESQ.

DEAR SIR,—I shall be happy to bear testimony upon any occasion that may be afforded me of such parts of your conduct as came within my observation during the late unhappy rebellion. In the first instance, I perfectly recollect that on the 27th of May last, you joined the corps of yeomanry to which I belong, but from appearing in coloured clothes in common with a few other persons who had offered their services, it was thought advisable by the officer commanding the party, that such persons as were not in military uniform should return to Wexford. For the space of fifteen days, I had frequent opportunities of seeing and hearing of your conduct, which I believe to have been strongly marked by mildness and humanity, and an abhorrence of the excesses that were daily committing, which you had it not in your power to prevent; nor did I ever see you carry arms during that period. I have to acknowledge many kind and friendly visits from you during my confinement, when you gave me, Mrs. Browne, her sister Mrs. Huson, and family, all the consolation in your power; but in particular, after I had been dragged down to gaol by a party of the rebels, you immediately repaired there, used your exertions, brought down General Roche, and happily for me you succeeded in effecting my release. After this I was advised to go to my own house in the country, but being again made a prisoner there, and being surrounded by numerous perils, in the midst of my distress you wrote a most friendly letter, which was delivered to Mrs. Browne in the most secret manner, communicating the violent threats you had heard against me in Wexford, and recommending me to return to town, in order to refute the charges that had been brought against me. Upon the whole, I am convinced that your conduct toward me was solely actuated by motives of esteem and regard for my preservation, for which I should be happy to render you any adequate kindness. I am well convinced that during the disastrous period of three weeks—while the rebels had the possession of Wexford—many loyal subjects were obliged to act in a manner repugnant to their feelings, in order to save their lives and please the multitude, who threatened vengeance against many persons for not aiding and assisting in their designs. Your letter dated the 18th ult. I assure you I never received till about one o'clock yesterday, when it was handed to me in the court-house, which will apologise for my not attending to in due time.

I am, dear Sir,
Your obliged and faithful humble servant,
ARMSTRONG BROWNE,
First Lieutenant Shilmalier Cavalry.

Wexford, 2nd April, 1799.
To EDWARD HAY, Esq.

No. XII.

TESTIMONY OF EBENEZER JACOB, ESQ., M.D.,

On the Trial of Edward Hay, at the Assizes of Wexford, on the 27th of July, 1799, produced and sworn as an Evidence for the Crown.

Examined by TIMOTHY DRISCOL, ESQ.

Recollects the time in 1798, when the rebels were in possession of Wexford; was in Wexford during that period; knows the prisoner; believes the first time he saw Mr. Hay after the rebels came into Wexford, was when he was inquiring where General Fitzgerald was; heard he was at Mr. Lett's where Mr. Bagnal Harvey lodged; went to Mr. Lett's and found him there; to the best of his recollection, he saw Mr. Hay, Captain Keugh, and Mr. Harvey; cannot say in what situation Bagnal Harvey acted during the rebellion; saw Keugh at the head of a party of rebels in arms; has seen Keugh act as an officer; has no positive knowledge of a committee existing in Wexford at that time; saw Mr. Hay again passing by with Mr. Harvey, said they were going to give circulation to bank notes; does not believe there was any one else in company with them; believes he saw them near the court-house, moving on to the left of the town; remembers the 21st of June, 1798; was called on by Robert Meyler, who told him several persons were at Keugh's, and requested he would go there; went accordingly, and saw the prisoner at Keugh's house; saw Keugh, Harvey, R. Carty, priest Roche and several others, whose names he does not recollect, in company with prisoner; Keugh asked if they should speak on the subject Doctor Jacob was sent for? Hay said yes, and he did so; Keugh said, it would be madness not to surrender the town, as there were great numbers of the king's troops marching in different ways to Wexford; one army he said was marching from Taghmon, another from Oulart, and a third from Enniscorthy; they all immediately agreed but priest Roche, who was overruled.——It was proposed that he and Robert Carty should go with a flag of truce to the Taghmon army, and that the prisoner and Captain M'Manus should go to the Oulart army; Captain M'Manus was selected as a loyalist; cannot tell why Mr. Hay was selected; cannot say whether Keugh gave any reason for coupling them; Captain O'Hea and ——— were sent to the Enniscorthy army; Mr. Hay consented to go; spoke to that effect and went; the persons he met at Keugh's were of a tolerable degree, persons he conceived of high situation, from opinion, not knowledge; does not recollect any others that were there; the persons so assembled assumed authority; it was mentioned in Mr. Hay's presence that he was to go with Captain M'Manus, and he consented; does not believe Mr. Hay was an officer; never saw or heard he carried arms; cannot say whether Carty was an officer or not; never saw Bagnal Harvey act in the capacity of an officer; Carty was a rich farmer; Harvey was a man of property; Keugh was an officer in the army, and always considered a gentleman.

Cross-examined by PETER BURROUGHS, ESQ.

It was after the town was surrendered to the rebels he saw Mr. Hay; believes he did not meet Mr. Hay in company more than once or twice before that day. Many loyal persons were desirous of being in the company of Harvey and Keugh, to afford themselves protection. Believes that the religion of a Catholic might make him more respected with the rebels, and might give a Catholic more influence than a Protestant; believes great bloodshed was prevented by those who had influence; believes that a loyal man might be glad to have influence with the rebels; does not actually know that Mr. Hay used his influence to save lives, but is confident he would do so if he could. The loyal inhabitants would have been in great danger had there been a battle in taking the town. A loyal and humane man ought to join in the terms of recapitulation, but he conceived a loyal Roman Catholic would be preferred to go to the army. Many persons favoured the rebellion that detested it. Q. Do you not believe that many Protestants submitted to be christened by priests? A. I do believe many loyal men did so, but no true Protestant need do so, if it was not his own choice. Q. Do you believe that Captain Hay was considered a rebel? A. I do. Q. Did you not hear that he was tried and honourably acquitted by a court-martial? A. I did.

No. XIII.

LETTER FROM MR. HAY TO THE REV. MR. GORDON.

REVEREND SIR,—As you have publicly professed a wish to be informed of any involuntary errors contained in your History, at a time when speculative opinions supply the place of fact, and are so prevalent, hearsay evidence—whether oral, manuscript, or even printed—is to be received with the greatest caution. The great superiority of ocular information to any other induces me from personal knowledge of facts to send you along with my own opinion auxiliary documents that cannot fail to convince you that the introduction of my name into your History is not such as I am entitled to, and I hope your professions of candour and liberality may be realised, by doing justice to my present communication.

According to the plan contained in Mr. Byrne's circular letter two persons deputed from each Catholic congregation in the county of Wexford, assembled at Enniscorthy, on the 29th of July, 1792, where they elected delegates to represent the county in the general committee of the Catholics of Ireland. I attended this meeting as a voter from the congregation I belonged to, and had the honour of being elected one of the delegates for the county of Wexford. So that the intermediate step of baronials, which you mention in your History, had but a speculative existence, invented I do suppose with a view of assimilating the Catholic committee with the system of United Irishmen—a circumstance totally devoid of truth, as no kind of communication existed between them. In order that the meeting of the general committee should be publicly attended, proposals were made to hire different public places, which could not be obtained, so that no other place but the Taylor's Hall, Back-lane, could be procured. This precluded the possibility of being able to admit any but the delegates, as it was scarcely sufficient to contain them, and thus was the committee frustrated in having their assembly publicly attended. The first meeting of this general committee took place in December, 1792, for seven days only, which you mention to be many weeks. The second and final meeting for eight days in April, 1793, and the meeting ended in a dissolution beginning on the 16th and ending on the 25th, as Saturday the 20th was taken up by the attendance of all the delegates in the Court of King's Bench, to take the oaths prescribed by a late Act of Parliament. The collections made by the Catholics of Ireland to defray the necessary expenses, attendant on the pursuit of their emancipation, were voluntary subscriptions, and not in any degree assessments. It is evident the entreaties, by no means orders, of the sub-committee, were not attended to, as two-thirds of the counties of Ireland never produced one farthing. I paid the collection of the county of Wexford to the treasurer in 1792, and no second collection ever was made there. The statue of the king could not be erected, although voted as a monument of Catholic gratitude, which, along with other honourable engagements, were superseded by the general and calumnious outcry raised at the time against our collections.

The petition of the Catholics of Ireland might be supposed to escape animadversion, when his Majesty was graciously pleased to signify his strongest approbation in his recommendation to the Parliament of Ireland, who, in consequence, repealed the greater part of the penal statutes against Catholics. The late Earl of Clare did assert, as you have done in your History, " that the Catholic petition was surprisingly fraught with misrepresentation." On this assertion being made, the petition was re-published, reciting the statutes on which the allegations contained in the petition were grounded, prepared by the Hon. Simon Butler, whose reputation as a lawyer the Chancellor was too well acquainted with, to attempt to expose his error a second time, and gave up the point. So that I imagine this public document will be equally convincing to you, which I send, along with all the proceedings of the Catholic Committee relating to this event, for your perusal, as I would wish your avowal to proceed from the most perfect information on the subject.

Although I profess the Roman Catholic religion, I should not be of that communion a single hour, were their tenets as they are represented, through that baneful prejudice, so prevalent in Ireland, that proves such an effectual draw-back to the otherwise infallible prosperity of my country; and I cannot sufficiently lament to see such so industriously circulated, as it only serves to keep alive those prejudices that all liberal men see through and reprobate as a pest to society.

A sloop which had been fitted up by the insurgents in Wexford, but had been twice condemned, as totally unfit for that service, was hauled on one side in the harbour, where she sunk within a foot of her deck, and remained in that situation for a month, when she was pumped out. I was the same day, without trial or inquiry, put on board along with those that had been tried and sentenced to transportation. The wet straw was left in her hold, and a little dry straw shook over, which our walking on soon made as bad as the rest; so that it was not possible to sit or lie down without imbibing the wet, nor had we even the satisfaction of resting against the sides of the ship, as the planks were water-soaked. The effervescence of the putrid malt was so strong as to turn money black in our pockets in the course of a few hours. We had also a profusion of rats that bit some of the prisoners. My health has been greatly impaired by five weeks' confinement on board this sloop, and I fear it will never be perfectly re-established. I should detain you too long, to enumerate the various hardships I suffered during the period of thirteen months that I was confined, which I was at last released from by an honourable acquittal, at the Summer Assizes in Wexford, in August, 1799, independent of the Amnesty Bill. Whereas, my persecutors could be punished by the fundamental laws of the Constitution, had they not the Indemnity Bills to screen their base and tyrannical conduct towards me. I have confined myself merely to the facts stated in your History, in which I have been in some degree concerned, and an eye-witness, which precludes the possibility of cavilling or contradiction. I hope you may be kind enough to set them in their proper colours. I request the favour of your answer, as I am anxious to learn your determination on a subject you have hitherto been so much uninformed about, as I do not mean to let such transactions go uncontradicted to posterity.

I have the honour to be, with great respect, reverend sir, your most obedient, humble servant,

EDWARD HAY.

Dublin, 6th July, 1802.
To the Rev. Mr. Gordon, Boro Lodge.

ANSWER OF THE REV. MR. GORDON.

SIR,—I have received your documents, and think you much aggrieved. I am satisfied of their veracity; they remove a mistake in my History. I shall publish them in my next edition with suitable acknowledgments.

I am, sir, your very humble servant,

JAMES GORDON.

Boro Lodge, July 18th, 1802.

APPENDIX.

While my work was at press, an edition of the Rev. Mr. Gordon's History was published in London, in which he certainly has noticed my communications, but not in the extent I think I shall be able to point out, deserving his attention in the supplement he has promised to the public.

From the pursuit I am at present engaged in, I consider it my duty to seek and unravel truth, and shall be happy to elucidate any circumstances that may be considered more useful in promoting public knowledge. In consequence of the progress I have already made with the Rev. Mr. Gordon, and in consideration of our communications being hitherto very circumscribed, I have offered him my services, and hope for his co-operation in the pursuit of my intention—THE UNION AND HARMONY OF ALL DESCRIPTIONS OF OUR COUNTRYMEN. This object is extensive enough to engage the attention of many. The public have already anticipated their favourable opinion of gentlemen employed in researches that are so likely to increase the high opinion entertained of their superior talents. If an humble individual can recommend himself by the sincerity of his co-operation, I shall hope to be included among those who are willing to point out the means of general happiness.

THE END.

www.ingramcontent.com/pod-product-compliance
Lightning Source LLC
Chambersburg PA
CBHW030603300426
44111CB00009B/1082